FORGOTTEN RAILWAYS

*Volume 11*

# Severn Valley and Welsh Borders

# FORGOTTEN RAILWAYS

### Editor: J. Allan Patmore

The master volume, Forgotten Railways by H.P. White, in larger format, has now also been published.

*Note:* The description of an old railway route does not imply that there is a public right of way along it, and readers must obtain permission to enter private land. Increasingly, railway land is passing into private ownership and often the owners of former stations do not want their privacy disturbed by casual visitors.

*Jacket illustration:* Railways were on top of the world in Shropshire long before the lorry arrived. The Severn Valley and Welsh Border was packed with lines of great charm, individuality and character. The Ludlow & Clee Hill branch even had a dual personality. It began with over four miles of steeply graded steam working to Bitterley Yard tucked into the lower slopes of the hill. From there, a rope-worked incline steepening to 1 in 6, ran to Clee Hill Top, where steam working was resumed to stone quarries. On a summer's day, 'Pannier' tank No 4678 pounds the final 1 in 20 gradient to Bitterley yard with empty wagons. Because of the gradient even short trains of twelve empty wagons were divided. 22 August 1956. (*Photograph: Geoffrey Bannister*)

FORGOTTEN RAILWAYS

*Volume 11*

# Severn Valley and Welsh Border

REX CHRISTIANSEN

DAVID ST JOHN THOMAS
DAVID & CHARLES

**British Cataloguing in Publication Data**

Christiansen, Rex
   Severn valley and Welsh border.—
   (Forgotten railways; v. 11).
   1. England. West Midlands. Railway services.
   Disused routes
   I. Title   II. Series
   385'.09424

ISBN 0–946537–43–7

Set in 11 on 13 Baskerville
by Typesetters (Birmingham) Ltd
and printed in Great Britain
by Redwood Burn Ltd
for David St John Thomas
Distributed by David & Charles plc
Brunel House Newton Abbot Devon

Published in the United States of America
by David & Charles Inc
North Pomfret Vermont 05053 USA

# Contents

# Acknowledgements

A writer may sometimes wonder if he has attracted nationwide attention when complaints and criticisms of his latest book start arriving! But while he is writing it, his is a solitary task. Nobody can write for him so it is always pleasant to receive the much valued help of friends.

I am especially grateful to Gordon Biddle, who accompanied me on some of my research visits, to John Marshall, who read part of the manuscript, and to Harold Forster MBE, retired station manager, Manchester Piccadilly.

I have appreciated help, too, from John Hughes, Project Officer of the Severn Gorge Countryside Management Project, John Mair, M.P.N. Reading, Jeffrey Williams, and the staff of British Rail's Press Office in Manchester, which closed in March 1988. I had valued their help for some thirty years.

I am grateful to a number of people for their help with illustrations and especial thanks are due to Geoffrey Bannister, Gordon Biddle and John Edgington. The plates have been supplied as follows: Plate 30, C. A. Appleton; 14, 16, 25 and 32, the author; 1, 4, 15, 19, 21 and 26, G. F. Bannister; 24, C. R. Berridge; 5, 6, 7, 9 and 11, J. Edgington; 8, N. Fields; 2, 3, 10, 18, 20, 22 and 28, L&GRP; 12, 13, 17, 23, 27, 29 and 31, R. E. G. Read (by courtesy of Gordon Biddle).

Chelford, Cheshire
Spring 1988

# CHAPTER 1

# Capri-cious!

*'Home to Ludlow in the evenings'*

Even amid the beauty of the Isle of Capri on a summer's day, it was hard to stop thinking about trains. Descending the modern funicular from the little town perched on the hill to the Marina Grande, having bought a thin paper ticket as blue as the Mediterranean far below, it occurred to me what a splendid funicular the former Clee Hill mineral branch might have made. Fanciful? Totally!

Shropshire is too beautiful a county for a project like that to be contemplated. Yet, once the Clee Hill branch was almost a funicular for railwaymen were once allowed to use the bottom section from Bitterley Yard to Ludlow in a way that sounded rather jolly if the weather was fine.

Page 65 of the *Sectional Appendix* to the Working Time Tables for the Chester & Birkenhead and Shrewsbury & Hereford sections of the LMS and GW Joint Railways was headed by three paragraphs concerning the operation.

When working of the branch will admit, the undermen going home to Ludlow in the evenings may make use of the (platelayers) trolley. The permission of the signalman must first be obtained, and when preceding the branch train a staff ticket must be taken, and when following the train the train staff must be carried. The trolley must be signalled in the same manner as the trains are dealt with . . . The speed of the trolley must not exceed 10 miles per hour.

7

The speed limit was emphasised in thick black type.

Allowed to run rather faster are trains that pass the windows of my den a field away from the Manchester and Crewe line at Chelford in the quiet South Cheshire countryside. Among them are the Manchester – Cardiff services which every day evoke memories of the Welsh Border route – the *Marches Country* as BR are currently marketing it.

I think of the hilly 'road ahead' south of Shrewsbury and wish I was travelling, for the Shrewsbury & Hereford route, despite having lost so many branches, is still a delight to use.

Doctor Beeching may have destroyed the Severn Valley railway as a through branch between Shrewsbury and Worcester, but the enthusiasts' revival of its core is a success story which only its visionaries would have thought possible when it began.

Does any other preserved railway join towns as historic and fine as Bridgnorth and Bewdley? Bewdley has always been noted for its black and white buildings and now at the station, across the Severn from the town, there are the pleasures of a variety of locomotive and carriage liveries not seen in GWR days.

Many of the trackbeds in this book are the graves of lines which linked the Welsh Border to Worcester and Stafford, Crewe and Chester. I have reconstructed their hey-day partly by using an 80 year old *Bradshaw's* and when I placed it beside a *Railway Clearing House* map only ten years younger, the pleasures of searching for old railways became heady and complete.

The map is that of *Staffordshire & District*, which might seem a curious choice for studying the Welsh Borders, yet it reached to Llandrindod Wells and Dinmore Ridge and tunnel on the Shrewsbury & Hereford Joint Line. The Joint Railways system is hatched red and yellow and covers far more miles than those between Shrewsbury & Hereford, often the limits by which it is remembered today as the years of its individuality slip deeper into the past. For the system also embraced Shrewsbury and Wellington, part of a route used by trains from Stafford to

Welshpool. West of Shrewsbury they ran over the Joint Railways to reach the Cambrian Railways at Buttington.

The Joint Railways also included the Minsterley branch (stemming from the Shrewsbury & Welshpool), the Clee Hill branch and the western tip of the long branch from Woofferton to Bewdley, comprising the five miles from Woofferton to Tenbury Wells.

In the offices at Shrewsbury station, so magnificently restored in the mid 1980s, was that of the joint superintendent who exercised direct control of the line to Hereford.

Shrewsbury is a place that gives the lover of only forgotten lines no cause to linger, for its losses have been confined to a short stretch of the Shropshire & Montgomeryshire, and the Shropshire Union goods yard beside station and prison. That is now a car park and can be viewed quickly.

Yet it would take hours to recall the glory of Shrewsbury in the hey day of steam when, to quote from *Through the Window Paddington to Birkenhead* 'The enormous number of rails here impresses every traveller'.

It is now more than two decades since the end of that service and of North to West expresses via Shrewsbury and the Severn Tunnel. The station atmosphere has changed little since the withdrawal of local services to Worcester, Stafford, via Wellington, and Minsterley.

Shrewsbury suffered a major loss through closure of the Western Region's rail welding depot at Hookagate, two miles out of town on the Welshpool line, in May 1986. It was the place where locomotive No 6000 *King George V* went for water after hauling the first leg of a memorable David & Charles steam excursion in 1972. Even without its welding depot, Hookagate was assured of a place in railway history for it was here that after years of wrangling, a junction was established between the Shrewsbury & Welshpool and the Shropshire & Montogomeryshire railways.

My *Bradshaw's* of 1908 makes no mention of the latter for it was still seeking rebirth. But the timetable was carrying an interesting note on the fortunes of the equally eccentric

# LONDON AND NORTH WESTERN RAILWAY

LONDON SUNDAY SCHOOL CHOIRS' FESTIVAL at the CRYSTAL PALACE, JUNE 29th.

## GREAT SPECTACULAR DRAMA OF "VENICE IN LONDON,"
### At OLYMPIA, Kensington (Addison Road).

Each holder of an Excursion Ticket to London by this Excursion may obtain a Ticket for a 2s. Seat (numbered and reserved) for "Venice in London" for 1s. 6d., on production of the Return Half of their Excursion Ticket at Olympia.

## International Horticultural Exhibition and Buffalo Bill's Wild West Show
### AT EARL'S COURT.

## MADAME TUSSAUD'S EXHIBITION, opposite Baker Street Station.

# SUMMER EXCURSIONS.

## On MONDAY, JUNE 27th,

# A CHEAP EXCURSION

| WILL LEAVE | | A.M. | WILL LEAVE | | A.M. |
|---|---|---|---|---|---|
| CREWE | ... | at 11.10 | SHREWSBURY | ... | at 10.20 |
| NANTWICH | ... | „ 10. 5 | WELLINGTON | ... | „ 10.34 |
| WHITCHURCH | ... | „ 9.40 | NEWPORT | ... | „ 10.50 |
| WEM | ... | „ 9.50 | STAFFORD | ... | „ 11.46 |

# FOR LONDON

### And the undermentioned places:

| FARES FOR THE DOUBLE JOURNEY TO | From Crewe, Nantwich, Whitchurch, Wem. | From Shrewsbury. | From Wellington, Newport. | From Stafford. |
|---|---|---|---|---|
| | Third Class. | Third Class. | Third Class. | Third Class. |
| LONDON (Euston) ... | 14/0 | 13/0 | 13/0 | 12/0 |
| CRYSTAL PALACE (including Admission) | 15/6 | 14/6 | 14/6 | 13/6 |
| OXFORD ... ... ... | 14/0 | 12/0 | 12/0 | 10/6 |
| BANBURY ... ... ... | 13/0 | 10/6 | 10/0 | 9/6 |
| LEAMINGTON, WARWICK, or KENILWORTH | 12/0 | 9/6 | 9/0 | 8/0 |
| COVENTRY ... ... | 10/6 | 8/0 | 7/6 | 6/6 |
| BIRMINGHAM ... | 7/0 | 5/6 | 4/0 | ... |
| WALSALL, WEDNESBURY, DUDLEY, DUDLEY PORT | 6/6 | ... | ... | ... |
| WOLVERHAMPTON | 5/6 | ... | ... | ... |

Returning on Friday, July 1st.

## CHILDREN UNDER TWELVE YEARS OF AGE, HALF-FARE.

Tickets not transferable. Personal Luggage under 60 lbs. Free, at Passengers' own risk.
The Excursion Trains to London call, both going and returning, at Willesden Junction, whence Trains are run at frequent intervals to Earl's Court, Kensington, Highbury and Islington Station on the North London Railway (which is within easy distance of the Agricultural Hall), the City, West End, and to all parts of the suburbs.

The issuing of Through Tickets is subject to the conditions and regulations referred to in the Time Tables, Books, Bills, and Notices of the respective Companies and Proprietors on whose Railways, Coaches, or Steamboats they are available; and the holder, by accepting a Through Ticket, agrees that the respective Companies and Proprietors are not to be liable for any loss, damage, injury, delay, or detention caused or arising off their respective Railways, Coaches, or Steamboats. The contract and liability of each Company and Proprietor are limited to their own Railways, Coaches, and Steamboats.

THE RETURN TRAINS on Friday, July 1st, will leave Euston Station, London, at 11.5 a.m.; Oxford at 9.50 a.m.; Banbury, 9.50 a.m.; Leamington (Avenue Station), 11.50 a.m.; Warwick (Milverton), 11.54 a.m.; Kenilworth, 12.2 noon; Coventry, 1.8 p.m.; Birmingham (New Street), 1.50 p.m.; Dudley, 1.40 p.m.; Dudley Port, 2.5 p.m.; Wednesbury, 1.29 p.m.; Walsall, 1.35 p.m.; and Wolverhampton at 2.20 p.m.
Tickets and Small Bills may be obtained at the Stations.

Euston Station, London, June, 1892.　　　　G. FINDLAY, General Manager.

Messrs. HENRY GAZE & SONS, CONTINENTAL TOURIST AGENTS of the Company, supply Tickets to PARIS, RHINE, BELGIUM, SWITZERLAND, &c., from all principal Stations on the LONDON AND NORTH WESTERN RAILWAY, for Direct Single or Return Journeys, Independent Travel, CIRCULAR TOURS, and EXCURSIONS, by all Best Services and Routes. Tickets may be obtained in advance of intended date of starting. For full particulars see GAZE'S TOURIST GAZETTE, 4d., Post Free, of
H. GAZE & SONS, Chief Office, 142. Strand, London.
McCorquodale & Co. Limited, Cardington Street, London, N.W.

CRYSTAL PALACE.—Passengers will be booked through to the Crystal Palace and back, and back from either London Bridge or Victoria, by their own conveyance across London, and the Crystal Palace.

L. B. & S. C. Co.'s route may travel, "their own conveyance across London," within any distance for one journey between.

Passengers holding Through Tickets to the Crystal Palace by the L. B. & S. C. or L. C. & D. route, and those holding Tickets by the L. C. & D. Ry.), may travel from either Victoria, Holborn Viaduct, or Ludgate Hill Stations (L. C. & D. Ry.), and the Excursion Tickets entitle the holder to remain in London, but will only be available by any Train on any of the days during which the Excursion Tickets are available. Passengers must, however, state at the time of booking by which route they elect to travel.

Bishop's Castle Railway, close enough in rural terms to be regarded as a neighbour.

Despite losing the Minsterley branch, the Shrewsbury & Welshpool has enjoyed strategic importance since it became the only route into Mid Wales and the Cambrian coast in the 1960s following closure of the Cambrian main line between Whitchurch and Welshpool; the Great Western secondary route between Ruabon and Barmouth and the LNWR between Bangor and Afon Wen. Shrewsbury's rail network benefitted from the three closures.

To the south, Craven Arms was the terminus of long withdrawn services on the Bishop's Castle Railway and, more importantly, to the Severn Valley and Wellington. North of the Severn, one small station has become the headquarters of the Telford Horsehay Steam Trust, and BR passenger trains are back in the valley, linking the West Midlands and Coalbrookdale.

Another line that ran into the Severn Valley was the branch between Woofferton and Bewdley. Between Newnham Bridge and Cleobury Mortimer lay the small and remote station of Neen Sollars, which Service Time Tables noted as being 15 miles 38 chains from Hartlebury and 13 miles 45 chains from Kidderminster, while in 'Milepost Mileage' it was 147 miles 26 chains. Long after closure it came to epitomise the fascination of remote branches. When 'Cam' Camwell gave his annual film show to the East Midlands branch of the Railway Correspondence & Travel Society in 1974, a writer in *The Railway Observer* said his film showed how much had been swept away since 1956 and asked: 'Who can now remember a station with the delightful name of Neen Sollars?'

The LNWR used the Stafford–Wellington branch for excursion traffic from Shrewsbury to London and far beyond. A summer 1892 handbill offers a variety of attractions in London, including Buffalo Bill's Wild West Show. The reverse side promoted 'cheap conducted parties' to Paris and Switzerland. Fares from Wellington and Newport were no cheaper than those from Shrewsbury.

The *Service Time Tables* (three words in title) for the West
Midland section headed Oxford, Worcester, (sic) and Wolverhampton noted the Cleobury Mortimer and Ditton Priors
branch as being

A single line. Worked by Train Staff. No Block Telegraph.
Only one Engine in Steam or two Engines coupled together
allowed on this Branch at the same time.

By then, they were rules that could be ignored for
beneath in thick black, funereal, capitals was 'SERVICE
SUSPENDED'.

Yet while BR suspended the service, lovers of forgotten
railways did everything but abandon collecting memories.
When I joined them for the first time, many years after I
should have done, the aftermath of the Falklands campaign
was in the news and one recalled that it was war that had kept
the former light railway alive for so long, serving Royal Navy
ammunition dumps scattered throughout the countryside.

Searching for the ever diminishing remains, mostly trackbed, can take infinitely longer I suspect than the time the
slowest of passenger trains used to occupy getting local people
in and out of the countryside via Cleobury Mortimer and the
Bewdley branch.

If you are visiting the area lying under the distant shadow
of the high hills of Shropshire, you will find countryside you
will never forget, once, that is, you are away from the high
banked lanes where clearance for vehicles is far less than that
enjoyed by the trains.

One can conveniently return now to the Marshes through
Worcester and recall the city's highly individual railway system. One of its main ingredients, the presence of the Midland
and LMS with expresses looped off the Bristol – Birmingham
main line, has long gone, although the route remains.

It is perhaps harder to recall the LMS presence at Worcester
than it is to remember that of the GWR in Birmingham. Of

course, many Bristol–Birmingham expresses used the direct line on the eastern outskirts of Worcester, roaring through a string of lonely, wayside stations which have been part of the forgotten railway scene for many years.

Passengers on expresses that did call at Worcester (Shrub Hill) might have caught sight of a Pannier tank and a handful of wagons departing from the goods yard just north of the station and, after running between the two locomotive sheds, disappear into the city's heart. They were beginning a short journey down stiff gradients, across a bascule bridge and between works before reaching the Vinegar works of Hill Evans and Company. They also crossed a main road where GWR lower quadrant main line type signals stopped vehicles, not trains.

No enthusiast worth his salt missed the 'Vinegar branch', surely one of the most recorded in British railway history.

Worcester had another goods branch entwining its heart: the Butts or Riverside branch, which dropped away from the Hereford line at the western end of Foregate Street station on a viaduct and squeezed between the Severn approach viaduct and the Royal Infirmary to reach ground level between the river and the Racecourse. It then shunted back along the river bank for nearly half a mile to serve tidal wharfs which were busy for years.

No-one who loves to be beside the river at Worcester, with the Cathedral on one bank and one of the loveliest cricket grounds in England on the other, can have been sad at the closure of the Butts branch.

The journey from Worcester to Leominster was always leisurely and so was that from Leominster to New Radnor via Kington, which in Victorian days came to be the hub of what were regarded as four branches. Leominster – New Radnor was the stem formed of two of them. The others ran north from Titley to Presteigne, County town of Radnorshire, and south to the Hereford Hay & Brecon at Eardisley. All were the haunts of small GWR tanks, notably Panniers and 0–4–2's.

The Kington branches had a distinctive ambience born of serving remote country and this was sensed especially by enthusiasts from the town. GWR *Holiday Haunts* for 1947 and probably other years, noted New Radnor as 'an ideal place for a quiet holiday'. A pub three miles away advertised one of its visitor comforts as 'Electric Light Throughout'.

Years earlier, soon after the end of the first world war, the same guidebook described Presteign (sic) as 'a charming little town which only requires to be better known to become a favourite holiday resort.' Alas it was not to be and the GWR timetable planners were troubled little with amendments to the running of three weekday only trains on the branches with a slightly more intensive service between Leominster and Kington, until summer 1940 when, as France was overrun, the Titley – Eardisley branch was closed completely. After the war, the branches suffered further economies for a time when passenger services were suspended because of a major shortage of coal in 1947.

Although these branches were never more than rural, they had their importance, as was reflected in Murray's *Handbook for Travellers in South Wales:* Kington (population 3,200) 'is a favourite starting place for tourists to Aberystwyth, whither a coach runs daily, conveying passengers who are brought to Kington by the railway from Leominster.' The coaches ran via New Radnor in a glorious valley, where the railway eventually terminated some little distance from the striking village, across what is now the A44 by-pass.

It must have been known to at least some of the ambitious railway promoters of the Victorian years. For decades they dreamed of a long tunnel under the mountains at the head of the Valley to reach Aberystwyth, a busy port for timber, slates and the products of the West Indies. They were mentioned in the prospectus of the Welch Midland Junction Railway – 'Welch' being a common form of spelling in the 1840s.

But the Kington railways as developed were never more than branches and in Victorian and Edwardian times were never as attractive to the tourist as other parts of the Border Country and the Cambrian coast.

The *Thorough Guide to South Wales* written by Ward and

Baddeley, 1908 edition, quickly dismissed the lines from Eardisley to Kington, New Radnor and Presteigne.

These branches traverse an undulating agricultural district of no interest to the tourist.

The single line north from Eardisley to Titley joined the Kington branches to the Hereford Hay & Brecon Railway of the Midland, which was rather more important because of being a through route between the Midlands and South Wales. Hereford (Barr's Court) and Swansea (St Thomas) were $79^1/_4$ miles apart yet for many years, two of the four trains over the HH & B ran that distance in charge of Midland 0–4–4 tanks. Just over an hour was allowed between Hereford and Three Cocks, where the station was noted for its refreshment room, and $4^1/_4$ hours for the entire journey. Tourists often changed at Three Cocks for the Mid Wales Railway, although in summer there were through carriages between Hereford and Aberystwyth via Llanidloes, a middle of the day journey taking about five hours.

It was mentioned in the *Thorough Guide to South Wales* which stated in 1908 that

The railway from Hay to Pontrilas has disappeared from *Bradshaw's*.

This was better known as the Golden Valley Railway, which despite its name, lived a rather precarious existence and had closed temporarily for several years. But it was back in *Bradshaw's* by 1901 and seven years later that timetable was showing the 18 $^3/_4$ mile branch, by then GWR owned, as having three weekday trains.

It can claim to have had a more successful, and certainly less eccentric existence, than the Bishop's Castle Railway, the last line mentioned in the chapter about lines in the Marches.

The final chapters are devoted to lines north of the Severn: Great Western to Nantwich and Crewe; Chester, and to the Irish Sea at West Kirby. A line which ran across the gentle countryside of North Shropshire for much of its route to feed traffic to and from Wales was the LNWR branch from Stafford to Wellington, a distance of almost 19 miles. Trains ran through to Shrewsbury, calling at three intermediate stations on the LNWR and GWR Joint Line. They closed on 7 September 1964 when passenger services between Stafford and Wellington ended.

The branch offered an alternative route between London and Shrewsbury to the GWR through the West Midlands, but it was never one likely to have been entertained by the sane traveller, and would have been something of an endurance test for the enthusiast.

About the time of Nationalisation in 1948, the London Midland Region offered five trains on weekdays and one on Sundays, with a change at Stafford. The first left Euston at two minutes past midnight. It was a sleeper to Crewe, which took a leisurely route through Northampton and Birmingham to reach Stafford at 4.21 am. The traveller then had a wait of two hours 59 minutes before departure of his connection, which after calling at ten intermediate stations, reached Shrewsbury at 8.32 am.

But it is possible to end mention of the Stafford branch on a satisfactory note for the service was in a table which extended from Stafford to Welshpool over, of course, the Shrewsbury & Welshpool Joint Line, which has survived into the age of 'Sprinters'.

Because the Shrewsbury & Birmingham has a passenger service, recently strengthened by the opening of Telford station, it is hard to recall the hey day of Wellington's passenger services. That to Stafford was the last of four to be withdrawn. First had been those to Coalport, over another LNWR branch, which stopped in 1952.

Ten summers later, GWR Prairie tanks, including the small wheel 44XX, were relieved of the need to work passenger trains to Much Wenlock over the branch which until the end of 1951 had taken them through to Craven Arms.

16

Wellington's three – road GWR shed was splendidly sited just across a handful of sidings from the station and carriage window 'cops' were possible.

Its run down was gradual and its workload was eased by the end of passenger trains to Nantwich and Crewe. Until 1937

**Table 87** WELLINGTON, OAKENGATES, and COALPORT (Third class only)

| Miles | Week Days only | a.m | a.m | | p.m | p.m | p.m | p.m | |
|---|---|---|---|---|---|---|---|---|---|
| | Wellington .......... dep | 8 4 | 10 2 | .. | 1 40 | 3 55 | 6 30 | 9 15 | .. |
| 1¼ | Hadley | 8 10 | 10 6 | .. | 1 44 | 3 59 | 6 35 | 9 19 | .. |
| 3¼ | Oakengates | 8 18 | 1014 | .. | 1 52 | 4 8 | 6 44 | 9 27 | .. |
| 4¾ | Malins Lee | 8 23 | 1019 | .. | 1 57 | 4 13 | 6 49 | 9 32 | .. |
| 6 | Dawley & Stirchley | 8 27 | 1023 | .. | 2 1 | 4 18 | 6 53 | 9 36 | .. |
| 7½ | Madeley Market | 8 32 | 1028 | .. | 2 6 | 4 23 | 6 58 | 9 41 | .. |
| 9½ | Coalport N .......... arr | 8 37 | 1033 | .. | 2 11 | 4 28 | 7 3 | 9 46 | .. |

| Miles | Week Days only | a.m | a.m | a.m T | a.m U | p.m | p.m | p.m |
|---|---|---|---|---|---|---|---|---|
| | Coalport .......... dep | 6 22 | 8 50 | 1123 | 1157 | 2 35 | 4 40 | 7 40 |
| 2 | Madeley Market | 6 28 | 8 56 | 1129 | 12 3 | 2 41 | 4 46 | 7 46 |
| 3½ | Dawley & Stirchley | 6 33 | 9 1 | 1134 | 12 8 | 2 46 | 4 51 | 7 51 |
| 4¾ | Malins Lee | 6 37 | 9 5 | 1138 | 1212 | 2 50 | 4 55 | 7 55 |
| 6¼ | Oakengates | 6 41 | 9 9 | 1142 | 1216 | 2 55 | 5 0 | 8 0 |
| 8¼ | Hadley | 6 47 | 9 15 | 1148 | 1222 | 3 1 | 5 7 | 8 6 |
| 9½ | Wellington .......... arr | 6 52 | 9 20 | 1155 | 1227 | 3 6 | 5 12 | 8 13 |

**N** About 200 yards to W.R. Station. **T** Thursdays only. **U** Except Thursdays.
For **OTHER TRAINS** between Wellington and Hadley, see Table 85.

**Table 88** SHREWSBURY and MINSTERLEY

| Miles | Week Days only | a.m | | | p.m | | | p.m | | | | | | | | | | | | | | | | | |
|---|---|---|---|---|---|---|---|---|---|---|---|---|---|---|---|---|---|---|---|---|---|---|---|---|---|
| | Shrewsbury .......... dep | 7 20 | .. | .. | 1 23 | .. | .. | 6 20 | .. | .. | .. | .. | .. | .. | .. | .. | .. | .. | .. | .. | .. | .. | .. | .. | .. |
| 5 | Hanwood | 7 33 | .. | .. | 1 34 | .. | .. | 6 30 | .. | .. | .. | .. | .. | .. | .. | .. | .. | .. | .. | .. | .. | .. | .. | .. | .. |
| 7 | Plealey Road | .. | .. | .. | 1 40 | .. | .. | 6 36 | .. | .. | .. | .. | .. | .. | .. | .. | .. | .. | .. | .. | .. | .. | .. | .. | .. |
| 8½ | Pontesbury | 7 44 | .. | .. | 1 44 | .. | .. | 6 40 | .. | .. | .. | .. | .. | .. | .. | .. | .. | .. | .. | .. | .. | .. | .. | .. | .. |
| 10 | Minsterley .......... arr | 7 49 | .. | .. | 1 49 | .. | .. | 6 46 | .. | .. | .. | .. | .. | .. | .. | .. | .. | .. | .. | .. | .. | .. | .. | .. | .. |

| Miles | Week Days only | a.m | | | p.m | | | p.m | | | | | | | | | | | | | | | | | |
|---|---|---|---|---|---|---|---|---|---|---|---|---|---|---|---|---|---|---|---|---|---|---|---|---|---|
| | Minsterley .......... dep | 8 5 | .. | .. | 2 0 | .. | .. | 7 15 | .. | .. | .. | .. | .. | .. | .. | .. | .. | .. | .. | .. | .. | .. | .. | .. | .. |
| 1½ | Pontesbury | 8 10 | .. | .. | 2 5 | .. | .. | 7 20 | .. | .. | .. | .. | .. | .. | .. | .. | .. | .. | .. | .. | .. | .. | .. | .. | .. |
| 3 | Plealey Road | 8 14 | .. | .. | 2 9 | .. | .. | 7 24 | .. | .. | .. | .. | .. | .. | .. | .. | .. | .. | .. | .. | .. | .. | .. | .. | .. |
| 5 | Hanwood | 8 21 | .. | .. | 2 14 | .. | .. | 7 29 | .. | .. | .. | .. | .. | .. | .. | .. | .. | .. | .. | .. | .. | .. | .. | .. | .. |
| 10 | Shrewsbury .......... arr | 8 31 | .. | .. | 2 25 | .. | .. | 7 42 | .. | .. | .. | .. | .. | .. | .. | .. | .. | .. | .. | .. | .. | .. | .. | .. | .. |

For **OTHER TRAINS** between Shrewsbury and Hanwood, see Table 85.

**Table 89** WOOFFERTON and TENBURY WELLS

| Miles | Week Days only | | a.m 3 | | a.m V | a.m 3 | a.m | a.m V | | p.m V | | p.m 3 | | p.m | | p.m | | p.m S | | |
|---|---|---|---|---|---|---|---|---|---|---|---|---|---|---|---|---|---|---|---|---|
| | Woofferton .......... dep | Dep Leominster 7 25 a.m. | 7 40 | Dep Ludlow 7 25 a.m. | 8 9 | 8 30 | 10 5 | 1150 | .. | 3 47 | Dep Ludlow 4 20 p.m. | 4 30 | .. | 5 55 | .. | 7 55 | .. | 9 45 | .. | .. |
| 2¾ | Easton Court B | | 7 46 | | 8 15 | 8 36 | 1011 | 1156 | .. | 3 53 | | 4 36 | .. | 6 1 | .. | 8 1 | .. | 9 51 | .. | .. |
| 5¼ | Tenbury Wells .......... arr | | 7 50 | | 8 19 | 8 40 | 1015 | 12 0 | .. | 3 57 | | 4 40 | .. | 6 5 | .. | 8 5 | .. | 9 55 | .. | .. |

| Miles | Week Days only | a.m 3 | | a.m 3 | | a.m | | a.m V | | | p.m V | | p.m 3 | | p.m C | | p.m D | | p.m V | | p.m S | | |
|---|---|---|---|---|---|---|---|---|---|---|---|---|---|---|---|---|---|---|---|---|---|---|---|
| | Tenbury Wells .......... dep | 7 58 | .. | 8 45 | . | 9 40 | .. | 11 9 | .. | .. | 3 10 | .. | 4 46 | .. | 5 28 | .. | 5 40 | .. | 7 14 | .. | 9 23 | .. | .. |
| 2½ | Easton Court B | 8 3 | .. | 8 50 | . | 9 45 | .. | 1114 | .. | .. | 3 15 | .. | 4 51 | .. | 5 33 | .. | 5 45 | .. | 7 19 | .. | 9 28 | .. | .. |
| 5¼ | Woofferton .......... arr | 8 8 | .. | 8 55 | . | 9 50 | .. | 1119 | .. | .. | 3 20 | .. | 4 56 | .. | 5 38 | .. | 5 50 | .. | 7 24 | .. | 9 33 | .. | .. |

**B** Station for Little Hereford. **C** Fridays and Saturdays. **D** Except Fridays and Saturdays.
**S** Saturdays only. **V** Third class only, limited accommodation. **3** Third class only.

Two LNWR services of almost equal distance closed down soon after nationalisation: Coalport and Minsterley. The tables are from early London Midland timetables of 27 September 1948 'until further notice'. Compare the much more generous service shown in the bottom table with that shown on page 77.

the local trains were often worked by *Barnum* class engines, which were the longest lived of Dean's 2-4-0 tender locomotives. At Crewe, the sight of GWR locomotives in the south bays on the down side provided a pleasant reminder that the LMS did not quite have a monopoly there. The Wellington – Crewe passenger service was (with Shrewsbury – Worcester), an autumn 1963 casualty.

Although Wellington shed closed in 1964, steam was seen on the Shrewsbury & Birmingham line for a year or two more.

One of the three intermediate wayside stations between Shrewsbury and Wellington was at Walcot, which achieved national prominence for a time when it was selected as a site for a major marshalling yard in the 1960s, only to be rather hastily forgotten when block trains came into fashion.

Part of its traffic would have been routed over the Wellington and Nantwich secondary line via Market Drayton. It was an unspectacular route which kept company for part of the way with the Shropshire Union Canal.

Audlem station was in a spectacular situation on a ledge looking across the Cheshire Plain towards Whitchurch. It is now the site of several detached houses. Railway and canal parted company at Audlem, being separated by a ridge.

The station proved troublesome in at least two ways. It was lit by gas, but in 1922 there was a note in a company report stating that 'owing to the bad quality of the gas and the high price, there is a proposal under consideration to use oil instead'. Parcels collection and delivery was 'performed by an Agent'. The Report explained that this could not be done by the station staff 'owing to the distance the village is from the station'.

Audlem, which keeps in the tourist eye with an ambitious and delightful colour leaflet of its history and trails, is on the southern boundary of Cheshire.

In Cheshire I am in my native County and so was delighted to discover that the GWR County class 4-6-0 proudly carrying that title outlived the rest of the class. I find it easy to draw from its railways immense pleasure and occasional inspiration, which are the compensations of middle age. No books, maps or timetables are needed to prod memories of *Cauliflowers* – LNWR 0-6-0 tender locomotives which looked ancient even when I was a boy – leaving the bays at the south end of Chester General for Whitchurch along a branch which, after closure, Cheshire County Councillors consigned to the railway wilderness by rejecting suggestions that it might become a walkway. It would be too uninteresting they said.

Quite right, for Cheshire has far better walking country, not least on the hills alongside the branch around Broxton.

Waverton, the only intermediate station on the Chester & Crewe used by the branch trains has long been closed, as have the four other stations on the main line, although Waverton's striking building has escaped demolition. The Whitchurch local trains were also pulled by LMS class 2 4-4-0's, stately locomotives which also added power and dignity to local trains which used the north bays at Chester (General) with trains to Mold, Denbigh, Ruthin and Corwen; other trains of my childhood, about which I wrote affectionately in *Forgotten Railways: North & Mid Wales* (volume 4).

The train shed they used at Chester has been preserved and restored and now you can park under a piece of Chester's Victorian history. Birkenhead – Paddington expresses which often reversed in the north bay have long gone, together with their terminal at Birkenhead (Woodside) closes 5 November 1967. Earlier that year, Chester lost its Paddington sleeping car service. It ran to and from Birkenhead (Woodside) via Birmingham (Snow Hill).

The former LMS and GWR scene at Chester that has long passed into history is compounded of things less obvious than the withdrawal of services. Gone is the control room on the first floor of the main building, where I sometimes used to pop in for a chat about the night's operating. Gone is the station's main buffet and bar, a stately home in miniature with a sense of the baronial enhanced by a roaring fire, a room in which I once waited to make a midnight footplate run with *The Irish Mail* down the Welsh coast.

The buffet is astonishingly well remembered, especially by men who used it in wartime. Home baked scones are as evocative to a friend as any of the trains he caught.

The only trains that ran non-stop through the station were goods, often bound to and from Saltney Yard, just beyond the junction of the Wrexham and Holyhead routes. It had a capacity, rarely taxed, of 2,000 wagons a day. For years the Lower Yard lay across the main road from Chester to North Wales and three keepers, who operated the gates by hand, were known to incur drivers' wrath. The crossing also provided access to the short Dee branch beside the river. Small ships had ceased using the wharfs by the early 1920's but traffic to works, including a shipbuilding yard, kept the branch open for many years.

The Dee branch must be among the most insignificant and unknown cross border branches. Tracing its route, including the bridge where it passed under the Chester & Holyhead, you are reminded of the border's presence at Saltney by the atmosphere of the village. Just over a mile into Wales, on the B5129 is the site of Saltney Ferry station and Mold Junction locomotive shed, now a scrap dealers. Immediately beyond the Mold branch curved away. Near Lower Kinnerton it crossed back into Cheshire for about half a mile before regaining Welsh soil for the rest of its route. *Forgotten Railways: North & Mid Wales* (volume 4).

Lament on a wider and grander scale than that for the scones, embraces the fortunes of a line, the start of which was on an embankment which could be glimpsed from the north end of Chester General. It was the Great Central route into North Wales which began at Chester East Junction, immediately west of where the Cheshire Lines route from Manchester crossed the Chester & Birkenhead at the tip of the triangle north of General station.

The very presence of the Great Central in North Wales, and its approaches to it, has excited enthusiasts for years. They revere it as a highly unusual outpost, full of character.

At Chester East Junction, Cheshire Lines passenger trains

from Manchester – often headed by *Director* class 4–4–0s – curved south into Chester Northgate, a barn of a station. What must environment conscious passengers, who joined trains amid the spacious glory of Manchester Central, have thought of Northgate?

Northgate's other passenger service was in the opposite direction to Shotton and Wrexham, and a most uninviting tin sheltered station at Central. But it had the advantage of being closer to the town's heart than the far pleasanter General station, which, since the end of passenger services between Wrexham and Northgate via Dee Marsh Junction, has been the station which Wrexham rail passengers have had to use for Chester.

Northgate station and the short curved and steeply graded curve to South Junction, round which Wrexham – bound trains squealed to reach the GC route begun at East Junction, closed in 1969. Manchester trains via Northwich were switched over a new junction at Mickle Trafford and ran to Manchester (Oxford Road) from General station.

Soon after closure Chester City Council spent £5 million on a leisure centre which retains the name Northgate, not because of the station, but rather because of the historic gateway through the City Walls close by.

Northgate as a station is not worthy of memory – better to rejoice in the pleasure of Chester General. Yet even the sight of a few old station railings and a dozen brick arches incorporated into the car park of the leisure centre are enough for me to recall it with affection. For it was my boyhood gateway to a city which, above all others, I have loved ever since.

A day's outing from home in Wallasey invariably meant a change at Hawarden Bridge or Shotton (High Level) – from where you could watch the North Wales expresses thundering by. You found yourself in the same type of compartment coach, but with a different engine at the head, although the C13 4–4–2 and N7 tanks were common to both routes.

The Dee Marsh Junction – Chester route opened in 1890,

21

just within the lifetime of my father, who outlived its passenger service by several years. I researched it after it closed
completely in 1984 when enthusiasts were attempting to reopen it to steam as a tourist attraction against the wishes of
local authorities which wanted part for a road and the rest for
a cycle track. The conflicting aspirations soon came to grief
because in September 1986, it was reopened to handle steel
coil trains between Shotton's modern mill and Scotland. The
future of the line remains a little uncertain for there is talk
that in several years time the route may be closed again.

Some years ago, the idea was mooted of building a spur
to allow trains from Chester General to be diverted to run
over the Great Central line to Wrexham, the attraction being
that it served intermediate stations in a number of growing
villages. There now seems little likelihood of that happening,
or of the reopening by British Rail of the Dee Marsh Junction
route to passengers so it qualifies for inclusion in this book as
a half-forgotten railway.

That footplate trip on the *Irish Mail* took me under the
Great Central at Shotton. In the excitement of enjoying the
night footplate, I never gave it a thought, but as we ran beside
the ever widening Dee estuary, intermittently illuminated by
a full moon as it played hide and seek with snow clouds, I
did think about the single branch that ran along the Cheshire
shore of the estuary on part of its 12 $^1/_2$ mile route between
Hooton and West Kirby.

It went to sleep every night until the 6.17 am stirred from
West Kirby and ran south, not stopping at Kirby Park, on
the outskirts of West Kirby, or its neighbour, Caldy, serving
a small and widely scattered village. It was not rail linked to
the day until almost 8 am.

The branch closed to passengers in 1956 and to goods
in 1962 and the scene was set for it to become one of Britain's best known forgotten railways in its role as The Wirral
Country Park, one of the first created under the Countryside
Act of 1968.

Nowadays it receives about half a million visitors a year

and the little station at Hadlow Road is busier as a restored example of a country station, than ever it was as a real one.

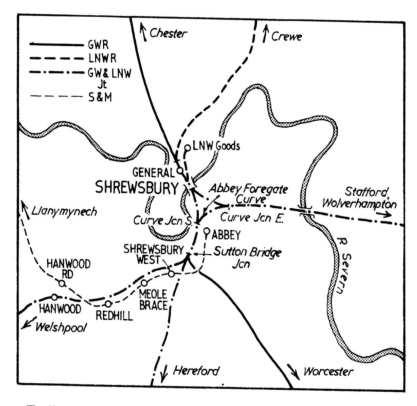

Traffic, rather than routes, has been the main economy at Shrewsbury, where the main-line network remains intact. As this book went to press, the section of the Shropshire & Montgomeryshire to Abbey oil depot closed (on 15 July 1988).

CHAPTER 2

# Shrewsbury & District

*Expresses – And Stations They Never Used*

Shrewsbury is a place where there are perhaps more forgotten services than branches: a visit to Severn Bridge Junction signal box made the point strongly. No longer did the long lever frames almost in the heavens overlooking the south end of the station, click and crash by the minute as a succession of trains, passenger and goods, rumbled by on the lines below. Periods of silence replaced 'paths' including those once occupied by expresses on two of Britain's notable routes; from Paddington to Birkenhead, and Scotland to the West of England via the Severn Tunnel.

No longer could a privileged visitor look down on *Castles*, often with pilot and tenders piled high with coal and roaring fires departing majestically to pound the banks of Shropshire and beyond.

Both services have been Shrewsbury's heaviest casualties, but not all has been lost, for the box still handles expresses arriving from Euston, not Paddington, to terminate in the station, and there are still semi-fast services on the Welsh Border route.

Shrewsbury's losses have been mainly of local passenger services. Minsterley branch trains ceased on 5 February 1951 and those to Bewdley through the Severn Valley on 9 September 1963. A year later, on 7 September 1964, Shrewsbury–Stafford services were withdrawn.

The last economy brought about the demise of two stations

on the Shrewsbury & Wellington Joint line: Walcot ($6^1/_4$ miles) and Admaston ($8^3/_4$). Upton Magna ($3^3/_4$) had closed a year earlier. The LNWR and GWR ran their own trains between Shrewsbury and Wellington, although some were regarded as Joint for what they termed 'local purposes'.

Complications did not end there because receipts for Joint traffic were unevenly divided. The GWR took $53^3/_4$ per cent, the LNWR the balance.

### Shrewsbury & Hereford: local stations

Shrewsbury's passenger traffic further declined, although not to any appreciable extent, with the withdrawal of local passenger services between Shrewsbury & Hereford from 9 June 1958. It was an economy that decimated Table 166 in Western Region timetables. Stations closed to passengers were Condover ($4^1/_4$ miles from Shrewsbury), Dorrington ($6^1/_4$), Leebotwood ($9^1/_2$), All Stretton Halt ($11^1/_4$) Little Stretton Halt ($13^3/_4$), Marsh Brook ($15^1/_4$), Onibury ($22^3/_4$), Bromfield (25), Berrington & Eye (35), Dinmore ($43^3/_4$), and Moreton-on–Lugg ($46^1/_2$).

Woofferton survived the end of the service to Tenbury Wells on 31 July 1961. There had been earlier economies, Wistanstow Halt ($18^1/_2$ miles from Shrewsbury) had closed on 11 June 1956, and earlier, on 5 April 1954, Ford Bridge ($40^3/_4$) had qualified for an asterisk in the timetable stating 'Station closed. Omnibus service available'.

Some of the stations which remained open to passengers until 1958 also had footnotes, which gave an indication that they were little used, for some trains only stopped at Condover, Leebotwood, All Stretton, Marsh Brook, Wistanstow Halt, Onibury and Bromfield on notice being given to the guard.

Shrewsbury & Hereford
The early hour service on the Welsh Border joint main line shows a traditional mixture of stopping services, semi-fasts and North-to-South expresses with restaurant cars in 1927.

**Crewe, Whitchurch,**     **486**     **Shrewsbury, and Hereford.**

UP.    CREWE, WHITCHURCH, SHREWSBURY, CRAVEN ARMS, and HEREFORD.—L. M. & S. and G. W.

Week Days.

| | | |
|---|---|---|
| | North and West Express. | **Fridays and Saturdays.** Restaurant Car, Liverpool (Lime Street) to Taunton. |
| | North and West Express. | Restaurant Car, Liverpool (Lime Street) to Plymouth. |
| | Through Carriage, Manchester (London Road) to Ilfracombe, see page 13. | Restaurant Car, Manchester (L. Rd.) to Paignton (arr. 5 20 aft.), see pages 13 and 24. |
| | **Saturdays only.** | |
| | North and West Express. | Restaurant Car, Liverpool (Lime Street) to Plymouth. |
| | Restaurant Car, Manchester to Kingswear, see pages 120, 13, and 24. | North and West Express. |
| | **Saturdays only.** | |
| | One class only. | Through Carriage, Manchester (London Road) to Aberystwyth, see page 136. |
| | **Saturdays only.** | North and West Express. |
| | **Except Mondays.** | **Mondays only.** |
| | **Except Mons.** | **Mondays only.** North and West Express. |
| | **Mondays only.** | **Mondays only.** North and West Express. |
| | Through Carriages, Glasgow to Penzance, via Carlisle and Severn Tunnel, see pages 732, 440, 120, 12, and 22. | **Except Mondays.** North and West Express. |
| | | **Except Mondays.** North & South Wales Express. |
| | Friday nights and Saturday mornings. | North and West Express. |

| Miles from Crewe. | |
|---|---|
| | 437 GLASGOW (Central) .... dep. |
| | 437 EDINBRO' (Princes Street) " |
| | 437 CARLISLE " |
| | 533 LEEDS (New) " |
| | 543 LIVERPOOL (Lime Street) " |
| | 522 MANCHESTER (Lon. Rd.) " |
| | 411 LONDON (Euston) " |
| | 499 BIRKENHEAD (Woodside) " |
| | 499 CHESTER (Gen. L.&N.W. " |
| — | Crewe (Central) .... dep. |
| 2¼ | Willaston |
| 4 | Nantwich |
| 9 | Wrenbury |
| 13¾ | Whitchurch 136, 619 .... arr. |
| | 518 BIRKENHEAD (Woodside) dep. |
| | 975 CHESTER (Gen. L.&N.W.) " |
| | Whitchurch |
| 19¾ | Prees |
| 22½ | Wem |
| 28 | Yorton |
| 29 | Hadnall |
| 32¾ | Shrewsbury A 108, 111 arr. |
| | 485 LONDON (Euston) .... dep. |
| | 98 " (Paddington) " |
| | 485 BIRMINGHAM (New St.) " |
| | 975 CHESTER (Gen. L.&N.W.) " |
| | 445 STAFFORD (Snow Hill) " |
| | 111 LIVERPOOL (Landing Stg) " |
| | 111 BIRKENHEAD (Woodside) " |
| | 111 CHESTER (General, G.W.) " |
| | Shrewsbury (General) .... dep. |
| 36½ | Condover |
| 39 | Dorrington |
| 43 | Leebotwood |
| 46 | Church Stretton |
| 48 | Marsh Brook |
| 51 | Craven Arms & Stokesay arr. / dep. |
| 59½ | Onibury |
| 57½ | Bromfield |
| 59 | Ludlow 97 |
| 64 | Woofferton 97 |
| 67 | Berrington and Eye |
| 70½ | Leominster 96, 130 |
| 73 | Dinmore |
| 78½ | Ford Bridge |
| 79 | Moreton-on-Lugg |
| 84½ | Hereford 79, 120, 123 arr. |
| 136 | MERTHYR |
| 129½ | NEWPORT (High Street) " |
| 117½ | CARDIFF (Temple Meads) " |
| 183 | BRISTOL (Temple Meade) " |
| 229½ | EXETER (St. David's) " |
| 281½ | PLYMOUTH (North Road) " |
| 22 | " (Millbay) " |
| 360 | PENZANCE " |

27

This procedure was not necessary on all trains to Bromfield for this was the station for Ludlow racecourse, alongside the line, and special services ran during meetings.

The prospect of a stopping train journey between Shrewsbury and Hereford must have been daunting, for while trains did not call at all stations, they still took 2 hours. Today, the Manchester – Cardiff services take half that time between Shrewsbury and Hereford, stopping at Church Stretton, Craven Arms, Ludlow and Leominster.

Until 1951, a single road engine shed at Ludlow stabled locomotives of both companies, working traffic from the Clee Hill branch and local passenger services. Some on the Joint Line ran only between Shrewsbury and Ludlow.

### Shrewsbury & Chester Local Services

The second day of May 1960 brought closure of Hadnall station, nearly five miles north of Shrewsbury. It remains the only one on the Shrewsbury & Crewe in the Shrewsbury area to have closed. Willaston, between Crewe and Nantwich, closed to passengers 6 September 1954, has been the only other station closed on that line.

More significantly, Shrewsbury lost its links with 13 stations and halts at the start of winter services from 12 September 1960. Seven were in North Shropshire in the eighteen miles to Gobowen and its ornate station, now restored to its former glory.

They were Leaton ($3^3/_4$ miles from Shrewsbury), Oldwoods Halt ($5^1/_2$), Baschurch ($7^3/_4$), Stanwardine Halt ($9^1/_4$), Haughton Halt (12), Rednal & West Felton ($13^1/_2$) and Whittington (Low Level) ($16^1/_4$), where the High Level station on the former Cambrian main line between Oswestry Ellesmere and Whitchurch was closed when passenger services were withdrawn on 18 January 1965.

Whittington was an unusual boundary in GWR terms for Low Level station was in the Chester Division while High Level was attached to the Central Wales. The Low

In Shropshire Hills: *Plate 1 (above)* Pannier tank No 4678 slowly pounds the 1 in 20 gradient to Bitterley yard with a train of empty wagons. *Plate 2 (below).* Bitterley. Line left middle leads to Yard, on a higher level. Rope worked incline, right.

Shropshire Variety: *Plate 3 (above)* The Shropshire & Montgomeryshire locomotive shed at Kinnerley, 1938. A scene epitomising the rural railway between the two World Wars. *Plate 4 (below)* Almost two decades later, the mid-morning scene at Buildwas on 29 April 1957 with two trains in the Severn Valley line platforms waiting to connect with two more. A streamlined railcar is working the 10.50 am Bewdley–Shrewsbury and Pannier tank No 4614, the 11.25 am Shrewsbury–Hartlebury.

Level station master supervised the staff and station at High Level.

Some of the character of lines that remain open was sapped away by the closure not only of stations, but of their goods yards and signal boxes. Typical, perhaps, was Rednal & West Felton, where two sidings for a total of 35 wagons, and accommodation for four horse boxes on the Down side, were considered inadequate at Grouping. Local goods trains had to cross from one main line to the other 'very frequently' to allow through trains to pass. Proposals were formulated for extra sidings, but it was felt that the cost could not be justified.

Goods traffic was often the reason why wayside stations were profitable: at Rednal, general merchandise, manure, cattle, horses and a considerable volume of timber produced receipts seven times greater than those for passengers, which were only a little ahead of receipts for parcels.

A mile and a half closer to Shrewsbury were Haughton Sidings with a Loop and Refuge able to take a total of 96 wagons. Two men worked the box under the supervision of the Rednal station master. The oil lamps were maintained by the Shrewsbury signal lampman.

There was nothing at Haughton Sidings to single them out for especial historic attention, but there might have been because before Grouping, the GWR

carried out boring operations near this place with a view to providing water troughs, but it has not been practicable to obtain an adequate supply of water.

The troughs would have been some 12 miles north of Shrewsbury and their value would have been in reducing station delays at Shrewsbury when locomotives had to take water.

The other six stations closed on 12 September 1960 comprised all the intermediate ones between Shrewsbury and Welshpool. Nearest Shrewsbury was Hanwood ($4^3/_4$ miles), which had lost its other passenger service, to Minsterley, nine years earlier. Yockleton, which became a halt in 1956, was at

$7^1/_2$ miles; Westbury, the only crossing place on the section today, 11 miles; Plas-y-Court Halt ($13^1/_4$); Breidden (14) and Buttington (17). Buttington's Cambrian platforms on the Welshpool Oswestry and Whitchurch route also closed on the same day, marking the disappearance of one of Britain's biggest, remotest and surely least used four platform stations.

All the stations closed in 1960 had survived far longer than two stopping places at the Shrewsbury approaches. Their closure many years ago never affected passenger traffic, except perhaps to reduce the number of fare dodgers. The economies were those of the ticket platforms at English Bridge for Welshpool and Minsterley and Hereford and Severn Valley trains, closed 31 May 1899 and Abbey Foregate, less than half a mile away, closed on 30 September 1912. It was used by trains on the Wellington line.

### Shrewsbury: Goods Yards

The only purely GWR goods yards were at Coton Hill, a quarter of a mile north of the station and half that distance from the end-on junction between the Shrewsbury & Chester and the Joint Line. Designated as Coton Hill (North), a yard survives, a shadow of its former size.

In GWR days, Coton Hill had a class 1 yardmaster who supervised Castle Foregate Yard, with which it was connected, and also Coleham, south of the station. Coton Hill was a veritable goods hub, handling 75 daily trains to and from Shrewsbury & Hereford, Welshpool, Minsterley, Severn Valley, Wellington and Chester lines, in addition to LMS traffic routed via Crewe.

Coton Hill was operated by the Traffic Department and had a staff of 80. One of its four shunting locomotives worked Castle Foregate Yard, which lay in the fork of the Chester and Crewe lines. It was run by the Goods Department with a staff of 63. Apart from general goods, mineral and timber traffic, it handled a large volume of cattle from twice weekly sales.

## Coton Hill Carriage Repair Shop

Most substantial relic of Shrewsbury's locomotive sheds is that which Brassey built for the Shrewsbury & Chester at Coton. After the GWR concentrated locomotives at Coleham, the shed became a carriage repair shop.

Monday mornings were among the busiest times for it was then that 'vehicles' – the GWR's terminology – were shunted in and out of the shop and its sidings using a 'special shunting engine provided by the Locomotive Department'. The Carriage Department staff helped the Traffic Department shunter with the work.

In the 1920s, nearly 400 carriages and wagons went through the Shop and 1,000 more needing less attention, were repaired in the Yard. About 100 road vehicles a year were repaired at the Shop, which had a permanent staff of 46 men under a C & W Department foreman. After closure, the Shop became a warehouse and later a National Carriers Depot.

Coton Hill marshalling yard was an important centre for the distribution of passenger and goods rolling stock and the Chester Division Rolling Stock Office used to telephone nightly orders for up to 190 vehicles.

The Coleham yard grew from being the Shrewsbury & Hereford depot and became a permanent way depot after closure to goods traffic in August 1966. It was awkward to work, London Midland *Appendixes* noting that

Trains must set back from the down main line with great care to avoid wagons becoming derailed. Any necessary shunting must be performed in the shunting neck and not through the crossings.

'Yard' was perhaps a misnomer in the sense that it had only a goods shed and six sidings, used for interchange traffic in Joint company days. The capacity was 194 wagons, according to a track alteration plan approved at the Chester Division superintendent's office on 22 February 1917. As a wartime paper economy, the plan was drawn on the back of the printed minutes of GWR Conciliation Board 'C' for guards, ballast guards, brakesmen, shunter, etc, which met at Paddington on 8 May 1914, less than three months before the outbreak of war.

The employee's side was drawn from men from all parts of the system, while that of the management was headed by Stanley Baldwin, MP, a future Prime Minister, who had inherited his father's seat on the GWR board.

Abbey Foregate to the east of the station on the Up side of the Shrewsbury & Birmingham within sight of Severn Bridge Junction box, was also a small yard. It handled a fair volume of exchange traffic with Coleham and the *Appendix* laid down detailed instructions.

It stipulated that traffic from Minsterley for Abbey Foregate, or LMS traffic for the Wellington direction, was to be taken to Abbey Foregate or Shropshire Sidings, immediately adjacent, by the engine working the Joint line freight train.

Part of the Abbey Foregate yard was made up of carriage sidings, much used until the advent of diesel sets, and it closed October 1968, within weeks of the steam sheds and the site was soon redeveloped.

### Shropshire Union Yard

Rail passengers and the traffic planners coping with the problems of a town where the road layout is restricted because of the Severn, benefitted from the abandonment of the Shropshire Union Goods Yard, for it immediately provided valuable and convenient car parking, beside the station and close to the town centre. I don't suppose many users think about its origins. It is not the happiest place in Shrewsbury. It is dominated by the jail. In one of his Shropshire Lad poems, A.E. Housman immortalised prisoners who listened to the trains through the night. For years, the building's presence was acknowledged in the *Appendix:*

If there is no engine in the yard the traffic for Wellington and beyond must be shunted on to the coal sidings adjacent to the horse landing, and the traffic for Shrewsbury proper must be shunted on the wall siding which runs parallel with the Gaol.

Conversion to a car park gave the site its third use, for the Yard was built by the Shropshire Union Railways & Canal Company on its original wharf.

The Yard, reached by a sharp curve beginning alongside the station's most easterly platform, and passing under Howard Street, consisted of a fan of six sidings for coal trucks, horse wagons and vans using a landing, and a warehouse. It closed on 5 April 1971.

Another building with LNWR associations which overlooks the Yard is the town's privately built butter and cheese market of 1836. This striking building was acquired by Euston in 1857 and converted into a grain warehouse, although this was not accomplished for some years. Measom's *Official Guide to the North-Western Railway* (sic), 1861 edition, still referred to the Butter and Cheese market. Shropshire Union was far from being the only local Yard to close. Harlescott, a small yard on the Crewe line opened in 1943 to relieve wartime congestion, is now but a memory, having closed in 1960, when its work was transferred to Crewe.

*Coleham Locomotive Sheds*

The side by side sheds at Coleham, south of the viaduct and opposite the small goods yard, held an especial fascination for many enthusiasts because of the usually large variety of locomotives stabled there. In summer 1938, the *Railway Observer* noted that apart from a few of Stanier's 4–6–0s and Moguls 'the LMS Shed contains a fine assortment of pre-Grouping types'. the LNWR was well represented, while there were also Midland 0–6–0s, tender and tank; Lancashire & Yorkshire 0–6–0s and even a Pug 0–4–0, with which the Caledonian Railway maintained a presence.

But it is by its GWR engines that Coleham is best remembered, especially the *Star* and later, *Castle* 4–6–0s which helped to turn into reality holidays on the Cornish Riviera and in 'Glorious Devon', which notherners booked after reading *GWR Holiday Haunts* on long winter evenings. Coleham's humbler locomotives handled goods as well as passenger trains. The allocation of smaller locomotives included, in the 1930s a brace of 10 Dean Goods 0–6–0s, and veteran Midland and Lancashire & Yorkshire 0–6–0s, subsequently replaced by Collett's *2251* class.

The Coleham sheds grew from a small one built by the Shrewsbury & Hereford which was taken over by the two large companies in 1862. Because of strained relations, the LNWR built its own shed alongside the original one in 1877 and soon afterwards the GWR added its own roundhouse alongside.

Eventually some 200 locomotives were shedded at Coleham, but by the time steam working officially ceased from 6 March 1967, less than 30 were left. The depot continued as a diesel depot for another three years. Subsequent demolition included the enginemen's lodging house in the south west corner of the site, between the turntable and the Severn Valley branch.

Rivalry had remained until the end, as Russell Mulford noted in the Bi-Centenary Souvenir of the *Shrewsbury Chronicle* of 23 November 1972

Each (company) established locomotive depots at Coleham, where, despite the joint arrangements at the station, there was great inter-company rivalry among the engine men, the pangs of which are felt by old timers to this day.

In its hey-day, the Shrewsbury shed – for the two were amalgamated on Nationalisation under Western Region, and later, London Midland control – had sub sheds scattered as far and wide from their parent depot as any in Britain. More than a dozen locomotives were often away at Craven Arms, Ludlow and Clee Hill, Coalport and Trench, Knighton and Builth Road.

Shrewsbury locomotives were sometimes stabled at the

GWR shed at Brecon, while servicing those arriving at Shrewsbury with trains on several routes including the Central Wales. A 50ft turntable on the LMS side was not its biggest in Shrewsbury for there was one 5ft longer in the triangle dominated by Severn Bridge Junction box. The turntable's disappearance left the triangle with a small yet tidy wilderness.

The end of steam on the *Cambrian Coast Express* and the Shrewsbury & Welshpool line, of course, took place on 4 March 1967 and presented enthusiasts with an unenviable dilemma. The *Railway Observer* reported that hundreds of enthusiasts thronged the station to glimpse two special trains, hauled by *Clun Castle* and *Pendennis Castle*, marking the end of Paddington – Birkenhead services.

Many diehards forsook the chance of a trip behind the Castles for the authenticity of a scheduled last run on the *Cambrian Coast Express*.

The depth of local feeling at the loss of steam was expressed in a commemoration booklet published by Shrewsbury & Atcham Borough Council called *Steam Railways in Shrewsbury*.

Another affectionate tribute is to be found in another booklet, *Shrewsbury in Steam Days* by Michael Griggs. Shropshire County Council publishes nostalgic railway books and reprints old guides while the County Record Office issues an extensive and informative list of deposited plans of canals and railways.

### *Shrewsbury – Minsterley*

Snow which was falling heavily outside my Cheshire window as I began to write about the Minsterley branch reminded me to look up the *Joint Sectional Appendix* of 1933 to find out the regulations applicable in bad weather. Fogmen, we learn, were not provided at the 'Distant Signal Posts' at Pontesbury, Plealey Road (Up and Down) and Minsterley (Down), and that they were withdrawn at Cruckmeole Junction Up distant (Minsterley Line) between 9 pm and 8.15 am – a few minutes before the first up train, the 8.5 am from Minsterley, was due.

The snow fell on 5 February 1986, which happened to be the 35th anniversary of the withdrawal of the three weekday only trains. They were allowed 26m for the 10 miles between Shrewsbury and Minsterley with three intermediate stops, the first at Hanwood near Cruckmeole Junction, where the branch trains left the single line of the Shrewsbury & Welshpool Joint, to make the last half of their journey through the quietly attractive valley of the Rea Brook, dominated by Pontesbury Hill, just over 1,000 feet above sea level and some 700 ft above the floor of the green and fertile valley.

The $9^1/_2$ miles between Sutton Bridge Junction with the Shrewsbury & Hereford at Shrewsbury, and Minsterley formed the first section of what became the Shrewsbury & Welshpool Joint.

It opened on 14 February 1861 and it was almost another year before the $11^1/_2$ miles from Cruckmeole Junction to the Oswestry & Newtown at Buttington opened on 27 January 1862. The company reached Welshpool with running powers over the Oswestry & Newtown. *Forgotten Railways: North & Mid Wales* (volume 4).

With the Earl of Powis as chairman, the Shrewsbury & Welshpool, including the Minsterley branch, had been incorporated in 1856 and was acquired jointly by the GWR and LNWR in 1865 when they began running through coaches between London and the Cambrian coast via the Cambrian Railways, formed by the amalgamation of several companies the year before.

Through the years, LNWR and LMS timetablers accorded the Minsterley branch better status than did the GWR and its successors. While the LNWR gave the branch its own table, the GWR lumped it as 'WELSHPOOL, MINSTERLEY & CAMBRIAN LINES' in a table stretching from Paddington to Aberystwyth. However, the four weekday trains which ran for many years were easy enough to dig out because the services between Paddington and North West England and Aberystwyth and Barmouth were not too intensive and the table included footnote 'D' which identified the first Minsterley branch train of the day as being mixed.

The treatment accorded by the timetablers was no doubt influenced by the branch being worked by LMS locomotives and coaches. LNWR 0–6–2 coal tanks did much of the work until displaced by Fowler 2–6–2 tanks in 1948. Two other Webb classes – 5ft 6in 2–4–2 tanks and his Cauliflower 0–6–0s were among classes authorised to work the branch.

Although never heavily used, the passenger trains ran through world war 2, partly because of petrol shortages facing rural bus services, only to stop when Britain was in the middle of a coal supply crisis in winter 1951. Some years earlier Minsterley suffered an economy with the closure of a ticket platform only yards short of the terminus. It lay close to where the single line broadened into the terminal layout which included cattle and horse docks, a milk wharf and goods shed and sidings. Hanwood station stayed open until al the intermediate stations between Shrewsbury & Welshpool closed in autumn 1960.

Minsterley, LNWR timetables noted by their usual asterisks, handled horses and carriages, but it was milk, agricultural, general and above all, mineral traffic, that kept the branch profitable. Cattle traffic was often heavy, especially on Tuesday mornings when 'an additional brake van must be sent by the 8.20 am Shrewsbury to Minsterley'.

There was a granite from the hill quarries and at Pontesbury, hopper wagons of the Snailbeach Railways tipped stone into standard gauge wagons. The Pontesbury exchange sidings were also used for many years for the transhipment of lead from local mines.

Branch goods traffic which was sorted at Coleham Yard, ceased in May 1967, but the line remained open, being worked under one engine in steam regulations by BR engineers for the testing of Sentinel industrial diesel locomotives built at the Rolls Royce factory beside the Crewe line at Harlescott. The company acquired the factory in 1958 and complete locomotives were produced until the early 1970s when the work was transferred to Rotherham, and the branch was lifted in 1973.

### Snailbeach District Railways

Sadness for lost railways takes many forms, but never is the symptom stronger than when recalling narrow gauge companies, so often the individuals extraordinary of all the glorious companies, great and small, and their lines which made up the railway map of Britain before Grouping.

Some were well publicised, if not used. The Lynton & Barnstaple was no doubt among memories taken home from Devon by holidaymakers who travelled through Shropshire on West to North expresses via the Severn Tunnel. In Staffordshire, the Leek & Manifold was a gem best known to ramblers, being too far off the beaten holiday track to attract crowds.

And tucked away in the Rea Valley of a little known part of Shropshire on the lower slopes of the Stiperstones was the Snailbeach District Railways, whose plurality of title did not mislead those who discovered it into thinking it was a line of major importance.

It received few visits from enthusiasts, partly because it never carried passengers. It was built by a company in which the Snailbeach Mine was a major shareholder. The Incorporation Act of 1873 provided for a 3 mile line of 2ft 4in gauge from the Minsterley branch at Pontesbury to the mine, plus an extension of nearly 2 miles to a mine owned by the Earl of Tankerton at the south end of the Hope Valley. The extension was never built but the authorised route was laid, conquering steeply rising ground on a ruling gradient of 1 in 37 and a zig-zag run-round, rather than curve, at Crow's Nest, only a quarter of a mile short of the terminus.

The company was unpretentious and in *Bradshaw's Manual* for 1923 it noted that it had four directors, offices in Oswestry, at 3 Upper Brook Street, and its financial problems. 'No dividends have been paid, and there was a debit balance to revenue at the end of 1920 of £3,627'. It also noted that: 'In 1922, the railway which had lain derelict for some years, was reopened.' The company then had two locomotives and 45 goods vehicles.

Subsequently the line closed again, but re-opened in 1928 after passing to the control of Colonel Stephens. When he died three years later, his partner, W.H. Austen, became director and engineer and it was he who was thanked by H.F.G. Dalston when he wrote about the line in the Railway Magazine in the November & December 1944 issue.

Eighteen months later the line closed, apart from the first mile from Pontesbury to Callow Hill Quarry, which was acquired by Shropshire County Council which worked the section not by locomotive, but a farm tractor, a mode of operation which continued until line closure in 1959.

The remains could still be found a quarter of a century later when brilliant sunshine suddenly dissolved fog through which I had driven on an autumn morning after exploring the route of the Bishop's Castle Railway, another line with which Colonel Stephens had been connected. The fog rolled away to reveal, behind a protective guard of young trees, the Snailbeach engine shed, its stout stone walls now a little battered, like the doors.

It was a delightful surprise, not least because most of the Snailbeach Mine buildings, by far the biggest in Shropshire, had long gone. Here was the shed enthusiasts used to visit to see two Baldwin 4–6–0 tanks, which arrived when the line re-opened in 1923, and a 0–4–2 Kerr Stuart tank of 1902. The Baldwins had come to this rural haven from France, where they ran from new in 1915. W.G. Bagnall rebuilt and regauged them from $3/8$ inch less than 2ft 0in to the Snailbeach width.

Close to the shed there were other satisfying manifestations of the line: heavily overgrown track which end at the site of the mine; track within the shed, track which ran past it and dropped away down the hill to what used to be the junction at Lords Hill, forming the dog's leg section.

## *Ludlow & Clee Hill Railway*

Another line built to serve Shropshire hill quarries was on a far grander scale. The standard gauge Ludlow & Clee Hill Railway was launched as a private venture in 1861 to provide an outlet for large quarries being developed high on the hill. It was leased to the GWR and LNWR in 1867 and absorbed jointly on 1 January 1893 when it became the most distinctive and far-flung section of the S & H Joint.

It had three sections, each with its own individual operation and character. The bottom section, opened in 1864, ran $4^1/_2$ miles over the lower slopes of the hill from just north of Ludlow station to Bitterley Yard, created almost in a bowl hewn out of the hillside. The half way point on this section was Middleton Siding, where trains of empty mineral wagons pulled by Pannier tanks were halved if the rails were wet or slippery for the final climb into the Yard was at 1 in 20. The Panniers often rushed the gradient, but a water tower built at the gradient foot was available to drivers if needed and then the climb was taken more sedately.

The Yard was at the foot of the Clee Hill Incline (official name), completed in 1867, which rose for $1^1/_4$ miles at 1 in 12, steepening to 1 in 6 shortly before the summit; the sharp change of gradient is a feature of the trackbed today. The summit at 1,250 feet above sea level was 600 ft above the Yard.

The Incline, single like the entire branch, included a passing 'loop' where there was a common central rail. Operation was by wire rope and four wagons, with brake truck attached, were raised and lowered in a balanced operation powered by a stationary steam engine working a large drum in a house at the summit. Operating instructions were copious:

The man at the drum brake must be careful to start the descending wagons without any jerk. On no account must the trip be started by means of an engine at the bottom giving the wagons a push.

Maximum speed was 6mph and train loads were limited to 85 tons, including a dummy truck.

From the Incline top, the track continued past the stone built brake house and spread into three sidings, one of which had a transhipment dock. Opposite was a small wooden engine shed, heavily buttressed against gales which swept the exposed hillside. Beyond the sidings, the line became partly a street tramway, passing close to the A4117 before turning towards Clee Hill quarry stacking ground and a private engine shed, again for only a single locomotive. The terminus was at a crushing plant a short distance beyond.

There was also a small goods shed 924 yards from the Incline top which Sectional Appendixes noted was, like the Incline top, 'not a block post, tablet or staff station'. But it did have features useful to local people, the *Railway & Commercial Gazetteer* 1917 edition stating that Clee Hill Goods was a station with a Post Office and Money Office with telegraphic facilities.

After World War I ended, the quarries were busier than ever, despatching about 6,000 tons of roadstone a week. Most of it began its journey to sites all over Britain by being lowered down the Incline, but in the 1930s as lorries became more reliable and powerful and roads better, rail traffic began falling away.

But it remained sufficient to keep the branch open through another world war and for a decade and a half beyond until 1960 when, having been little used, it was vandalised and closed instantly, without ceremony on 10 May. Closure left the last of BR's steam locomotives marooned in the shed. It was no 1143, one of two former Swansea Harbour Trust 0-4-0 saddle tanks which found a home in the Shropshire hills. It was brought down on 14 November and, noted the Railway Observer, 'removed to Shrewsbury for disposal'. Its final journey, a month later, was, perhaps appropriately, back to South Wales and Caerphilly Works, where it was scrapped.

Clee Hill was always a fascinating place for enthusiasts, as much for the variety of the hill – top locomotives as the

Incline. The locomotives were out-shedded from Shrewsbury and all have been well documented historically by enthusiasts who spent hours at winter firesides recording details of their visits to the hill, always an occasion because until the advent of the car, it often meant a slow journey from Ludlow. The stud included an LNWR saddle tank, No 3243 of 1892. Later a vertical boilered locomotive was at work. This was no 7184 delivered from the Sentinel works at Shrewsbury in 1928. The locomotive shed was demolished soon after closure and the track lifted.

Once the Incline closed in 1960 there was little traffic between Ludlow and Bitterley Yard and it closed at the end of 1962, having fallen into disuse in mid-October.

The hill-top formation can be easily traced to a point close to the Clee Hill hotel. Beyond, its route merges into rough roads to the still-busy quarry.

### *Titterstone Quarry Incline*

Until 1952 Bitterley Yard handled traffic brought down from another major quarry high on the hill. Titterstone Quarry, belonging to British Stone Quarries, was connected by a one and a quarter mile self-acting incline with a 3ft 0in gauge line, which ran to the quarry faces and crushing plant.

The incline followed a route still shown on OS 1: 50,000 maps and the remains of the system are worth visiting. The trackbed is easily found by taking a lane climbing away from the north side of the overgrown site of Bitterley Yard.

Just beyond a row of cottages are the remains of a stone bridge that carried the incline across Benson's Brook. Shortly before the hamlet of Bedlam you reach the point where the incline crossed the lane at right angles, plunging steeply downhill to the west, climbing the steepening hillside on the opposite side. It ended on a plateau with wide views and assorted, though not particularly beautiful, quarry remains lying below.

To reach the plateau by road you will have to make a detour back downhill from Bedlam to Bitterley, and then use the A4117 and the lane that humps the main incline trackbed almost at the summit.

The lane is busy, used by vehicles taking laundry and other supplies to the Civil Aviation Authority radar station with golf balls dominating the Clee Hills. The station controls the path of airliners and occasionally I have looked down and fleetingly remembered the railways of Clee Hill – and some, if not all, of the little lines that one veined the Welsh Border.

### *Shropshire & Montgomeryshire Light Railway*

Llanymynech is now quite the centre of railways. One called the 'Potteries Junction' was projected as a portion of the West Midland scheme to develop a new Welsh port (for the Irish traffic at Porthdinlleyn). All that has come of it is sixteen miles connecting Llanymynech and Shrewsbury, with a spur of a mile or so to Llanyblodwell. Between Llanymynech and Shrewsbury, Nescliff (sic) Hill and Kynaston's Cave, the site of Knockin Castle, and other places – of which much legendary gossip might be narrated – can be visited by a run over the line.

That is what *The Gossiping Guide to Wales* stated in 1879. But it was wrong because by then the line had been closed for seven years after the start of a history that was to be well chequered.

The first route, which was never built, was that of the Shrewsbury & North Wales Railway, authorised on 29 July 1862 between Westbury on the Shrewsbury & Welshpool, which had been completed to the Oswestry & Newtown at Buttington Junction, the previous January, to Llanymynech, a distance of $13^3/_4$ miles. It was promoted by R.S. France, owner of quarries on the distinctively shaped Llanymynech Hill, and secretary of the Mid Wales Railway, then under construction.

The route constructed was promoted as the Potteries

Shrewsbury & North Wales Railway – the Potts. This company was formed by the amalgamation of the S & NWR and the Shrewsbury & Potteries Junction, authorised in 1865.

Its line, opened 13 August 1866, is that which is now so well remembered. It had a terminus at Abbey Foregate, Shrewsbury, below the level of the Joint Station, which dominates so much of the town centre, and ran to Llanymynech and west to quarries at Nantmawr, crossing the Oswestry & Newtown on the level.

A six mile branch opened in 1871 served quarries at Criggion on Breidden Hill 'a conspicuous object from every line of railway in this district', said the *Gossiping Guide*. Today, it is still conspicuous from the oblong windows of Sprinters on the Shrewsbury – Aberystwyth link, now the only line of railway in the area.

The countryside served by the Potts was too sparsely populated to support a line and a Board of Trade Order of 1880 put an end to its activities between Shrewsbury and Llanymynech for some 30 years, although the Llanymynech – Nantmawr section survived rather better, as I relate in *Forgotten Railways: North & Mid Wales* (volume 4).

Revival came with a Light Railway Order of 11 February 1909 on the initiative of an engineer whose passion for rural and down and out railways brought an 'empire' into being as a result of the Light Railway Act of 1896. Holman Fred Stephens, stated a biographical note in the *Railway Year Book* 1914, 'has had an unusually eventful experience in connection with railway work'.

He was shown as being 'manager and engineer of the S & M Light Railway, Kent & East Sussex'.

He had reopened the S & M with financial and sympathetic help from local councils in April 1911, the day, once again, being 'the 13th'. The Criggion branch was not used until the following year and the section between Shrewsbury (Abbey) and the junction with the Shrewsbury & Birmingham was never relaid. The GWR and LNWR did not oppose the Potts revival, although Paddington representatives might have had

Shropshire Variety – 2: *Plate 5 (above)* Coalport station 30 May 1970. The scene before the trackbed was incorporated into the Severn Valley Way. The station house is in private use. *Plate 6 (below)* Wellington was the terminus of two Severn Valley services. Ex GWR 2–6–2 tank No 4406 heads a Much Wenlock train while ex LNWR coal tank, 0–6–2 No 58904 is about to depart with a Coalport East train. 15 July 1950.

Small Stations: *Plate 7 (above)* Gas-lit Ketley was one of the intermediate calls for local trains on the Wellington & Severn Junction route. 2–6–2 tank No 4158 on the 5.45 pm Much Wenlock–Wellington service. 1 May 1957. *Plate 8 (below)* Much Wenlock became a terminus in 1951 following the withdrawal of Wellington–Craven Arms through services. Wellington–Much Wenlock trains survived another twelve years. Pannier tank No 9741 seen after arrival at Much Wenlock. 25 October 1955.

second thoughts for a GWR Divisional Report of 1924 noted of the situation at Baschurch, 'the S & M Railway compete for traffic, their station being at Kinnerley'.

That was six miles cross country, and the Report was perhaps not taken too seriously, especially as the competition noted at Rednal, five miles up the line, was that of the Shropshire Union Canal Company.

A few years earlier, links between the GWR and the S & M had been strengthened by the GWR's prelude to Grouping take-over of the Cambrian Railways which gave the GWR its own junction with the S & M at Llanymynech. The GWR also gained a junction with the Nantmawr branch, but by then that was of no concern to the S & M, for after the revival, the branch had remained under the control of the Cambrian.

The LRO had provided for a new spur between the Shrewsbury & Hereford and the S & M close to where they crossed just south of Shrewsbury but it was not started and the interchange for goods, mineral and livestock traffic remained at Meole Brace, where, stated a GWR *Appendix* of January 1913, 'Traffic will be exchanged once daily'. It was also laid down:

> Should there be Live Stock from either Company consigned to Stations on the S & M Railway, the Joint Yardsman, at Coleham, must arrange for it to be taken to Meole Brace Junction, and put in the S & M Sidings. An advice to Abbey station of such Traffic must be sent by the Company conveying the Traffic'.

There was, of course, no exchange passenger traffic and GWR Cambrian section timetables never acknowledge Llanymynech as an exchange station. Not that S & M passenger trains frequently appeared there – Charles F Klapper in a two-part history in the *Railway Magazine* 1934, noting that apart from Saturdays when return facilities were available to local passengers, the service had obviously been 'unsuitable for the ordinary course of travel.' His article was a valediction to the passenger service, withdrawn from 6 November 1933.

An occasional goods service continued and, more significantly, 1934 saw the opening by a company that later became Esso of a depot at Abbey Foregate yard and so began a service that kept alive a short section of the S & M into the late 1980s.

F.H. Stephens became a Lieutenant Colonel in World War I, and can be thought of as the first 'military man' to be associated with the S & M, the first of a long line for in 1940, as Britain was experiencing its 'finest hour', the S & M beginning its own, being requisitioned by the War Department in 1941. It was relaid and revamped to serve what was a well-spaced huge ammunition dump from where, as the tide of war turned in the Allies' favour, shells were dispatched for the North African campaign and later D Day and the advance through Europe.

The line was worked from both ends and stretches were added to the main line including a branch to a four platform station, Lonsdale, serving the main cap at Nesscliff. Troop halts were added and Abbey Foregate echoed again to passengers as weekend leave specials arrived and departed. Left to soldier on in its own fashion was the Criggion branch, used by quarry trains until December 1959. They made their way along the S & M in between WD trains. The line closed officially on 29 February 1960. Three days earlier, construction began on the connection which survives to Abbey Foregate depot from the stub of the Severn Valley branch. On 20 March 1960 there was a farewell in 'Camwellian' style: an SLS Midland Area special train, with black edged Photographic Souvenirs for the mourners.

Did they include, I wonder, people who had followed the S & M's fortunes through the years as recorded in notes in the *Railway Magazine* where in December 1937, R.K. Cope wrote of various remnants of engines and carriages, which had been cut up on the Criggion branch.

A correspondent of the *Railway Observer* noted at Kinnerley on 12 December 1938 that the bracket signal at the west end of the down platform had an unfamiliar appearance as the main line signal arm had been blown off in a recent gale.

Several months later, the same magazine was reporting on Gazelle, which was 0–4–2 tank No 1 and its carriage, in a siding near the engine shed. It appeared that parts of the carriage were once part of a Wolseley railcar which Colonel Stephens used as a mobile shooting box.

That was in the days when *Hesperus* an 1875 *Ilfracombe Goods* locomotive worked the daily train, a duty shared with ex-LNWR coal engines. Those veterans were joined in WD days by Dean 0–6–0s. But Gazelle was perhaps the most eccentric of all, remembered by H Walker of Doncaster, who wrote to *Rail News* in 1983. He was one of the first servicemen to be associated with the S & M as a military railway.

Our pride and joy was the Gazelle, a miniature loco, complete with its glass coach and wheels the size of dinner plates, together with the hand propelled platelayers' trolley, which we used for our trips down the line to the local!'

Much of the trackbed is now in agricultural use. Melverley viaduct on the Criggion branch was reconstructed as a road in the 1960s, with the trackbed adapted as approaches. The work provided a valuable extra road crossing of the Severn in a remote area where bridges were miles apart. It remains a useful short cut for enthusiasts who go in search of the line.

### Hookagate Rail Welding Depot

The return of steam to the Cambrian Coast in May 1987 when *Hinton Manor* ran between Machynlleth and Barmouth and occasionally, Pwllheli, was a happy occasion. Yet for me it was tinged with regret for the dmu carrying our party from Birmingham to Machynlleth ran past the remains of the Hookagate Rail Welding Depot on the outskirts of Shrewsbury, closed just over a year earlier.

It was developed by the Western Region in 1959–60 on the

# CHAPTER 3

# Severn Valley Railway

## *The Living and the Dead*

How many enthusiasts and tourists who enjoy the Severn Valley Railway of today think about, or go in search of the Severn Valley Railway of Victorian days? The $12^1/_2$ miles between Bridgnorth and Bewdley (plus the Kidderminster Branch) which enthusiasts revived represent only a third of a splendid GWR secondary route of almost 40 miles between Shrewsbury and Hartlebury.

Interesting forgotten stretches lie at both ends of the restored route. They comprise some 22 miles between Shrewsbury and Bridgnorth and just over 5 miles between Bewdley and Hartlebury, via Stourport, part of which is owned by the Severn Valley Railway.

Shrewsbury featured in two Acts of 20 August 1853. They were those of the Shrewsbury and Crewe, completed in five years as the LNWR thrust towards Central Wales, and the Severn Valley Railway, which did not open until nine years after authorisation.

Its birth included financial problems, an Act of 30 July 1855 allowing reduction of capital. The company stated at the time:

Power is taken to use part of the Shrewsbury & Hereford, also the Shrewsbury station, and the Wellington & Severn Junction is to afford facilities for the transmission of traffic.

The SVR contractors, Sir Morton Peto and Brassey and

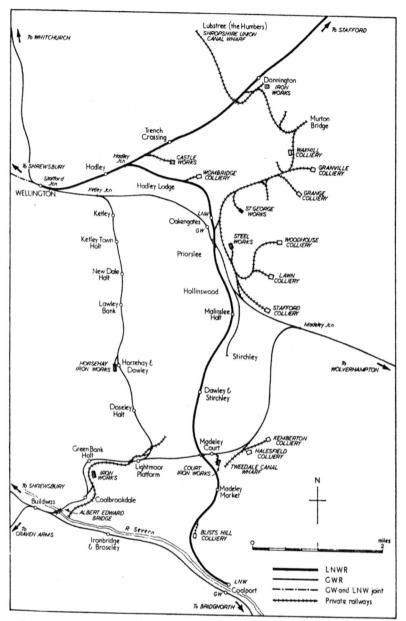

Severn Valley – cradle of the Industrial Revolution, where the first cast iron rails in the world were laid. GWR dominated, but the LNWR had a foothold

54

# HOLIDAY RUNABOUT TICKETS

ISSUED ON ANY DAY FROM

## APRIL 27th to OCTOBER 31st, 1952
## Available for one Week from date of issue

PROVIDE

## UNLIMITED TRAVEL IN HOLIDAY AREAS

# SHAKESPEARE COUNTRY, COTSWOLD and MALVERN HILLS
# SEVERN, WYE and USK VALLEYS

### THIRD CLASS FARES
### Areas Nos. 9, 10, 12 and 22
# 16s. 6d. *each*

Children under Three years of age, Free; Three and under Fourteen years of age, Half-fare.

### SEVERN VALLEY. — Area No. 22.

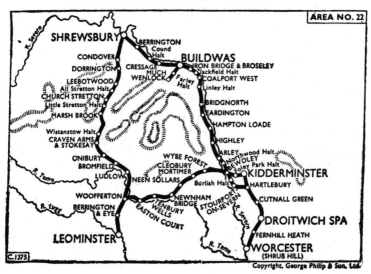

Holiday Runabout Tickets of 1952, area no 22, covered the Severn Valley Railway, Kidderminster to Woofferton and the truncated Buildwas – Craven Arms branch only to Much Wenlock. But it was still possible to use a number of halts on the Shrewsbury & Hereford Joint line.

Betts, proposed a double track, but shareholders rejected the plan. The line was leased to the West Midland in 1860 and became part of the GWR 12 years later.

The branch never had great development potential, primarily because the towns and villages it served were better reached by good bus services, more directly linked to Shrewsbury and to towns in the West Midlands.

Worcester bound trains left the Shrewsbury & Hereford at what was finally known as Sutton Bridge Junction. The first quarter mile of the branch to Burnt Mill Junction was doubled in 1894.

Burnt Mill was the site of what the company called an 'old carriage shed.' A Report stated:

Owing to its inaccessibility it is rarely used except for stabling the Engineer's coach. It is in a bad state of repair and the Engineer has the question of its renewal in hand.

That was in 1924 when the GWR were considering the more pressing matter of increasing passenger traffic on the Severn Valley line but it was a decade before it was sufficient to support four halts. One, opened 4 August 1934, was at Cound, three miles east of the first station, Berrington. Ten years earlier, a Company report regarded Berrington as serving the village of Cound, even though it was much closer to Cressage.

Though passenger traffic was never intense, there was quite a good service with six weekday through trains augmented by several south from Bridgnorth. They were used by people making connections at Buildwas and Bewdley. Both were junctions of services which ran only short distances to large towns. Wellington – Buildwas was 8 miles; Kidderminster – Bewdley 3 $1/2$ – before pursuing routes of 20 miles through mainly lonely countryside to connect with the same main line: the Shrewsbury–Hereford. Trains from Buildwas reached it at

Marsh Farm Junction, and ran another four miles to Craven Arms, those from Bewdley joined it at Woofferton.

Buildwas became a junction from the opening of the line, which coincided with that of a short branch from the small, rather pretty, market town of Much Wenlock in the hills above the Valley. The junction was completed by the Much Wenlock Railway which, in 1864, extended across the river on the Albert Edward Bridge to meet the GWR branch from the Shrewsbury & Birmingham at Madeley, and connect with the Wellington and Severn Junction.

Buildwas had platforms at two levels and they were much photographed through the years. It was a busy junction and the station master (class 4) had a staff of ten.

There were three sidings on the Down side of the Severn Valley line for 107 wagons and another in which the engineer kept sand wagons. A fifth led to the pump house of the locomotive department.

There was also an engineer's siding for sand wagons at Meadow Wharf and another for getting coal to the locomotive department pumping house near the river. From 1932 Buildwas station was dominated by the original Ironbridge Power Station and then the area was later almost swallowed by the much larger 1,000 MW 'B' Station. The most easterly of its four 375 ft high cooling towers was built on the branch trackbed, but the branch survives in a layout used by merry-go-round coal trains, which reach the station from the Shrewsbury & Birmingham at Madeley Junction.

The demise of Buildwas removed from the railways of Shropshire and of England, one of those small, off the beaten track junctions that for years were as much a part of the landscape as the black and white houses and churches which were built before them and live on today, long after them.

Buildwas was one of those places that attracted and excited and delighted the enthusiast. It was, of course, purely GWR and so lacked the variety of some other junctions in this book used by more than one company; Three Cocks and its neighbour, Talyllyn, both come immediately to mind.

## 'Brunel's Wonderful Railway'

Travel writers were quick to appreciate the beauty of the area and a 50 page Handbook to the Severn Valley Railway by J Randall FGS, appeared about a year after opening. It is among several similar publications published in facsimile in recent years by the ever enterprising Shropshire Libraries.

*Darlington's Handbook to The Severn Valley* dating from the 1930s highlights the most spectacular section, even though its reference to Brunel is wrong since he had died three years before the opening and had had no direct connection with the branch.

Brunel's wonderful railway sticks to the side of the gorge, with the help of tunnels and rock platforms and buttressed built-up terraces. And perhaps the railway train is the best methods of travelling through it all.

Darlington, who was also wrong in mentioning tunnels, suggested walks in Shrewsbury commencing from the station. A revised edition of today could offer attractions, too, on the outskirts for the half mile tip of the line from the junction has been adapted as a footpath and cycleway through a modern residential area. After reaching a busy road, it continues south to the A5 as a shale path.

But the gorge is the place to ramble because there the trackbed forms The Severn Valley Way. For about three quarters of a mile from where the power station planners released the trackbed back to nature, close to the Albert Edward Bridge, downstream to Ironbridge, the way incorporates the Benthall Edge Railway Trail.

Created by the Severn Gorge Management Project, the Trail takes walkers over the 'rock platforms,' which were in fact, a viaduct. Across the river is the restored Severn Warehouse, one of the Museum's best known buildings. Another part of the project is a nature trail through the dense hillside woods. A useful Guide to both (price 20 pence in 1988), is more parochial than Darlington, telling of the love of wild strawberries for the lime they find in the mortar of stone walls, and of long forgotten inclined planes between hillside clay pits and quarries and the river bank.

The Severn Valley Way runs past the site of Ironbridge station beside the historic bridge. Now it is one of the best sited car parks of Shropshire. At the entrance is a centre where you can buy information sheets including No 8 Coalbrookdale Locomotives, a useful aid to study and nostalgia.

The Way continues along the river bank to Coalport, where the station buildings are in private occupation. In between lies Jackfield Works and Tile Museum. It was established as part of the Ironbridge Gorge Museum to commemorate Jackfield having for many years two of the biggest decorative tile works in the world. Their products were dispatched from short sidings and a GWR Appendix of March 1914 laid down instructions for the works of Maw & Coy. 'No Engine must pass the Notice Board which is fixed 30 yards inside the Gates leading to the works.'

Jackfield was also interesting as a place which had two halts. One opened by the GWR on 3 December 1934 had to be replaced because of the danger of landslip. Its sucessor opened a quarter of a mile nearer Bridgnorth on 1 March 1954.

For a time there were hopes that the Severn Valley Railway could be reopened north from Bridgnorth as an extra attraction, as well as an additional and pleasant way of access to the Gorge Museum sites, but that proved impossible because of trackbed developments carried out after BR closed the branch. A stretch was converted into a track to give better access to isolated farms, and a housing estate has been built on the trackbed at Bridgnorth.

After the issue was under public discussion in late 1987, the Chair of Wrekin Council Tourism Group, Councillor Phil Davis, wrote to Railway World describing such a scheme as 'a non-starter.'

He said that more realistically local authorities were assisting rail connections to the Ironbridge Gorge via existing routes. If any realistic extension of preserved rail was likely it rested on possible Council support for relaying the Lightmoor branch to Telford Horsehay Steam Trust headquarters.

There seems no reason to doubt that never again will Bridgnorth Tunnel (559 yds) echo to the sound of a gong positioned about 250 yds from the station end to signal drivers during shunting operations.

### Bewdley – Hartlebury

Some lines are best forgotten. Certainly drivers and pedestrians never lamented the end of Bewdley – Hartlebury trains, passenger and goods, which so often held up traffic at a level crossing on the fringe of Stourport-on-Severn. It was as much a problem for the railways as for road planners. Operating instructions for the Severn Valley Line in GWR Appendix to the working timetables contained a note which was in force for years:

To prevent complaint of detention to vehicles crossing the line by the Level Crossing at Stourport, all Wagons on Down Trains for Stourport must be formed next to the Engine...

That was the rule in March 1914... and so it was until the line closed. The five miles of the Severn Valley Railway between Bewdley, Stourport and Hartlebury were in some ways different from the rest of the line because of the Bewdley – Kidderminster branch.

Passenger services between Kidderminster, Bewdley, Stourport and Hartlebury, which were shown in a separate timetable to those of the Severn Valley, were not withdrawn until 5 January 1970. Bewdley – Stourport closed completely, but the rest of the line was retained until 1980 for traffic to the Stourport Power Stations. The last coal train is thought to have run in March 1979.

Meanwhile, in 1972, the Severn Valley Railway bought the trackless one-mile northern tip between Bewdley South Box and Burlish, through Mount Pleasant Tunnel (123 yd) for a stock siding. The price, quoted in the Severn Valley Guide was £100. But the company was not interested in buying the line to Stourport because of road improvement schemes, including the crossing by Stourport station.

The purchased trackbed includes the stretch which, with the Kidderminster line, crosses Sandbourne Viaduct, Bewdley (101 yd).

The GWR developed one halt between Stourport and Bewdley, to serve the growing area of Burlish. It was beside the B4195, nearly a mile north of Stourport station. It dated from 31 March 1930.

Stourport was one of Britain's few 'canal' towns, being strategically placed at the head of the Severn navigation. There was some interchange between rail and canal at the Stourport basin of the Staffordshire & Worcestershire Canal but it was limited and Stourport remained of no especial importance in railway terms, although the branch provided a useful power station connection from the mid 1930s until the late 1970s.

# CHAPTER 4

# Severn Valley : The Branches

*Madeley – Buildwas: Merry Go Round*

The Severn Valley Railway and the Ironbridge Gorge Museum are two of the best examples of living history to be found in Europe, but few people realise that within a few miles of them are a rich variety of forgotten railways rewarding to visit and enjoy.

Shopshire's 'railway' history goes back much further than the Shrewsbury & Birmingham route for several wooden railways were associated with Coalbrookdale, which cradled the Industrial Revolution. Their success led to the development of them in other areas of Britain. See; *Early Wooden Railways* M.J.T. Lewis (1970). Three forgotten routes stem from the one line that survives through Coalbrookdale. It forms the last six miles of the route of merry-go-round coal trains to Buildwas Power Station. The first four miles from Shifnal to Ironbridge were authorised on 2 July 1847 as the only branch of the Shrewsbury & Birmingham Railway, incorporated 11 months earlier. The four single track miles opened on 1 June 1854, three months before the S & B amalgamated with the GWR. The branch left the main line at Madeley Junction, 2 miles west of Shifnal and there was one intermediate station at Madeley, almost 3 miles from the junction, which became the railhead for an area stated to stretch to Bridgnorth, and, more closely, Ironbridge and Dawley.

It was timetabled as Madeley (Salop) to distinguish it from Madeley, on the West Coast main line; neighbouring Madeley

Market on the LNWR Coalport branch, and Madeley Road on the NSR between Stoke and Market Drayton.

All survived far longer for Madeley (Salop) closed in 1915. It reopened experimentally in summer 1925, but closed permanently to passengers two months later. But it continued to handle goods – mainly castings, hay, straw, potatoes and general merchandise. There was also parcels traffic, concentrated at Shifnal and worked forward on the 6.15am Oxley – Buildwas goods. 'The traffic,' stated a company report, 'is light and conveyed in the Guard's van. It is delivered within the area served by the LMS company's Madeley Market station by the Goods Carting Agent.'

The heaviest volume of branch traffic was coal and the station master or porter at Madeley assisted in shunting at Kemberton Colliery of the Madeley Wood Colliery company, which produced about 40 wagon loads a day in the 1920s.

The Shrewsbury & Birmingham branch was not completed until 1864 when the GWR extended it $1^1/_2$ miles from Lightmoor to join Railway No 2 of the Wenlock Railway, built across the river from Buildwas. It included the shapely Albert Edward Bridge, constructed by the Coalbrookdale Company in 1863. It is often called the Royal Albert Bridge and one GWR report even recorded it as the Royal Albert Edward Bridge. Its virtues are extolled in *The Railway Heritage of Britain*.

### Wellington & Severn Junction

By the time the S & B branch was extended, it had been joined by the Wellington & Severn Junction Railway. It was a rather grandiose title for a single line of only $5^1/_2$ miles, yet it did have the merit of forming the northern section of a delightful cross country route of $24^1/_4$ miles. From Wellington, it served industry as far as Buildwas and ran through the Wenlock Edge country, immortalised by the poet A.E. Housman, to Marsh Farm Junction.

The junction at Lightmoor was named after an area which got its name from the workings of numerous blast furnaces.

The W & S J was incorporated in 1853 with the Coalbrookdale Company owning at least three quarters of the shares. Engineered by Henry Robertson, whose offices were in Shrewsbury, the section of nearly four miles between Ketley Junction, a mile east of Wellington station, and Horeshay were used for passengers from 1857, but it seems that goods trains did not work south of Horsehay until 1860.

Horsehay was the largest of the intermediate stations. There was a house for the station master who had a staff of five: two signalmen, two male crossing keepers and a porter 'who assists at Lawley Bank for the greater portion of his time', to quote a GWR Report.

Goods work was supervised not by the station master, but the Coalbrookdale goods agent. Access to the goods yard was by ground frame locked by the key of the Ketley – Horsehay token.

It was a busy yard with 10 sidings accommodating up to 150 wagons and a spur which could take another 30. Two sidings led from the yard to Horsehay Ironworks. For years the station was known as Horsehay & Dawley.

The GWR continually fought road competition, although its attitude seems to have been a little half-hearted since it took four years to develop three halts. The first, Doseley, opened on 1 December 1932 – seven years after a company Report had noted:

The district has recently been covered by the Midland Motor Omnibus Company and schemes have been submitted showing how the Great Western Company could inaugurate services to meet the competition.

Doseley Halt was followed by New Dale on 29 January 1934 and, only half a mile to the north, Ketley Town on 6 March 1936.

Stiff gradients and closely – placed stops meant that 21 minutes were needed between Wellington and Lightmoor Halt, and another 10 minutes to Buildwas. Two coach trains were always in charge of tanks: 2–6–2s or *Panniers*.

Small stations – 2: *Plate 9 (above)* Harton Road, one of the more remote of Shropshire stations photographed 3 April 1955 more than three years after complete closure. *Plate 10 (below)* Malins Lee on the LNWR Coalport branch looking towards Coalport.

Small stations – 3: *Plate 11 (above)* In the final years of its existence, Coalport, ex LNWR, became Coalport East to avoid confusion with the GWR station just across the river. Coal tank No 58904 awaits to depart for Wellington. 15 July 1950. *Plate 12 (below)* Tenbury Wells had a station some distance from its centre. It was demolished to make way for an industrial estate.

Not all trains were in Public timetables. The 5.20am Wellington – Buildwas was, in the words of the working time table of the Chester District, 'not advertised'. It was shown as 'ECS and Workmen's'.

It was followed from Wellington, 10 mins later, by a light engine scheduled to run non-stop to Much Wenlock 'to work 6.50am Much Wenlock to Wellington'.

Its return journey took an extra 11 mins because of the numerous stops. In 1953, a writer in *The Railway Observer* noted that trains paused 'at a phenomenal number of modest platforms, most with rude wooden or iron shelters . . .'

Passenger trains continued to do that until withdrawal between Wellington and Craven Arms in July 1962. Ketley Junction – Lightmoor Junction remained open for goods for another two years, and Horsehay works – Lightmoor Junction reopened experimentally about a year later and survived until 1981, although latterly traffic was confined to occasional workings of heavy bridge sections.

*Telford Horsehay Steam Trust*

Soon afterwards the section was lifted, a little too soon for enthusiasts who have since established Telford Horsehay Steam Trust and apart from site relaying, have a noted reputation for locomotive restoration. They have official support from Telford Development Corporation, which took over ownership of the line after closure. They leased on and three quarter miles from Heath Hill tunnel (59 yds) under the A442, to Lightmoor to the Trust. Operating between Horsehay Yard and the Tunnel began in May 1984 and Horsehay & Dawley Station was reopened in December 1985.

The Horsehay section may be the most interesting and satisfying place where redevelopment has occurred since the branch closed, but it is not the only one. Close to the M54, a short footpath leads north towards the site of Ketley Junction from Ketley Town Halt. A short distance further south the *Wrekin Way* picks its path on the route of the trackbed across

Lawley Common, between the sites of New Dale Halt and Lawley Bank station.

### *Lightmoor – Buildwas*

Lightmoor to Buildwas, two and a half miles, was double tracked – the only section destined to be so between Wellington and Marsh Farm Junction. Coalbrookdale received a two – platform station with the main buildings, including a ladies' waiting room on the Up side, and only a wooden shelter on the opposite platform.

The station master (class 5) was in charge of the two porter signalmen who manned the box on the down platform; two porters and a gatewoman. He also supervised two signalmen at Lightmoor, where a 'platform' opened on 12 August 1907, under his supervision. The porters worked at both places. Although Lightmoor was not officially a halt until the late 1950s, it was referred to as one in many GWR documents.

There was no such confusion over the designation of Green Bank Halt opened between Lightmoor and Coalbrookdale on 12 March 1934.

The problem there was operating, Service timetables emphasising Ministry of Transport requirements: 'All trains using the halt must be fitted with continuous brake throughout. No coupling or uncoupling of engines or vehicles is permitted.'

The site can be occasionally glimpsed from the carriage window of special services running between Birmingham (New Street) and Coalbrookdale, where a temporary three-car dmu platform was built of wood and tubular scaffolding.

A summer service was run to mark the bi-centenary of the Iron Bridge in 1979, but it was not revived until 1987, again for visitors to the Ironbridge Gorge Museum. One reason, said BR, was to keep the area free of road traffic 'giving visitors the chance of touring this lovely spot without the worry of parking their cars.' The recently restored Coalbrookdale station, a Grade II Listed Building is the headquarters of the Green Wood Trust, a charity promoting the educational, social and commercial value of small woodlands.

### *Buildwas – Much Wenlock – Craven Arms*

The occasional delight of seeing a preserved small ex-GWR 2-6-2 tank is compounded by memories of what they achieved working two-coach trains between Wellington and Craven Arms. They did their most sterling work in the Severn Valley, not least on the 1 in 40 climb between Buildwas and Much Wenlock.

The $3^1/_2$ mile stretch was on the east side of a narrow and pleasant wooded valley, and its course can be traced from the B4378, a field or so away. Until Farley Halt, almost half way, opened on 27 October 1934, the run was non-stop. It lay beside a crossing of a minor road and the keeper, who had an adjacent cottage, 'attended to' Bradley Siding, where lime, cement and stone traffic was handled.

The section was built by the Much Wenlock & Severn Junction Railway, incorporated in 1859. Four of the six directors lived in Much Wenlock.

The line west from Much Wenlock to the Shrewsbury & Hereford at Marsh Farm Junction, north of Craven Arms, was built by the Wenlock Railway as railway No 1. (No 2 was Buildwas – Coalbrookdale).

The Wenlock Railway – incorporated as the Much Wenlock Craven Arms & Coalbrookdale Railway in 1861 – was opened in two stages. Much Wenlock to Presthope was completed on 1 November 1864 (on the same day as the line across the Severn on the Albert Edward Bridge), and the 11 miles from Presthope to Marsh Farm Junction opened on 16 December 1867.

The company made radical improvements at Much Wenlock, converting the Much Wenlock & Severn Junction station into a goods shed and building a much more spacious one, which survives in private use today. Although having only a single platform, the station building had a booking office, two waiting rooms and accommodation for the station master whose staff grew to 13.

Opposite the station was a small signal box of 31 levers, an overadequate provision as many remained spare. Between platform and box lay a loop: 'Two Goods Trains, or one Passenger Train and one Goods Train may be allowed to cross at this Station.'

Thus stated Service Time Table Appendice whose authors revelled in every opportunity to use capital letters, presumably to give added authority to their edicts.

The yard and goods shed, which lay across the B4378, bridged by the line, have gone. The yard included three sidings, the longest for 26 wagons, and had two landings, the main one for coal and horses and a stone warehouse. The other was used by farmers.

Also of stone was the single road engine shed, which housed two small tanks, generally class 44 2–6–2s, or Panniers from Wellington. All took water from a column inside the shed fed from a small GWR – owned reservoir, fed by streams between Much Wenlock and Presthope.

Opposition from landowners at Presthope, three miles west of Much Wenlock, meant a costly deviation for it included building a tunnel of 207 yds under Wenlock Edge.

Presthope was a busy station, though only for goods, including lime from the Knowle works, and horse and cattle traffic. It had a passing loop capable of taking trains of up to 57 wagons, and sidings another 78 wagons. There was a staff of only two: the station master and a signalman 'who also assists generally with station work.'
Their drinking water supply was from a pump in the oil-lamp room or one in the yard, opposite the single platform.

Longville was the smallest of five scattered villages served by its station, which dealt mainly with farm produce, timber, horses and cattle providing jointly an annual revenue seven times greater than that of passengers. It was an intermediate non-crossing station on the 6 mile Presthope – Rushbury block section.

Rushbury handled only about a third of the amount of traffic dealt with at Longville, yet it had more facilities, including a cart weighbridge, signal box and a water column at the Craven Arms end of the single platform, on the Up side.

Harton Road. $2^1/_2$ miles west of Rushbury, was the least used of the branch stations, with traffic receipts for 1924 under £600, including those for passengers of £82 – half the parcel revenue. Horse and cattle pens were provided, but an 'old covered van body in the yard' was considered to be an adequate lock up for goods traffic.

Because the volume of passenger and goods traffic between the Shrewsbury & Hereford route and the Severn Valley never grew to expected proportions, economies were often considered, not least a reduction in the status of crossings where the gatekeepers were often the wives of railway workers.

The Longville station master's wife lived in the cottage at the neighbouring Coates Crosses on a bridle road between Church Stretton and Bridgnorth. Wolverton Crossing was looked after by the wife of a sub-ganger. A gatewoman's pay was three old shillings a week – only four old pence less than the weekly rent for the crossing cottage. But they did get bonuses of three and sixpence a week.

Two halts were added as bus competition grew: Westwood, between Much Wenlock and Presthope in December 1935 and Easthope, four months later. It lay almost half way along the four mile stretch between Presthope and Longville.

Longville began a 12 year spell as terminus of the branch after Much Wenlock – Craven Arms passenger services were withdrawn on New Year's Eve, 1951, and Longville – Marsh Farm Junction closed to goods as well. Buildwas – Longville closed completely on 4 December 1963. Today, a line that was open for just under a century has been dead for a quarter of that time.

## The Appeal of Wellington

Wellington was never regarded by enthusiasts as a rail centre in the same class as Shrewsbury, yet it had an appeal of its own. Although the LNWR asserted its presence through partnership with the GWR of the Shrewsbury & Birmingham main line west to Shrewsbury, and with the Stafford and Coalport branches, the atmosphere was strongly Great Western.

The Joint Line extended west from Wellington No 1 box (Stafford Station) and although the station was Joint, the locomotive shed opposite the Up platform, an island, was GWR. A typical allocation through the years was of six or seven 2–6–2 tanks of the 44XX and 51XX classes and a similar number of Pannier tanks.

Their diagrams included shunting Hollinswood Sidings (Stirchley Yard), which closed on 2 February 1959 and became the site of Telford Central station, opened 12 May 1986, at the town centre, beside the M54.

The Yard lay on both sides of the S & B and its 14 sidings and two refuge loops had a capacity of more than 500 wagons. The main source of traffic was to and from Lilleshall steel works.

The company's own locomotives worked to the Up sidings under an agreement of 1 January 1872. The Yard also dealt with traffic for the asphaltic slag works of Willliam Shepherd & Sons, the British Basic Slag Company, the Brownhills Chemical Company, the Lilleshall Coal Distillation Company an the Centrifugal Concrete Blocks & Poles Company. Traffic was also sent from the Yard over the Lilleshall company's private line to the Midland Iron Works of C & W Walker. In addition there were large quantities of limestone and ore for the Lilleshall blast furnaces.

## Stirchley Branch

The down sidings in the yard provided access to the $1^1/_4$ mile Stirchley branch, which ran parallel to the Wellington & Severn Junction line less than a $^1/_4$ mile to the east. The

GWR began working the branch in 1908 and it survived for just over half a century longer before closing with the Yard.

Purely for goods, it served Randlay brickworks, where there was a tramway which ran across the branch. Gates were normally positioned across the branch and the shunter who had to accompany all trains had to remove the tramway rails and replace them once his train had passed. There was also exchange sidings with the Haybridge Company, which had its own locomotives.

Branch gradients were average, but there was a siding to a brickworks falling at 1 in 27 and another to a chemical works, which dropped away down a short gradient at 1 in 33.

### LNWR: Wellington – Coalport

The LMS and GWR both called their stations on opposite banks of the Severn 'Coalport'. *Bradshaw's* clarified the situation a little with footnotes that the stations were about 200 yds apart: there was no mention of the river in between. Understandable, perhaps, because, apart from space considerations, mention of it might have confused the casual traveller or tourist even more.

In later years the position was made a little clearer when Coalport of LMS ilk became Coalport East and as such it passed into memory as a passenger station only four years after Nationalisation, which led to the branch locomotives being transferred from Shrewsbury LMS to Wellington Western Region shed. For years the branch was worked by 'Cauliflower' 0–6–0s and Webb Coal tanks and the *Coalport Dodger* was regarded by enthusiasts as the epitome of branch line services which, it seemed likely, would soon disappear.

It was goods which sustained the branch, which stemmed from the Stafford – Wellington line at Hadley Junction and ran eight miles to Coalport. A string of private sidings between Wellington and Stirchley, including those of the Lilleshall Company, provided traffic which helped to keep the branch alive for 10–12 years after the passenger service ended.

A century earlier, the LNWR worked traffic on the independent Shropshire Canal and when its condition deteriorated, Euston got powers, under an Act of 1857 to buy it and convert the section almost to Dawley into a railway, which then continued along an independent route to the riverside at Coalport, reached in 1861.

It dropped into the valley on steep gradients which included a stretch at 1 in 31. A councillor who drove the Dodger for the last ten years of its life later said the service was so infrequent that people forgot there was one. Yet before the creation of Telford New Town the area did not have a population sufficient to support more than three or four weekday trains.

Complete closure of the branch released land for use by planners of Telford New Town and the southern four miles, the most scenically promising, were incorporated into The Silkin Way, named in honour of the new town pioneer, Lord Silkin and opened 1 April 1977. It runs for 14 miles from the site of Coalport East station to Bratton, the most northerly section from Admaston to Bratton being over the route of the Wellington and Nantwich branch (page 114). Near Coalport, a tunnel infilled to a height only passable by walkers and cyclists, takes it under the entrance to Blists Hill Open Air Museum part of the Ironbridge Gorge Museum. Here the railway enthusiast is likely to be most content for it includes a reconstruction of Blists Hill siding from which bricks and roofing tiles were dispatched over the Coalport branch.

The Countryside Wardens of Telford Development Corporation have written an informative, clearly illustrated guide to the Silkin Way, which is issued free.

The Coalport branch trackbed was used for several years as the route of the 2ft 0in Telford Town tram, operated by the Telford Horsehay Steam Trust.
Its public debut, of one day only, was on 8 September 1979 and it again carried passengers during the Wrekin and Telford Festival in April 1980. Motive power was a vertical boiler 0–4–0 which hauled a single open coach over 400 yds

74

of the former branch beside Randlay Lake, between Malins Lee and Stirchley.

There were plans for major extensions, including a line to The Silkin Way close to the Ironbridge Gorge Museum, but they were never built and the line was closed some years ago. One problem was that Telford Development Corporation was not allowed to run public transport.

*Woofferton – Tenbury – Bewdley*

Far removed in character, though not distance, from the industrialised branches which ran into the Severn Valley further upstream was the branch from Woofferton to Bewdley, and a highly individual line that will forever be associated with it: the Cleobury Mortimer & Ditton Priors Light Railway.

The character of the area was well captured in a Victorian guide.

From Woofferton Junction, the line proceeds in an easterly direction for about five miles before reaching Tenbury, a small town of about 1,200 inhabitants, situated in the pretty agricultural district, given to the growth of orchard fruit and hops. The beautiful Teme, a confluent of the Severn, passes Tenbury, and gives a great charm to the district. Leaving Tenbury the train passes through the minor stations, called Newnham Bridge, Neen Sollars, Cleobury Mortimer and Wyre Forest to Bewdley, a more considerable town of over 3,000 inhabitants prettily situated on the banks of the glorious Severn.

This lyrical description of the 20 miles of a branch line is from a publication not of the GWR, which owned three quarters of the route, but the LNWR, which had a half share in the other quarter. The quote is taken from the 1876 edition of the *Tourists' Picturesque Guide to the London & North Western Railway* sub-titled 'and other railways with which it is immediately in connection'. It was also stated to be 'specially prepared for the use of American tourists'.

The company boundaries were well defined in *Railway Clearing House* maps, with the 5 miles from Woofferton hatched red and yellow as part of the LNWR/GWR Joint line, while the rest of the route was shown in unblemished GWR yellow.

Tenbury or Tenbury Wells? The GWR called it simply Tenbury in public timetables, but Tenbury Wells (which was also the LNWR designation) in working ones. The route was shown in passenger timetables as being extended beyond branch limits to Kidderminster, an overall distance of 24 miles. I am dividing it into two sections to bring out the original flavour of rural railway enterprise.

Exploring the branch was great fun, even though I had to wait half an hour at Woofferton for the clearance of fog so thick that I could only just see from the roadside the squat and attractive signal cabin. It is among the best of those on the S & H Joint to survive.

I was 25 years too late to wait at Woofferton station for that was closed to passengers on the same day as the branch closed as far as Tenbury on a summer's day in 1961, having had a life span three years longer than many of the S & H intermediate stations, including those near Shrewsbury.

A small group of landowners led by Lord Northwick began the active promotion of a branch to Tenbury Wells two decades after it had become established as a small spa following the discovery of saline springs.

They established an office in the town and worked closely with the Joint company, which gave it part of the Leominster Canal, which had been closed for some years by the time the Tenbury Railway was incorporated in 1859. With the flat valley of the river Teme presenting no constructional problems, the line was completed in two years.

It was surprising to find the only intermediate station, Easton Court, a single platform with substantial building, shown in two timetables. It was in GWR branch timetables and those of the S & H North to West through services. Both

**G.W. & L.N.W.] WOOFFERTON, TENBURY & BEWDLEY.—Weekdays only.—For Footnotes see page 104.**

*(railway timetable — Woofferton, Tenbury & Bewdley, weekday services; with stations including Hereford dep, Leominster, Ludlow, Woofferton, Easton Court, Tenbury, Newnham B'ge, Neen Sollars, Cleobury Mort'r, Wyre Forest, Bewdley arr/dep, Kidderminster arr/dep, Birm. (S.H.) arr, Birm. (N.St.) arr, W'hpton (L.L.) arr)*

**G.W. & L.N.W.] SEVERN VALLEY TO BIRMINGHAM.—Weekdays only.**

*(railway timetable — Severn Valley to Birmingham, weekday services; with stations including Shrewsbury dep, Berrington, Cressage, Buildwas, Much Wenlock dep, Iron Bridge dep, Coalport, Linley, Bridgnorth, Eardington, Hampton Loade, Highley, Arley, Bewdley arr/dep, Stourport, Hartlebury arr/dep, Kidderminster arr, Birm. (S.H.), Birm. (N.S.), Wolv. (L.L.) arr)*

For Sunday Trains see page 100.     For Notes see foot of page 104.

*(vertical side text:)* SAMES SWEET TONED PIANOS CORPORATION ST OPPOSITE COBDEN

Journeys long and short: The *Birmingham Gazette & Express* Railway Guide of February, 1907 showed a service between Woofferton Tenbury Bewdley and Birmingham, which included some 'Rail Motor Car' services between Bewdley and Kidderminster. The Severn Valley service was shown as Shrewsbury – Hartlebury: no mention of Worcester.

noted it as the station for Little Hereford, yet only the main line timetables revealed that the hamlet, beside the Teme, was half a mile away. Before World War I, its population was 425, according to *The Railway & Commercial Gazetteer* which noted Easton Court as being 144 miles from London.

The countryside was empty enough for Ordnance Survey map makers to squeeze 'E.C.Sta' between the black an white hatching of the line and the pale blue showing the river. Yet the map was too small a scale at one inch to illustrate an interesting facet of railway operation. It came under the heading in working *Appendixes* 'Five Occupation Crossings near Easton Court Station.' It ordered 'Drivers to whistle to warn users of the crossings'!

Like Easton Court, Tenbury station was half a mile from

the town centre. The station was actually at Burford – the seat of Lord Northwick – and the town across the Teme, spanned by an ornate road bridge.

Tenbury is a rewarding and pleasant town to explore, especially as the station site now holds little interest for even the explorer of old lines. Its two – platform layout with a dominating signal box, which befitted a town of Tenbury's ranking, has been replaced by an industrial estate, which has been hidden from the surrounding countryside, partly by utilising a high earth embankment which lay on the north side of the station.

*Tenbury – Cleobury Mortimer – Bewdley*

My pleasure in discovering old lines was renewed by finding a splendid bridge in the Wyre Forest section of the purely GWR line to Bewdley. To reach it, I drove east along the A456, eyeing the trackbed on a low embankment to my left until Newnham Bridge, where the station buildings have been restored as a village shop and part of the area as a nursery. The rest is a Hereford & Worcester County Council road depot, its hallmark, salt mountains. At the eastern end, where the trackbed heads north east to bury itself in the Forest, a bridge with a single span just about as long as it was possible to build, carries a minor road over the site of the station sidings.

It is of Horsehay origin, and although I could find no date, it must originate from the creation of the Tenbury & Bewdley Railway, which was promoted by the same local landowners as the Tenbury Railway.

Incorporated in August 1860, the T & BR took four years to complete and on opening it was worked by the GWR, which absorbed it in 1869.

The river Rea had to be bridged several times in Wyre Forest and construction involved excavation of a deep cutting and a high bridge carrying the B4202, south east of Cleobury Mortimer. The curving trackbed, now hidden by tightly packed

78

trees, lies far below the bridge, which provides a grandstand for outstanding views towards the Clee Hills.

Cleobury Mortimer station was another hopelessly distant from the town it was supposed to serve, two miles away along twisting roads. Timetables never warned passengers.

The junction station, as opposed to Cleobury Mortimer Town, was converted into holiday apartments, advertised as 'retaining many of the station's original features.'

Bridges which carried the Bewdley branch and the CM & DP across the A4117 have long gone, though abutments are still to be seen. Wyre Forest station may have disappeared from timetables, but because of the 'nature' of the trackbed today, it is now found in country books, where it is noted as the base of the Wyre Forest Nature Reserve. The Nature Conservancy Council owns $2^1/_4$ miles of the trackbed stretching almost to the eastern edge of the Forest.

The single tract through the Forest was unspectacular, although *Darlington's Handbook to the Severn Valley* introduced a quasi-poetical note:

It skirts the south side of Wyre Forest, showing its wide area of brush and shrub and oak trees, amongst which there is hardly a single road, and through which the Downes brook finds its sequestered way to the Severn above Bewdley.

The brook is in fact the Dowles, which gave its name to a three span viaduct across the Severn. The two pillars in the stream can be glimpsed from Telford's bridge in the centre of Bewdley. After crossing it, Bewdley bound trains curved and climbed a steep gradient to reach the Severn Valley line. The stretch between the viaduct and Bewdley can be studied enjoyably and at leisurely pace from the carriage window.

Woofferton – Bewdley passenger services were in the customary mould of GWR branch lines. Speeds were slow: 10 minutes being allowed from Woofferton to Tenbury, another

23 minutes to Cleobury Mortimer and 13 minutes to Bewdley. The one or two coach trains were in charge of a variety of tank locomotives including 2–6–2s, *Panniers* and class 1400 0–4–2s. Diesel railcars were also used and timetables had notes that most trains carried only third class accommodation, and that was stated to be 'limited' between Woofferton and Kidderminster.

BR hopes of closing the entire route to passengers in summer 1961 were so strongly opposed that a morning service from Tenbury to Bewdley and an evening return was maintained Mondays to Fridays. They were handled by locomotives which could be used also for goods traffic. The arrangement lasted until 1 August 1962. Freight withdrawal followed in two stages, the service from Bewdley being cut back from Tenbury to Cleobury Mortimer in January 1964. Complete line closure took place in February 1966.

Every autumn I try to visit the Severn Valley Railway, almost as an act of thanksgiving that it, too, is not a forgotten railway. Sometimes, towards sunset, I sight the Dowles viaduct abutments and piers and the Forest beyond and dream of how wonderful it would be if the line could reopen.

For, in contrast to the Severn Valley with its many open views, the line through the Forest took the passenger to seemingly secret places, so near, yet so far from outlying towns of the West Midlands just over the hill, notably Stourbridge and Kidderminster.


*Cleobury Mortimer & Ditton Priors Light Railway*
Somewhere on the B4364 road that rolls over the hills between Bridgnorth and Ludlow, there is a cricket ground. I stopped briefly once and watched a match in which players were back-clothed by hills that stretched for miles and looked glorious in the midsummer sun.

I am not sure where the ground was, except that it was near where the Cleobury Mortimer & Ditton Priors Light Railway used to cross that road. My efforts to find the railway's

**G W** **128**

### ROSS-ON-WYE, MONMOUTH, and PONTYPOOL ROAD—(One class only)

| Miles | Down. | Week Days. | | | | | | | | | | | | | | | | | | Sundays. | | |
|---|---|---|---|---|---|---|---|---|---|---|---|---|---|---|---|---|---|---|---|---|---|---|
| | | mrn | mrn | mrn | mrn | mrn | mrn | mrn | aft | aft | aft | aft | aft | aft | aft | aft | aft | aft | aft | mrn | | aft |
| | Ross-on-Wye ¶ ..........dep. | 6 40 | 7 13 | 8 22 | B | 1057 | B | 1148 | .. | 1 50 | 3 1 | B | 4 30 | .. | 5 10 | B | 7 25 | B | | 1010 | .. | 7 15 |
| 4 | Kerne Bridge A ........ | 6 50 | 7 23 | 8 32 | .. | 11 7 | .. | 1156 | .. | 2 0 | 3 11 | .. | 4 40 | .. | 5 20 | .. | 7 35 | .. | | 1019 | .. | 7 25 |
| 5½ | Lydbrook Junction ........ | 6 51 | 7 26 | 8 36 | .. | 1111 | .. | 1159 | .. | 2 4 | 3 15 | .. | 4 44 | .. | 5 24 | .. | 7 39 | .. | Saturdays only. | 1024 | .. | 7 29 |
| 7½ | Symonds Yat ........ | 6 59 | .. | 8 41 | .. | 1116 | .. | | .. | 2 8 | 3 20 | .. | | .. | 5 29 | .. | 7 44 | .. | | 1029 | .. | 7 34 |
| 12½ | Monmouth (May Hill) ........ | 7 8 | .. | 8 50 | 9 20 | 1125 | 1158 | Saturdays only. | .. | .. | 3 30 | .. | Except Saturdays. | .. | 5 38 | 6 43 | 7 53 | .. | | 1040 | .. | 7 45 |
| 13 | " (Troy) 89.. arr. | 7 14 | .. | 8 55 | 9 22 | 1128 | 12 0 | | .. | .. | 3 37 | .. | | .. | 5 42 | 6 44 | 7 58 | .. | | 1043 | .. | 7 50 |
| | dep. | 7 28 | .. | .. | 9 25 | 1155 | .. | | .. | .. | .. | 3 51 | | 5 25 | .. | .. | .. | 8 48 | | 1050 | .. | 8 0 |
| 16½ | Dingestow ¶ ........ | 7 34 | .. | .. | 9 31 | 12 1 | .. | | .. | .. | .. | 3 57 | | 5 31 | .. | .. | .. | 8 54 | | 1056 | .. | 8 6 |
| 19½ | Raglan ¶ ........ | 7 42 | .. | .. | 9 37 | 12 9 | .. | | .. | .. | .. | 4 3 | | 5 39 | .. | .. | .. | 9 1 | | 11 5 | .. | 8 15 |
| 21½ | Llandenny ........ | 7 49 | .. | .. | 9 43 | 1216 | .. | | .. | .. | .. | 4 9 | | 5 46 | .. | .. | .. | 9 6 | | 1112 | .. | 8 22 |
| 25 | Usk ........ | 7 57 | .. | .. | 9 50 | 1223 | .. | | 1 58 | .. | .. | 4 16 | | 5 53 | .. | .. | .. | 9 13 | 9 50 | 1120 | .. | 8 30 |
| 27 | Glascoed Halt ........ [125 | 8 2 | .. | .. | 9 55 | 1228 | .. | | 2 3 | .. | .. | 4 21 | .. | 5 58 | .. | .. | .. | 9 18 | 9 55 | 1126 | .. | 8 36 |
| 29 | Little Mill Junction ..[122, | 8 7 | .. | .. | 9 58 | 1233 | .. | .. | 2 8 | .. | .. | 4 25 | .. | 6 3 | .. | .. | .. | 9 21 | 10 0 | 1130 | .. | 8 40 |
| 31 | Pontypool Road 80, arr. | 8 11 | .. | .. | 10 3 | 1242 | .. | .. | 2 12 | .. | .. | 4 30 | .. | 6 7 | .. | .. | .. | 9 26 | 10 4 | 1134 | .. | 8 44 |

| Miles | Up. | Week Days. | | | | | | | | | | | | | | | | | | Sundays. | | |
|---|---|---|---|---|---|---|---|---|---|---|---|---|---|---|---|---|---|---|---|---|---|---|
| | | mrn | mrn | mrn | B | mrn | B | aft | aft | aft | aft | aft | aft | aft | aft | B | aft | aft | | aft | | aft |
| | Pontypool Road ........dep. | .. | .. | 7 42 | 8 33 | .. | 1114 | | .. | 1 30 | .. | 2 30 | 3 56 | .. | .. | 6 2 | .. | 9 30 | .. | 1 52 | .. | 5 15 |
| 2 | Little Mill Junction ........ | .. | .. | 7 46 | 8 37 | .. | 1118 | | .. | 1 34 | .. | 2 34 | 4 0 | .. | .. | 6 6 | .. | 9 34 | .. | 1 56 | .. | 5 19 |
| 4 | Glascoed Halt ........ | .. | .. | 7 50 | 8 41 | .. | 1122 | Saturdays only. | .. | 1 38 | .. | 2 38 | 4 4 | .. | .. | 6 10 | .. | 9 38 | .. | 2 0 | .. | 5 23 |
| 6 | Usk ........ | .. | .. | 7 59 | 8 47 | .. | 1128 | | .. | 1 44 | .. | 2 44 | 4 10 | | .. | 6 15 | .. | 9 44 | .. | 2 6 | .. | 5 29 |
| 9½ | Llandenny ¶ ........ | .. | .. | 8 6 | 8 53 | .. | 1134 | | .. | .. | .. | 2 51 | .. | Except Saturdays. | .. | 6 22 | .. | Saturdays only. | .. | 2 13 | .. | 5 36 |
| 11½ | Raglan ¶ ........ | .. | .. | 8 12 | 8 59 | .. | 1140 | | .. | .. | .. | 2 57 | .. | | .. | 6 27 | .. | | .. | 2 20 | .. | 5 43 |
| 14½ | Dingestow ........ | .. | .. | 8 21 | 9 6 | .. | 1147 | | .. | .. | .. | 3 5 | .. | | .. | 6 34 | .. | | .. | 2 26 | .. | 5 51 |
| 18 | Monmouth (Troy) 89.. arr. | .. | .. | 8 26 | 9 12 | .. | 1153 | | .. | .. | .. | 3 12 | .. | | .. | 6 40 | .. | | .. | 2 32 | .. | 5 57 |
| | dep. | 7 24 | .. | 8A28 | 9 14 | 9 46 | 1154 | | 1240 | .. | .. | 3 51 | .. | | 6 20 | 6 41 | 8 43 | | .. | 2 36 | .. | 6 0 |
| 18½ | " (May Hill) ........ | 7 27 | .. | 8A30 | 9 16 | 9 50 | 1156 | | 1244 | .. | .. | 3 54 | .. | | 6 24 | 6 42 | 8 47 | | .. | 2 39 | .. | 6 3 |
| 23½ | Symonds' Yat ........ | 7 37 | .. | .. | .. | 10 0 | .. | | 1254 | .. | 2 20 | 4 4 | .. | | 6 34 | .. | 8 57 | | .. | 2 49 | .. | 6 13 |
| 25½ | Lydbrook Junction ........ | 7 42 | 8 0 | .. | .. | 10 7 | .. | 1210 | 1259 | .. | 2 24 | 4 9 | .. | 4 50 | 6 39 | .. | 9 2 | | .. | 2 54 | .. | 6 18 |
| 27 | Kerne Bridge A ¶ ........ | 7 46 | 8 4 | .. | .. | 1011 | .. | 1214 | 1 3 | .. | 2 29 | 4 13 | .. | 4 54 | 6 43 | .. | 9 6 | | .. | 2 58 | .. | 6 22 |
| 31 | Ross-on-Wye (below) ....arr. | 7 55 | 8 13 | .. | .. | 1020 | .. | 1223 | 1 12 | .. | 2 38 | 4 22 | .. | 5 3 | 6 52 | .. | 9 17 | | .. | 3 8 | .. | 6 32 |

**A** Station for Goodrich Castle. A Not during School Holidays.
**B** One class only. Limited accommodation.
¶ "Halts" at Walford between Ross-on-Wye and Kerne Bridge; at Elms Bridge, between Dingestow and Raglan; and at Raglan Road Crossing between Raglan and Llandenny.

### GLOUCESTER, ROSS-ON-WYE, and HEREFORD.

| Miles | Down. | Week Days. | | | | | | | | | | Sun. | |
|---|---|---|---|---|---|---|---|---|---|---|---|---|---|
| | | mrn | mrn | mrn | | mrn | mrn | aft | aft | aft | | | |
| | 74 London (Pad.) ........dep. | 12A55 | 12A55 | 5 30 | .. | 9 15 | 1045 | 12V45 | 3 15 | 6 35 | .. | .. | .. |
| — | Gloucester ........dep. | 5 32 | 7 15 | 9 45 | .. | 1235 | 2 5 | 3 47 | 6 10 | 9 24 | .. | .. | .. |
| 5½ | Oakle Street ........ | .. | 7 24 | 9 54 | .. | 1244 | 2 14 | 3 56 | 6 19 | 9 30 | .. | .. | .. |
| 7½ | Grange Court ¶ ........ | Aa | 7 29 | 9 59 | .. | 1249 | 2 19 | 4 2 | 6 24 | 9 36 | .. | .. | .. |
| 11 | Longhope ........ | .. | 7 42 | 10 9 | .. | 1259 | 2 29 | 4 12 | 6 34 | 9 45 | .. | .. | .. |
| 14 | Mitcheldean Road ¶ ........ | .. | 7 51 | 10 16 | .. | 1 6 | 2 36 | 4 19 | 6 42 | 9 53 | .. | .. | .. |
| 18 | Ross-on-Wye (above) ¶ ........ | 6B10 | 8B5 | 10 27 | .. | 1B20 | 2 48 | 4F35 | 6 54 | 10 3 | .. | .. | .. |
| 22 | Fawley ........ | .. | 8 16 | 10 37 | .. | 1 33 | 2 58 | 4 46 | 7 6 | 1012 | .. | .. | .. |
| 23 | Ballingham ........ | .. | 8 19 | 10 41 | .. | 1 37 | 3 1 | 4 49 | 7 9 | .. | .. | .. | .. |
| 26 | Holme Lacy ........ | .. | 8 27 | 10 49 | .. | 1 45 | 3 11 | 4 58 | 7 18 | 1022 | .. | .. | .. |
| 30 | Hereford 122, 490, 699 arr. | 6 35 | 8 35 | 10 58 | .. | 1 53 | 3 18 | 5 6 | 7 27 | 1031 | .. | .. | .. |

| Miles | Up. | Week Days. | | | | | | | | | | Sun. | |
|---|---|---|---|---|---|---|---|---|---|---|---|---|---|
| | | mrn | mrn | mrn | | aft | aft | aft | aft | E | S | | |
| | Hereford ........dep. | 7 5 | 7 35 | 1020 | .. | 1 15 | 2 20 | 4 10 | 6 48 | 8 55 | 9 35 | .. | .. |
| 4 | Holme Lacy ........ | 7 13 | 7 43 | 1028 | .. | 1 23 | 2 28 | 4 18 | 6 56 | 9 4 | 9 43 | .. | .. |
| 7 | Ballingham ........ | .. | 7 49 | 1034 | .. | 1 29 | 2 34 | 4 24 | 7 2 | .. | 9 49 | .. | .. |
| 8 | Fawley ¶ ........ | 7 21 | 7 52 | 1037 | .. | 1 34 | 2 37 | 4 27 | 7 8 | 9 13 | 9 52 | .. | .. |
| 12 | Ross-on-Wye (above) ¶ ........ | 7 29 | 8B6 | 1051 | .. | 1 47 | 2 49 | 4 39 | 7 23 | 9B26 | 10 5 | .. | .. |
| 16 | Mitcheldean Road ........ | 7 39 | 8 17 | 11 1 | .. | 1 58 | 3 0 | 4 50 | 7 34 | 9 36 | 1017 | .. | .. |
| 19 | Longhope ¶ ........ | 7 44 | 8 23 | 11 7 | .. | 2 3 | 3 6 | 4 56 | 7 40 | 9 45 | 1023 | .. | .. |
| 22½ | Grange Court 74 ........ | 7 53 | 8 33 | 1118 | .. | 2 13 | 3 14 | 5 5 | 7 48 | 9 54 | 1030 | .. | .. |
| 24½ | Oakle Street ........ | 7 57 | 8 37 | 1122 | .. | 2 17 | .. | 5 9 | 7 52 | Cc | Cc | .. | .. |
| 30 | Gloucester 75, 76, 656 arr. | 8 6 | 8 46 | 1131 | .. | 2 25 | 3 25 | 5 17 | 8 2 | 10 8 | 1043 | .. | .. |
| 144½ | 75 London (Pad.) ........arr. | 1030 | 1230 | 2 30 | .. | 5 0 | 7H0 | 8 45 | 2D40 | 3 25 | 3 25 | .. | .. |

A Except Mondays.
Aa Stops to set down on notice to Guard at Gloucester.
B Arr. 5 mins. *earlier*.
Cc Stops when required to take up
D Sunday mornings only.
E Except Saturdays.
F Arr. 8 mins. *earlier*.
H Arr. 8 10 aft. on Sats.
m One class only.
S Saturdays only.
V Via Kingham and Cheltenham Spa (Malvern Road), see pages 116, 136, and 76.

¶ "Halts" at Blaisdon, between Grange Court and Longhope; at Weston-under-Penyard, between Mitcheldean Road and Ross-on-Wye; and at Backney, between Ross-on-Wye and Fawley.

For **OTHER TRAINS** between Gloucester and Grange Court, see page 74.

### CLEOBURY MORTIMER and DITTON PRIORS HALT.

| Miles | Down. | Week Days only. | | | | | | |
|---|---|---|---|---|---|---|---|---|
| | | mrn | | | aft | | aft | |
| | Cleobury Mortimer.dep. | 9 30 | .. | Wednesdays only. | 2 24 | .. | 5 20 | .. |
| 2 | Cleobury Town Halt arr. | 9 40 | .. | | 2 34 | .. | 5 28 | .. |
| | dep. | 9 48 | .. | | 2 39 | .. | 5 29 | .. |
| 4½ | Detton Ford Siding ........ | 9A58 | .. | | 2A48 | .. | 5A36 | .. |
| 5½ | Prescott Siding ........ | 10A5 | .. | | 2A53 | .. | 5A40 | .. |
| 6½ | Stottesdon Halt ........ | 10 11 | .. | | 3 1 | .. | 5 45 | .. |
| 8½ | Aston Botterell Siding ... | 10A20 | .. | | 3A13 | .. | 5A50 | .. |
| 9½ | Burwarton Halt ........ | 10 29 | .. | | 3 19 | .. | 5 57 | .. |
| 10½ | Cleobury North Crossing.. | 10A40 | .. | | 3A27 | .. | 6A4 | .. |
| 12 | Ditton Priors Halt..arr. | 10 48 | .. | | 3 36 | .. | 6 11 | .. |

| Miles | Up. | Week Days only. | | | | | | |
|---|---|---|---|---|---|---|---|---|
| | | mrn | | | aft | | aft | |
| | Ditton Priors Halt ....dep. | 11 10 | .. | Wednesdays only. | 3 50 | .. | 6 23 | .. |
| 1½ | Cleobury North Crossing ... | 11A16 | .. | | 3A53 | .. | 6A25 | .. |
| 2½ | Burwarton Halt ........ | 11 23 | .. | | 4 3 | .. | 6 32 | .. |
| 3½ | Aston Botterell Siding ..... | 11A27 | .. | | .. | .. | .. | .. |
| 5½ | Stottesdon Halt ........ | 11 35 | .. | | 4 13 | .. | 6 43 | .. |
| 6½ | Prescott Siding ........ | 11A40 | .. | | .. | .. | .. | .. |
| 7½ | Detton Ford Siding ........ | 11A48 | .. | | 4A24 | .. | 6A52 | .. |
| 10 | Cleobury Town Halt.. arr. | 12 5 | .. | | 4 34 | .. | 7 2 | .. |
| | dep. | 12 10 | .. | | 4 44 | .. | 7 4 | .. |
| 12 | Cleobury Mortimer 135 ar. | 12 20 | .. | | 4 58 | .. | 7 14 | .. |

A Stop when required.

**Directions for using the Guide,** see page ii

The ultimate GW backwater branch had nothing but halts, sidings and a crossing as calling points, even the terminus being a halt. There were few patrons of the 1938 CM & DP service. Rather busier was the Gloucester, Ross and Hereford branch. The withdrawal of passenger services in 1964 reduced Hereford's importance as a junction.

remains led to an unusual clue on another road – the B4363 where it is on a hillside overlooking Cleobury Mortimer to the west. For on an electricity pole I found a small letterbox with the tag 'Cleobury Town Station'. That was more than four decades after a regular passenger train had called at the modest station.

The line has too many admirers to be forgotten. Among their ranks may be some of the enthusiasts who 'invaded' Cleobury Mortimer station on Saturday 24 September 1938. According to the *Railway Magazine* 'this invasion apparently took the Great Western Railway by surprise'. The two four-wheeled gas-lit carriages, dingy but comparatively comfortable, which formed the branch train that day had to be augmented by two 'in a more delapidated condition' which were requisitioned from a siding.

The magazine also reported that the booking clerk was 'running to and fro issuing excess tickets' needed by most passengers as there were no through bookings to and from the branch.

It might have been a different situation had the hopes of the promoters been realised. In Edwardian days, the Rea Valley was one of the largest areas of Britain without railways. There was a demand for the transporting of valuable Dhu stones from the Clee Hill quarries owned by Lord Boyne to expanding urban districts, especially as the stone was regarded as excellent for tramway setts. A Light Railway Order was obtained in 1901, but it was another seven years before trains ran. A goods service began on 19 July 1908, and then two or three weekday only mixed trains were introduced from 20 November. The last train of the day from Ditton Priors was shown in a footnote to GWR timetables as running to Cleobury Town, only continuing to the junction 'when required for the convenience of Passengers from Stottesdon and beyond'.

A rope-worked incline brought stone down from Brown Clee Hill to Ditton Priors and an aerial ropeway linked quarries on Titterstone Clee with a siding at Detton Ford, $4^1/_2$ miles from the junction. In addition the railway carried a growing volume

Deep in the Country: *Plate 13 (above)* Few stations were more isolated than Neen Sollars, five miles east of Tenbury on the branch to Bewdley. *Plate 14 (below)* And few stations were more primative than Detton, a few miles north of Neen Sollars, on the Cleobury Mortimer & Ditton Priors Light Railway.

Worcester: Town and Country: *Plate 15 (above)* The Vinegar branch penetrated the city's heart to serve several industries. Pannier tank No 1661 fitted
with spark-arresting chimney, crosses the Worcester & Hereford main line as
it leaves the branch. Shrub Hill station is in the background, left. *Plate 16
(below)* Leigh Court station on the Worcester–Leominster branch has a
noticeboard for anglers – not passengers. The fenced shell of the station
building is used by an angling club whose members fish the river Teme
alongside.

of agricultural produce and there were hopes of developing a tourist industry. The *Railway Magazine* of April 1909 pointed out that Brown Clee Hill (1,792 ft) and the highest in Shropshire, commanded magnificent views.

> Now that it is possible to get by train to the base, there will be many seeking health on the heights of this mountain, on the slope of which in time, a new health resort may spring up, out-rivalling even Malvern and Church Stretton.

But those places were far more accessible by rail and the only tourists to the Rea Valley seem to have been rail enthusiasts.

The CD & MP lost some of its appeal with the passing of mixed trains, although its locomotives, two Manning Wardle 0–6–0 saddle tanks, remained the hallmark of the line's individuality. They worked a dwindling volume of freight until World War II brought a new role to the line, the one for which it is best remembered.

For like the Shropshire & Montgomeryshire, it became the feeder for a huge and scattered ammunition dump. The Admiralty built it in the lonely countryside around Ditton Priors. Locomotives and brake vans were fitted with spark arresters. Those of the locomotives, including GWR Pannier tanks, resembled large buckets or small balloons.

Sturdy locomotives were needed to conquer six stretches at 1 in 60 and sharp curves. Speeds were low because of crossing 13 roads. It was only within an Admiralty depot that diesel locomotives handled wagons.

The return of peace marked the start of gradual rundown of traffic and in 1957 the Admiralty took control of the line from the Western Region. It began its own operation in September of that year and continued until the branch closed on 16 April 1965, together with the last section of the Tenbury Wells – Bewdley branch east of Cleobury Mortimer, which provided the only access to the line for its entire life, although it would not have done so had extensions been made to

Bridgnorth or Coalport, and to Presthope. They never reached the planning stage.

*Railway Clearing House* maps marked the CM & DP in deep purple – still appropriate today because the railway is mourned so much.

# CHAPTER 5

# Railways of Worcester

*Down by The Riverside: The Butts Branch*

There are classic instances of places where the closure of railways, long or short, has immeasurably improved the environment. At Newquay in Cornwall, conversion of the cliff top section of the Harbour branch into a footpath made the resort centre a much pleasanter place to enjoy. And, inland, at Worcester, the riverside scene was improved by closure of the Butts branch from the Racecourse to the Riverside terminus on North Quay, about half a mile closer to the Cathedral.

That happened about 1930: the precise date is uncertain because it took place in an age when railway closures were few, through growing, and little notice was taken of them. Not so, three decades later when the stem of the branch between Butts Branch Junction, almost at the western end of Foregate Street station, and the Racecourse passed into history. That was an event fully recorded.

I discovered the birthright of the branch in *Bradshaw's Shareholders' Guide Railway Manual and Directory* for 1859, bought in Worcester, as it happened, while enjoying The Three Choirs Festival in 1969. I sat with it on my knee in seat 137 in Block B in the Cathedral listening to Elgar's *Dream of Gerontius*, rather than leave it in the car.

In the Oxford Worcester & Wolverhampton section I noted an Act of 23 July 1858 by which

the company is authorised to abandon the Diglis branch

and (make) the prospective substitution of a short branch from the Worcester and Hereford to the Severn, called the Butts branch.

To provide a perspective of the OW & W at that time it is worth noting that the Act also allowed the replacement of the Stourbridge branch of 1855 'by a shorter and cheaper line'; abandonment of part of the Kingswinford branch, and extended the time for 'formation of the Stratford branch'.

The Diglis branch would have served the Basin, where the Worcester & Birmingham canal locks into the Severn. This is now the only industrialised area on the City waterfront and well hidden from the eyes of tourists who now stroll along the area where the Butts branch once ran.

From the main line, the single-line branch dropped steeply on an arched embankment tucked between the Royal Infirmary and the W & H, and the viaduct, also arched on the approach to its bridge across the river. Once clear of the hospital grounds, the Butts branch swung and fell towards the Racecourse. Here there was a dog legged shunt back to the remaining section which ran south for almost three quarters of a mile alongside the river and wharves, used by barges and small vessels bigger than those able to lock into Diglis Basin. Its route took it under the arch of the W & H viaduct closest to the river.

The stub of the branch which had opened about 1862, again on a date unknown, closed in the mid nineteen fifties, officially 1 February 1957, although it had not been used for the previous two years. An earlier economy had been the withdrawal of horse box facilities by BR in Spring 1953. Although classed in *RCH Station Handbooks* as a 'siding' the line had adequate claim to be a branch. Today, the only remains are those of the arches near the Royal Infirmary. They are very matter of fact and it is far more pleasant to contemplate the old branch while walking on its route beside the river, and watching the sunset over the Malvern Hills.

## The Vinegar Branch

Another branch which penetrated deep into the heart of Worcester's thriving and tightly packed industrial area was the Vinegar branch, officially called The Worcestershire Railways, truly a grandiose title for a line of no more than 29 chains. It was also known as the Lowesmoor Tramway because it served the Lowesmoor vinegar works, which Hill Evans & Company founded in 1830. The line was owned by the Company and worked by the GWR under a maintenance agreement of 28 May 1872. It had been authorised under the Worcestershire Railways & Tramway Act of 1870.

For years the branch's fame rested on an ungated crossing at Shrub Hill Road, because it was guarded by two lower quadrant signals. From about 1930 until branch closure in 1964 they were of standard main line pattern. The crossing was the sort of topic innocuous enough to be allowed mention in the *Railway Magazine* in wartime.

There was a photograph and description in the October 1940 edition, which must have been in preparation during the Battle of Britain.

The crossing was never a danger to the Germans, but it was to historians because its fame tended to obscure the branch's importance in serving not only the vinegar works, but several others as well. Their presence was conveniently summarised in Western Region Service Time Table of summer 1954:

Trips to and from Messrs. Heenan and Froudes (including Thomasson's), Tower Manufacturing Company's sidings, and Hill Evans and Co., must not exceed 12 ordinary wagons. On trips from the Works, the gross weight of the 12 wagons must not exceed 104 tons.

Working instructions covered nearly four pages of *Appendix* to Section 15 of WR Service Time Tables a seemingly inordinate amount until operating problems and difficulties were realised, the branch gradients included two short sections at 1 in 29 and 1 in 40.

The branch started inside the Shrub Hill triangle and ran between the two engine sheds. It then crossed the Worcester & Hereford line on the level and operating instructions were precise:

> No engine or train may pass on to the line of the Worcester Railways without first stopping dead at the stopboard at a point short of the crossing. . . .The maximum speed of trains over this branch is five miles per hour; the speed of trains over Shrub Hill Road, Padmore Street and Pheasant Street Crossings must not exceed four miles per hour.

Trains first reached the private siding of the large engineering works of Heenan & Froude and sprags had to be inserted in the wheels of any wagon left standing: 'Sprags will be kept for the purpose alongside the siding in the vicinity of Tolladine Road Bridge'.

A short distance beyond, after passing the Tower Manufacturing Company's siding, trains reached Heenan & Froude (formerly Thomasson) & Company's Gateway. It was, in fact, another siding, where clearance was so tight that shunters were warned not to move alongside moving wagons.

Hill Evans provided a man to control traffic at Pheasant Street when a train was due. 'He will be equipped with the necessary flags and hurricane lamps with red glasses for stopping road traffic,' railmen were informed.

Trains were often short, especially in later years and usually they were in charge of Pannier 0-6-0 tanks, ideal for the duty. One was in charge of the last train, now nearly a quarter of a century ago. Few lines are remembered as much as this.

## Rainbows and Whistles

Worcester was City where there was an end to the spotter's rainbow: Railway Walk on Rainbow Hill, which overlooked the Shrub Hill triangle, which encompassed the two locomotive sheds, the Shrub Hill - Tunnel Junction avoiding line, the wagon works, London marshalling yard and, at further distance, other sidings, including those serving the Sheet Shops.

It was a fascinating scene almost equal to the footbridge that used to span all the tracks at the North end of Crewe station. Yet unlike Crewe, it never had an air of immortality about it.

Because the character of the Butts and Vinegar branches make them memorable, other economies in the area have been largely forgotten, especially as Worcester's main route network has remained intact, apart from the loss of local stations. Foregate Street retains its character, not least because of the refurbishment of its railway bridge, and Shrub Hill's main station building and eastern platform are grade II listed, because of strikingly ornate and attractive tiling.

There were no such refinements on three halts just across the Severn towards Hereford, which made timetable appearances between 1924 and 1965: Henwick, $1/2$ mile from Foregate Street; Boughton Halt, $3/4$ mile further west, beside the A44 Bromyard and Leominster road and still within the City boundary, and Rushwick. This was just under two miles from Foregate Street.

Henwick and Rushwick were used by Leominster trains, but Boughton was only in the Malvern and Hereford table, as was Bransford Road, which closed at the same time as the other halts. This lay west of the Leominster branch junction.

A casualty close to the northern outskirts of Worcester was Astwood Halt, not opened until 1936 and closed only three weeks after the start of World War II, although it was used by Blackpole workmen's trains. Its opening coincided with the introduction of a frequent local diesel railcar service and it was also the first stop of local trains between Worcester and the Severn Valley. They also called at Fernhill Heath, the only intermediate station between Worcester and Droitwich Spa. That, too, closed when Worcester local services were cut back in April 1965.

South of Shrub Hill, there are now no intermediate stations

before Pershore, Norton Halt and Stoulton having both closed.

At Worcester, change has been continual rather than spectacular.

### Goods Avoiding Line

Those economies simply added two more to the long list of Britain's closed stations. Far more sad, although the event passed without too much notice, was the closure of a third line in Worcester's heart: the Goods Avoiding Line between Tunnel Junction and Worcester Goods Yard Box. The rest of the route continued south for nearly half a mile, passing between Shrub Hill station and the large goods shed before reaching the Oxford Worcester & Wolverhampton main line at Wyld's Lane Box. It was known as 'Five Whistle' Road because of the beats on bell which were 1-5. The name was official, enshrined in the *Appendix* to section 15 of the Service Time Table.

After the Avoiding Line closed on 18 August 1968, the connection at Tunnel Junction was severed, but part of the middle section was retained as sidings.

Just east of London Yard lay Worcester Sheet Shop, about which the GWR *General Appendix* noted

'The Company make and maintain their own Wagon Cartage and Station Sheets. The principal part of this work is performed at Worcester, and the Sheet Works Manager who has charge of the Making and Repairing of Sheets is at that Station.

The Worcester Shop fronted Tolladine Road and was headquarters for Area No 2, covering a wide geographical section of the GWR, which had only three others - Saltney, Chester, covering Area No 1, Cathays and Bridgwater.

The Worcester triangle shrank further with the closure of the Wagon Works on 4 August 1968, but the economy was not as emotional for enthusiasts as had been the end of steam, which had taken place with the closure of the locomotive shed in December, 1965, when its status was reduced to that of a signing-on point.

The code of Worcester - WOS - crept into my World War II spotter's notebooks when I saw two of its Grange class 4-6-0s, nos 6851 *Hurst Grange* and 6877 *Llanfair Grange*, on goods trains at Birkenhead docks. They were among the final GWR allocation of 91 locomotives to Worcester, recorded in *An Historical Survey of Great Western Engine Sheds* 1947, by Edward Lyons.

Worcester GWR had two sheds, that for goods locomotives being separated from the carriage and wagon works by the Avoiding Line and several sidings. A few more sidings closer to Rainbow Hill was the slightly larger passenger shed. The diesel traction which arrived progressively to replace steam was not so much a novelty as it was in some areas, for Worcester had known diesel railcars from pre-war days, although they were outnumbered more than eight to one by steam locomotives.

Worcester's importance as a locomotive centre was best assessed by its being the headquarters of a division which had 17 sheds, including Gloucester and Cheltenham. Worcester used to repair locomotives from a wide area and the *Railway Observer* was hardly divulging state secrets when it reported in June 1940 that they included several LNER class J 25 0-6-0s. What it did not reveal was what LNER engines were doing in the area. Steam locomotives repairing at Worcester ended with closure of the repair works on 2 November 1964, after a run down lasting several years during which only locomotives from the near-area were handled.

Resignalling and rationalisation took place at Worcester in the early 1970s and the Worcester & Hereford lost intermittent permanent way trains following the closure of Newlands permanent way depot.

Much of London Yard was recovered and carriage sidings shortened in the early 1980s and a factory has been built on the site of the Midland locomotive shed, which closed about 1930.

Economies on the former Midland system in the Worcester area have an air of antiquity about them. Take Spetchley

on the Birmingham - Bristol main line, on the Evesham road, about three miles east of Worcester.

It closed to passengers in 1855, three years after completion of the Worcester Loop, by which the Midland was able to serve the city using running powers. Spetchley survived for parcels and goods until 2 January 1961, becoming one of the few stations in Britain where more than a century separated passenger and goods service withdrawals. Now it is among ten stations closed on the main line between Bromsgrove and Cheltenham.

Two other once prominent features of the Worcester railway scene are deserving of memory: the Worcester Engine Company, which built locomotives in the 1860s for several British companies, including the Great Eastern and Bristol & Exeter, and exported to Russia and other countries; and McKenzie & Holland, the signal engineers, which had their general office and works in the city, and other other works in Melbourne and Brisbane.

The company was formed as McKenzie Clunes & Holland on 21 June 1861, John McKenzie and Thomas Clunes being engineers and Walter Holland a financier. They acquired Clunes existing business at the Vulcan Ironworks in Shrub Hill. From the mid 1870's until closure in 1921. McKenzie & Holland were one of the three main signalling companies in Britain. The McKenzie Holland & Westinghouse Power Signal Company was formed on 29 August 1907 and many of the Worcester men moved to its Chippenham, Wiltshire, works in 1921.

In 1918 the signal engineers, McKenzie & Holland, projected themselves in London rather than a provincial setting, central London offices taking preference over the Worcester works.

# CHAPTER 6

# The Marches

*Worcester - Bromyard - Leominster*

It is many years since steam animated the lonely countryside between Worcester and Leominster, where country airs are as full of fragrance as the after-shave sachets offered to passengers on *The Manchester Pullman*. For this was a single branch on which economies began well ahead of Beeching.

The westerly 12 miles between Leominster and Bromyard were closed when passenger and freight services were withdrawn in September 1952, and the remainder of the 23 miles between Leominster and the Worcester & Hereford at Bransford Road Junction survived only until 1964, a year after the *Beeching Report*

The Worcester - Leominster branch and the Woofferton - Bewdley branches bear comparison, not least because of their birthright, each by two local companies destined, from the start, to join the GWR fold.

At closest they were about six miles apart (at Fencote and Tenbury Wells) and, at farthest, about twice that distance, Wyre Forest station lying about 13 crow-flying miles north of Knightwick. The Worcester orientated branch was firmly in that County, while its neighbour flirted with the Worcester - Shropshire border. Bromyard was the only intermediate place of any size between Worcester and Leominster, but the other branch served Cleobury Mortimer and Tenbury Wells.

That is partly the reason why they received railways well ahead of Bromyard, the through route to Bewdley having been completed in 1864, a decade before the first seven miles of the branch from Worcester, and three decades ahead of establishment of the through route.

Did passengers who used the branches ever realise, or care, that their services formed the first two tables in the *Hereford ABC Railway Guide* of summer 1935 (and, no doubt, many other issues)? The reasons why the compilers decided to give preference to humble branch trains rather than the expresses on the North to West route will remain one of the little mysteries of local railway history.

Worcester - Leominster trains used Shrub Hill station at the start and finish of their journeys and called at Foregate Street. Journey times were leisurely, almost 1hr 20mins being allowed between Worcester and Leominster, where connections were offered to Hereford reached anything up to 1hr 25mins later.

Not all passenger trains were shown in public timetables. Notable exceptions were those run from Birmingham and the Black Country to Worcestershire for hop pickers.

Their stock make-up was special, for, according to the GWR *General Appendix:*

Only *THIRD* Class coaches of the oldest type must be used for the conveyance of Hop-pickers. In no circumstances are lavatory carriages or carriages with first class compartments to be provided.

A meeting of the Great Western Railway (London) Lecture & Debating Society in January 1948 was told of 'the colossal number of people moved in a very short time'. The speaker said the problem of running hop pickers specials was particularly acute before World War II, on Saturdays and Sundays when there was a heavy programme of day and half-day excursions.

Once roads were improved, the branch was vulnerable to competition. The A44 closely follows the Worcester - Leominster trackbed and by-passes Bromyard, although that section was not built until some years after the branch had gone.

The types of locomotives allowed to use the branch were

severely restricted. 'Yellow' group locomotives were common for many years and the branch passenger trains were usually in charge of 0-4-2 tanks at the head of a trailer coach.

After closure between Leominster and Bromyard, the track was used for six years for condemned wagon storage - more than 600 of them. They were marshalled in batches with rail removed between them to prevent runaway accidents on the steep gradients. That was an age when no-one was quite sure whether railways were in decline to the extent that the industry feared.

Track, narrow gauge, returned to Bromyard under the auspices of the Bromyard & Linton Light Railway Association, using mainly diesel locomotive stock. I enjoyed exploring the route enormously on a glorious day in early autumn.

The branch with a strong feeling of remoteness and there were rewards for going in search of it. John Mair, an enthusiast, wrote in 1977 about his personal quest. At Steens Bridge, where a housing estate has replaced the station, he met a

> very charming old lady who remembered the station very well and told me that her own bungalow (no. 25) had been built on the site of the booking office.

He was particularly struck by Fencote station and its setting;

> It lies in a beautiful but isolated hollow - it is remarkable that someone thought it worthwhile to build a substantial two platform station there! The main building has been converted into a private house, and the platform on which it stands is linked by a small footway across the trackbed to the other platform. There were flowers and conifers usually found at GWR stations. Seen in mellow evening light, Fencote was undoubtedly the gem among the stations I saw during the trip.

John Mair ended his letter with a lament surely widely shared by enthusiasts: 'I find that these visits to closed stations are partly rewarding and partly melancholy, so I usually take just a few at a time.'

There are reminders of the branch close to both its main line junctions. Bransford Road on the Worcester & Hereford is worth spotting from the carriage window because it had three names in its lifetime: Bransford Junction, Leominster Junction, and finally, from 1950-64, Bransford Road. Compilers of railtour itineraries over the Shrewsbury & Hereford generally noted the remains of the branch trackbed running parallel for more than a mile south from Leominster, until it was largely absorbed by the A49 Leominster by-pass, constructed 1987-88.

After the branch trackbed climbs away east, crossing the river Arrow on a short bridge, the by-pass follows the S & H for several miles to the ridge pierced by Dinmore Tunnel.

I noted the by-pass under construction from *Y Cymro - The Welshman* (Cardiff - Holyhead), pulled by a class 47 named after Henry Ford.

### *The Kington Branches*

For ramblers living near Worcester, the branch to Leominster offered a useful and pleasant escape route into the heart of the Welsh Border country. For by catching the 8.5am from Shrub Hill, they could be in New Radnor or Presteigne by 10.45am.

The journey involved a 26mins wait at Leominster, hub of the Kington branches. Collectively, the Kington branches totalled three or four, depending on how you choose to interpret railway history. The stem was built by two independent companies, which took a line from Leominster to the small yet busy market town of Kington, and then west for a few more miles to New Radnor.

The other two 'Kington' branches ran north from Titley to Presteigne and south to the Hereford Hay & Brecon at Eardisley. All had very much the same character being GWR and all ran through some of the quietest country found anywhere in Britain.

Quarries first attracted canal promoters to the area and the Leominster Canal of 1791 was planned as a 46 mile link from the Severn at Stourport. Only about half had been completed before tramroads came into vogue. By 1816, the Hay Railway had reached Hay and was being extended to Eardisley when Kington businessmen embarked on what was effectively an extension from there to expanding limeworks at Burlinjobb, three and a half miles west. Built to 3ft 6in gauge, the same as the Hay Railway, the section to Kington quickly thrived, but it was some years before it was extended beyond.

It was regarded locally as part of the Hay Railway, Murray's *South Wales Handbook* of 1860 noting that the road west from Kington to Aberystwyth ran parallel to the tramroad: 'It is used for supplying this district with coal, and conveys in return lime and agricultural produce into Breconshire.'

By then its useful life was drawing to an end for the Leominster & Kington Railway, authorised in 1854 and opened in 1857, was beginning to thrive. The line was leased to the contractors Brassey and Field and although there was a cash shortage, the company was able to report from its offices in Corn Square, Leominster, in 1859 that traffic was steadily increasing along the $13^1/_4$ mile route.

Three years later the Company was leased to the West Midland Railway and, in 1865, to the GWR, with which it amalgamated in 1898. In the interim it completed the Presteigne branch, which was opened in 1875.

More significantly perhaps, that was the year which saw completion of the 'main stem' from Kington $6^1/_2$ miles west to New Radnor, a village which had been replaced as County Town of Radnor by the more conveniently situated and less isolated village of Presteigne. The line was built by the Kington & Eardisley Railway, which had been authorised in 1862 to acquire the Kington Railway and build a branch to link Kington and Eardisley.

Herefordshire Contrasts: *Plate 17 (above)* Bromyard was a small station on the Worcester–Leominster branch, yet adequate for the village and surrounding area that it served. *Plate 18 (below)* Leominster is still a busy, unmanned station, although only a shadow of its former self when it was called 'Leominster Junction' and was the grand junction of the Marches. Trains to Worcester and over the Kington branches departed from the platform on the east side of the Shrewsbury & Hereford main line.

The Kington Branches: *Plate 19 (above)* Kingsland lay on the main stem of the branches. Pannier No 7416 returns east with the daily Kington–Leominster freight. 11 April 1956. *Plate 20 (below)* Titley, junction for the Presteigne and Eardisley branches, lay in the middle of the countryside. The scene in August 1932.

### Presteigne Branch

*Murray's Handbook* noted that Presteigne - then spelt without a final 'e' - was 'more suited from position and importance' to handle the business of Radnorshire, yet even with the arrival of the railway in 1875, it did not grow and Kington remained the hub of the area.

Presteigne was reached at the third attempt by the Leominster & Kington, which took powers in 1871 after the lapsing of those obtained by the Kington & Eardisley Railway in its Act of 1864 and re-stated by another four years later.

The branch left the Leominster & Kington near Titley station and ran to a terminus close to Presteigne jail, later replaced by one more than a quarter of a mile nearer the centre. No intermediate stop appeared in the timetables until Forge Crossing halt opened in 1929.

The passenger service never took up much space in timetables. In table 14 in the *Hereford ABC Railway Guide* of summer 1935, there was a panel $3^1/_4$ inches wide by $^3/_4$ inch deep, comfortably adequate for the three weekday trains each way between Kington and Presteigne, even allowing for the extravagance of showing a minute separating arrival and departure at Titley.

### Kington & Eardisley Railway

Alongside the Presteigne table, was Kington - Eardisley, also of three weekday only trains, with the first departure from Kington at 9 am almost an hour and a half after the first to Presteigne. The Eardisley service ended earlier, the last train of the day returning to Kington just after 5 o'clock.

By 1935 the Eardisley branch had only five more summers to live for it closed completely on 1 July 1940 as Hitler over-ran France. The wartime setting meant that history was repeating itself for the seven mile branch had been a casualty of World War I. It closed on 1 January 1917 and did not reopen until four years after hostilities ended.

When World War II broke out, the passenger service was

down to two trains each day. The *Railway Observer* commented: 'It is difficult to see how such a service could possibly pay', and noted that it was worked by Worcester 58XX 0-4-2 tanks working from Kington sub-shed.

So it became the shortest lived of the Kington branches. It was not opened until August 1874 as the first part of the K & E for the Kington - New Radnor section was not ready for another year. The company worked between them exercising running powers over the GWR from Titley to Kington - a 'bond' which continued until the GWR absorbed the company in 1897.

The GWR had, of course, worked the K & E lines from their opening, although not, it would seem, to the entire satisfaction of the small company. It reported in *Bradshaw's Manual* the situation in 1896: 'The Great Western continue to work the line, but have rendered no accounts of such working. The directors, therefore, were unable to furnish any revenue accounts for the half-year ended 30th June 1896'. At that time, the K & E had three directors, all local men. The company bankers were at Kington - a branch of the Birmingham District & Counties Banking Company Ltd. - but the offices were in the City of London.

Like the Presteigne branch, which the L & K built with gradients which stiffened to 1 in 43, that to Eardisley was steep, the drop into the Wye Valley at Eardisley being for three miles at an average of 1 in 45.

Another feature, as John D Hewitt described in the *Railway Magazine* of September 1939, was the setting: 'The descent gives a magnificent panoramic view of the broad basin of the Wye, with Hay Bluff and the Black Mountains beyond.'

The branch curved sharply west to join the HH & B at Eardisley, but to reach the station with a spacious layout,

The *Hereford ABC Railway Guide* of summer 1935 included a number of branches that have long passed into history. Among them were the Kington branches and those that linked much of rural Shropshire with Wellington.

**15**

## LEOMINSTER, KINGTON & NEW RADNOR.—G.W.R. WEEK DAYS ONLY.

| | A.M | A.M | P.M | P.M | P.M | P.M |
|---|---|---|---|---|---|---|
| 71 HEREFORD (S.Hill) dep | 9 15 | 1145 | 4 15 | 5 15 | 7 30 | 9 35 |
| 1 WORCESTER(S.Hill) | 8 5 | 1025 | 3* 2 | | 7 55 | 7 13 |
| | | | *Sats.* | | *Sats.* | |
| | | | *excepted* | | *only.* | |
| Leominster ........ dep | 6 18 | 9 52 | 1235 | 5 0 | 6 0 | 9 10 8 |
| Kingsland ......... | 6 28 | 10 1 | 1250 | 5 9 | 6 9 | 14 1017 |
| Pembridge ......... | 6 37 | 10 9 | 1 25 | 5 17 | 6 22 | 22 1025 |
| Marston ........... | | 1014 | 1 9 | | 6 29 | 31 1031 |
| Titley ............ | 6 51 | 1022 | 1 18 | 5 26 | 6 31 | 37 1038 |
| Kington 14 ... arr | 6 56 | 1026 | 1 23 | 5 33 | 6 35 | 41 1042 |
| Stanner ........... dep | | 1031 | | 5 38 | | |
| Dolyhir ........... | | 1035 | | 5 45 | | |
| New Radnor ... arr | | 1045 | 2 13 | 5 55 | | |

| | A.M | P.M | P.M | P.M | |
|---|---|---|---|---|---|
| New Radnor ...... dep | 1050 | | | | |
| Dolyhir ........... | 1056 | | | | |
| Stanner ........... | 11 6 | | | | |
| Kington .... arr | 7 22 | 1110 | 2 0 | 3 6 | 6 5 |
| Titley ............ | 7 25 | 1114 | 2 4 | 3 6 | 6 11 |
| Marston ........... | 7 30 | 1119 | 2 10 | 3 21 | 6 15 |
| Pembridge ......... | 7 36 | 1124 | 2 16 | 3 36 | 6 21 |
| Kingsland ......... | 7 44 | 1134 | 2 25 | 3 77 | 6 27 |
| Leominster ... arr | 7 54 | 1141 | 2 32 | 3 87 | 6 52 |
| 1 WORCESTER(S.Hill) arr | 1011 | 40 | 15* | 2 87 | 8 6 |
| 71 HEREFORD ... arr | 8 35 | 1215 | 3 7 | 35 | 9 2 |
| | | | | | 10 2 |

* Via Hereford.
‡ Foregate Street.

---

**14**

## KINGTON and PRESTEIGN.—WEEK DAYS ONLY.

| | A.M | P.M | P.M | P.M | P.M | P.M |
|---|---|---|---|---|---|---|
| Kington ......... dep | 1029 | 1 5 | 5 23 | 1050 | 2 38 | 6 3 |
| Titley ............ | 1032 | 1 9 | 5 27 | 1068 | 2 48 | 6 13 |
| Forge Crossing .. dep | 1033 | 1 25 | 5 32 | 11 2 | 2 54 | 6 19 |
| Presteign ... arr | 1040 | 1 38 | 5 49 | 11 7 | 3 2 | 6 24 |

| | A.M | P.M | P.M |
|---|---|---|---|
| Presteign ....... dep | 1050 | 2 38 | 6 3 |
| Forge Crossing .. arr | 1068 | 2 48 | 6 13 |
| Titley ........... dep | 11 2 | 2 54 | 6 20 |
| Kington 15 ... arr | 11 7 | 3 2 | 6 24 |

*Sats. only.*

---

**16**

## KINGTON and EARDISLEY.—WEEK DAYS ONLY.

One class only.

| | A.M | A.M | P.M |
|---|---|---|---|
| Kington ......... dep | 9 0 | 1117 | 3 30 |
| Titley ............ | 9 10 | 1121 | 3 35 |
| Lyonshall ......... | 9 25 | 1125 | 3 40 |
| Eardisley ... arr | 9 38 | 1134 | 4 55 |

| | A.M | no'n | P.M |
|---|---|---|---|
| Eardisley ....... dep | 10 2 | 12 04 | 4 48 |
| Almeley ........... | 10 7 | 12 64 | 4 53 |
| Lyonshall ......... | 1014 | 1215 | 5 5 |
| Titley ............ | 1018 | 1222 | 5 6 |
| Kington 15 ... arr | 1022 | 1226 | 5 9 |

---

**17**

## CRAVEN ARMS, MUCH WENLOCK and WELLINGTON.—G.W.R. WEEK DAYS ONLY.

| | A.M | A.M | A.M | | P.M | P.M | P.M | J | S |
|---|---|---|---|---|---|---|---|---|---|
| Craven Arms ...... dep | | 7 50 | | 11 5 | | 4 50 | | | |
| Harton Road ...... | | 8 1 | 11 23 | | 5 117 | 107 | 17 | | |
| Rushbury ......... | | 8 6 | 11 28 | | 5 187 | 177 | 17 | | |
| Longville ........ | | 8 15 | 11 35 | | 5 257 | 257 | 25 | | |
| Presthope ........ | | 8 34 | 11 43 | | 5 357 | 457 | 48 | | |
| Much Wenlock 23 ... | 7 10 | 8 41 | 11 52 | | 5 437 | 547 | 48 | | 0 |
| Buildwas ......... arr | 7 19 | 8 52 | 12 4 | | 5 56 6 | 586 | 8 15 | | |
| Coalbrookdale .... dep | 6 30 | 8 57 | 11 58 | | 5 36 4 | 596 | 586 | | |
| Horsehay & Dawley | 6 45 | 9 11 | 12 18 | | 5 41 6 | 218 | 33 | | |
| Lawley Bank ...... | 6 47 | 9 19 | 12 27 | | 6 83 6 | 238 | 368 | | |
| Ketley ........... | 6 45 | 9 21 | 12 33 | | 6 28 6 | 298 | 428 | | |
| Wellington 5 ... arr | 6 17 | 6 39 | 11 12 | 12 32 | 6 183 | 348 | 478 | | 47 |

| | A.M | A.M | | P.M | P.M | P.M | S |
|---|---|---|---|---|---|---|---|
| Wellington ....... dep | 7 10 | 8 17 | 10 3 | 1 35 | 3 5 | 7 40 | 9 30 1035 |
| Ketley ........... | 7 14 | 8 27 | 1124 | 1 39 | 4 34 | 2 44 | 934 1040 |
| Lawley Bank ...... | 7 20 | 8 32 | 1013 | 1 45 | 4 05 | 5 50 | 940 1046 |
| Horsehay & Dawley | 7 25 | 8 43 | 1029 | 1 50 | 4 65 | 7 55 | 945 1051 |
| Coalbrookdale .... arr | 7 36 | 8 48 | 1035 | 3 2 | 5 6 | 8 6 | 956 1101 |
| Buildwas ......... dep | 7 41 | 6 30 | 9 0 | 2 63 | 5 85 | 6 68 | 20 1110 |
| Much Wenlock 23 | 7 45 | 6 45 | 9 20 | 2 03 | 6 20 | 8 20 | 35 1116 |
| Presthope ........ | | 6 88 | 9 30 | 3 3 | 6 30 | 8 35 | 1123 |
| Longville ........ | | 6 45 | 9 40 | 4 5 | 6 40 | | |
| Rushbury ......... | | 6 50 | 9 45 | 4 10 | 6 45 | | |
| Harton Road ...... | | 7 5 | 10 5 | 4 15 | | | |
| Craven Arms 71 ... arr | | | | 4 30 | | | |

*Sats. only*

---

Halts at Wistanstow, Farley, Green Bank, Lightmoor, Doseley and New Dale.

§ Does not call at Wistanstow Halt.

‖—Arr. 9.6    J—Sats. excepted
P—Sets down on informing Guard.

§—Sats. only.
T—Thurs. & Sats.

105

it had to exercise running powers over the Midland for just 5 chains.

The layout at Eardisley can still be appreciated today, as well as the beauty of the Wye Valley, although the river is more than a mile to the south of the trackbed.

Kington was always the focal point of the system, not least because it had the busiest passenger service of six trains a day from Leominster, of which only half ran through to New Radnor. Service timetables gave a fascinating insight to workings to meet local conditions and needs. Take the 6.18 am mixed from Leominster: 'The Passenger Brake third must be formed next in front of the Guard's Van and used for Mails only, under the control of the Guard'. For all that, the 6.18 am lacked the urgency of the night mail, its progress being better remembered as leisurely.

The booked time of 39 mins included 1 min each at Kingsland, Pembridge and Titley, a similar time for departing from each of the stations and another minute on arrival at Kington.

Signalmen who handled it booked on well in advance at intervals. Kingsland box was open at 6 am; Pembridge, $3\frac{1}{2}$ miles further west, 10 min later and those at Titley junction and Kington, 20 mins after that. The early morning routine of the signalmen was not arduous, the Kingsland man having a break of 1hr 17min between the mixed train going 'Down' the branch and returning to Leominster at 7.55 am.

Twenty five minutes later the first freight was due away on a diagram which included 20 mins at Kingsland and 15 mins at Pembridge on a schedule that allowed 1hr 26mins to Kington. The class 'K' diagram also included trips to Presteigne and the quarries at Dolyhir, four miles west of Kington.

Dolyhir became the end of the line when the goods service was cut back from New Radnor on New Year's Eve 1951. The passenger link between the village and Kington had ceased the previous February, when because of a coal crisis, passenger services were temporarily suspended west of Leominster.

When they were restored two months later, the service ran only to Kington. New Radnor and Presteigne never had a regular passenger service again while that to Kington survived only until February 1955.

Three years later, the Dolyhir - Kington goods link ceased but that to Presteigne survived until 1964 when it was withdrawn with the Leominster - Kington link. The Kington branches were no more.

One of the best memorials to them is to be found at Kington. A second station needed when the New Radnor line opened as demolished some years ago, but just across the road on what is now an industrial estate at the east end of the town, is the original one of 1857, maintaining a distinctly Victorian air among modern factories and ambulance station.

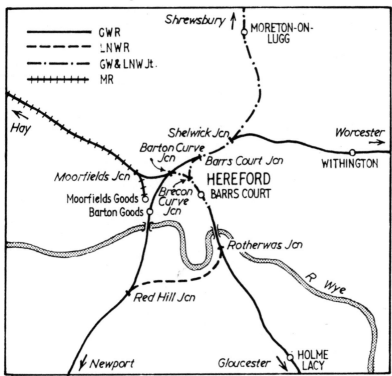

Hereford: LNWR loop and other developments

The railway connection is obvious at a glance and confirmation is available from plaques outside the well maintained house. One of the estate factories lies slewed across what was the goods yard.

Close to the industrial estate is the mile long Kington By-Pass which curves west through the widened railway cutting to rejoin the A44 west of the town. Further west near Dolyhir another stretch of trackbed has been used for A44 improvements.

New Radnor is a pleasant place in a narrowing valley, snug beneath hills rising to about 2,000 ft. Only the A44 climbs them to reach Rhayader and Aberystwyth, the goal of promoters during the 1845 Railway Mania. Hopes of extending to the Cardigan Bay coast which were alive when the single branch line reached the valley soon faded. It never got even to the village because, to avoid the cost of bridging the A44, the terminus was built among fields within sight of it. Today it is a pleasantly sited caravan park.


*Hereford: City of Change*

Like Shrewsbury, Hereford nurses its economy wounds discretely and many changes are not obvious to the casual traveller. A service from Paddington via Worcester keeps it as a terminal on the Inter City map and the North to West route lies a rank below that.

The only local services to have gone, apart from those on the Shrewsbury and Newport route, are those to Brecon at the end of 1962, and the Gloucester, via Ross, which ended in November 1964. *Regional History of the Railways of Great Britain, Vol 13: Thames & Severn.*

Brecon trains ran $38^1/_2$ miles, including 27 over the former Hereford Hay & Brecon metals. Those to Gloucester covered 30 miles over a secondary route which up to closure remained a diversionary route for North to West expresses.

More locally, the original Barton 'direct line' which avoided the loop through the station between Red Hill and Barr's Court junctions has been severed in recent years and mostly destroyed. Hereford GWR engine shed, known locally as Barton, was on the west side of the direct line. For years it had a small, but rather select allocation. For among its 40 plus engines in the last days of the GWR, eight *Saint* class 4-6-0 and one other locomotive with the same wheel arrangement: no 4079 *Pendennis Castle*. But it was the *Saints* that were the stars, especially because they were to be found stabled among much lesser engines, notably a brace of Pannier tanks.

There were no *Star* turns from Hereford's other and generally forgotten shed, a three road one which the LNWR built opposite Brecon Curve Junction. It closed on 4 July 1938 and its locomotives, a handful sub-shedded from Abergavenny, were transferred to the GWR shed the same evening, according to Chris Hawkins and George Reeve, authors of *LMS Engine Sheds* Volume 1.

*Hereford Hay & Brecon*

History repeated itself at Brecon 24 years later when an enthusiast found that 'Brecon shed was empty as all locomotives had been sent away late on Saturday night, some to Merthyr and some Llanidloes'. Those last sad journeys were noted in the *Journal* of the Stephenson Locomotive Society.

They were the prelude to the final act of Brecon's farewell to railways, accomplished the next day, Sunday 30 December 1962, when 400 enthusiasts on the Society's 'Farewell to the Brecon Lines of the former Cambrian and Midland Railways,' were given black-edged photographic souvenirs.

A quarter of a century later mine and other copies are collector's items, sought after and much valued not only by those lucky enough to have known the Brecon lines before closure, but by people who were not born until after they had gone. The route of the SLS special was from Moat Lane on the Cambrian to Brecon and then, in early evening from Brecon back to Shrewsbury, via the Hereford Hay & Brecon.

### Shrub Hill → Neath (Down)

| Shrub Hill, | A.M. | A.M. | P.M. | W (Weds. only) | P.M. | P.M. | S (Sats. only) | P.M. |
|---|---|---|---|---|---|---|---|---|
| WORCESTER dep | 7 15 | 1138 | 3 2 | | | 7 13 | | .... |
| " (F.S.) " | 7 19 | 1141 | 3 6 | | | 7 18 | | .... |
| MALVERN, GT. " | 7 41 | 1154 | 3 21 | | | 7 34 | | .... |
| LEDBURY .. " | 8 9 | 1210 | 3 14 | | | 7 56 | | 8 11 |
| HEREFORD arr | 8 40 | 1227 | 3 54 | | | 8 15 | | 8 43 |
| Hereford dep | 9 25 | 1246 | 4 10 | | 5 20 | 8 45 | | 1015 |
| Credenhill | 9 36 | 1257 | 4 21 | | 5 31 | 8 56 | | 1026 |
| Moorhampton | 9 45 | 1 6 | 4 30 | | 5 40 | 9 5 | | 1035 |
| Kinnersley | 9 53 | 1 14 | 4 38 | | 5 48 | 9 13 | | 1043 |
| Eardisley | 10 0 | 1 20 | 4 43 | | 5 53 | 9 18 | | 1048 |
| Whitney-on-Wye | 10 9 | 1 27 | 4 50 | | 6 0 | B | | 1056 |
| Hay 74 .. arr | 1019 | 1 35 | 4 59 | | 6 10 | 9 33 | | 11 4 |
| Glasbury | 1027 | 1 46 | 5 9 | | 6 20 | B | | |
| Three Cocks Jn. arr | 1034 | 1 50 | 5 13 | | 6 24 | 9 49 | | |
|    dep | 1038 | 1 55 | 5 15 | | 6 28 | 9 50 | Sats. only | |
| Talgarth | 1043 | 2 2 | 5 20 | | 6 34 | 9 56 | | |
| Trefeinon | K | U | H | | 6 40 | | | |
| Talyllyn Junc. arr | 1059 | 2 13 | 5 35 | | 6 47 | 10 7 | | .... |
|    dep | 11 2 | 2 21 | 5 38 | | 6 49 | 10 9 | | .... |
| Brecon arr | 1110 | 2 29 | 5 46 | | 6 57 | 1017 | | .... |
| NEATH, G.W. arr | 1 0 | .... | 7 37 | | .... | .... | | .... |

### Riverside → Worcester (Up)

| Riverside, | A.M. | A.M. | W | A.M. | A.M. | A.M. S | P.M. |
|---|---|---|---|---|---|---|---|
| NEATH, G.W. dep | .... | .... | | 8 25 | 1125 | .... | 4 10 |
| Brecon dep | 6 50 | 8 50 | | 1050 | 1 10 | .... | 5 58 |
| Talyllyn Junc. arr | 6 58 | 8 59 | | 1058 | 1 18 | | 6 6 |
|    dep | 6 59 | 9 0 | | 11 11 | 1 22 | | 6 7 |
| Trefeinon | U | 9 7 | U | | | | |
| Talgarth | 7 13 | 9 13 | | 1113 | 1 33 | | 6 18 |
| Three Cocks Jn. arr | 7 18 | 9 18 | | 1117 | 1 41 | | 6 23 |
|    dep | 7 30 | 9 21 | | 1118 | 1 50 | Sats. only | 6 25 |
| Glasbury | 7 34 | 9 28 | | 1123 | 1 57 | | 6 30 |
| Hay 74 | 7 44 | 9 38 | | 1132 | 2 7 | 5 26 | 6 40 |
| Whitney | 7 52 | 9 48 | | 1143 | 2 16 | 5 32 | 6 49 |
| Eardisley | 7 58 | 9 59 | | 1152 | 2 23 | 5 39 | 6 57 |
| Kinnersley | 8 3 | 10 3 | | 1156 | 2 28 | 5 45 | 7 3 |
| Moorhampton | 8 9 | 10 9 | | 12 2 | 2 35 | 5 52 | 7 10 |
| Hereford 70 arr | 8 31 | 1029 | | 1224 | 2 56 | 6 15 | 7 31 |
| HEREFORD dep | 9 56 | 1115 | | 1250 | 3 45 | 6 35 | 7 50 |
| LEDBURY arr | 10‡43 | 1138 | | 1 13 | 4 14 | 6 58 | 8 22 |
| MALVERN, Gt., " | 10 28 | 1152 | | 1 27 | 4 31 | 7 16 | 8 37 |
| WORCESTER (FS) | 10 43 | 12 8 | | 1 40 | 4 55 | 7 31 | 8 52 |
| " (S.H.), " | 11 30 | W | | 1 46 | 5 1 | .... | 8 57 |

‡ Dep. Hereford 10.10
B—Sets down on informing Guard.
H—Sets down on Weds. only
K—Picks up for Brecon on Tuesdays & Fridays.
U—Calls on Weds. only.
S—Sats. only.
W—Wednesdays only.

---

### Hereford → Aberystwyth / Barmouth (Down)

| | M A.M. | A.M. | P.M. | J P.M. | P.M. | S P.M. |
|---|---|---|---|---|---|---|
| 81 HEREFORD dep | 9 25 | 9 25 | 1246 | 4 10 | | 8 45 |
| Three Cocks dep | 1037 | 1052 | 1 56 | 4 44 | 5 42 | 9 52 |
| Boughrood | 1043 | 1057 | 2 1 | 4 50 | 5 48 | 9 58 |
| Llanstephan | 1047 | 11 3 | 2 6 | 4 54 | 5 52 | 10 2 |
| Erwood | 1053 | 11 9 | 2 12 | 5 1 | 5 59 | 10 9 |
| Aberedw | 1059 | 1114 | 2 17 | 5 7 | 6 5 | 1015 |
| Llanfaredd | 11 3 | 1119 | | 5 11 | | |
| Builth Wells arr | 11 7 | 1123 | 2 24 | 5 15 | 6 12 | 1022 |
| Builth Wells dep | | 1215 | 2 26 | 3 0 | | 6 15 |
| Builth Road arr | | 1218 | 2 29 | 3 3 | | 6 18 |
| LLANDRINDOD arr | | 1240 | 3 3 | | | 7 20 |
| Newbr'ge-on-Wye | a 1258 | | 3 13 | | | 6 27 |
| Doldowlod | 1 6 | | 3 23 | | | K |
| Rhayader | 1 15 | 2 52 | 3 31 | | | 6 43 |
| Marteg | 1 24 | | 3 47 | | | N |
| St. Harmon's | K | | 3 54 | | | N |
| Pantydwr | 1 36 | | 3 59 | | | 7 2 |
| Glanyrafon | 1 40 | | 4 4 | | | N |
| Tylwch | 1 45 | N | 4 8 | | | 7 10 |
| Llanidloes arr | 1 51 | 3 20 | 4 15 | | | 7 18 |
| Moat Lane Junc. " | 2 8 | 3 35 | 4 35 | | | 7 37 |
| ABERYSTWYTH arr | 3b55 | 5 5 | | | | |
| BARMOUTH " | 4b38 | 5 34 | | | | |

### Barmouth / Aberystwyth → Hereford (Up)

| | A.M. | P.M. | P.M. | Fridays only / Not Fridays | A.M. |
|---|---|---|---|---|---|
| BARMOUTH dep | | 7 28 | 1220 | | .... |
| ABERYSTWYTH " | | 7 50 | 1 0 | | .... |
| Moat Lane Jn. dep | 5 13 | 9 55 | 2 40 | | |
| Llanidloes | 5 32 | 10 15 | 2 58 | | 8 0 |
| Tylwch | 5 39 | 10 23 | 3 5 | | 8 7 |
| Pantydwr | | 10 27 | 3 9 | | 8 11 |
| Glanyrafon | | 10 33? | 3 16 | | 8 16 |
| St. Harmon's | K | 10 39 | 3 28 | | 8 20 |
| Marteg | | 10 45 | 3 34 | | 8 26 |
| Rhayader | 6 0 | 10 51 | 3 41 | | 8 32 |
| Doldowlod | 6 10 | 11 0 | 3 49 | | 8 41 |
| Newbr'ge-on-Wye | 6 18 | 11d 8 | 3 58 | | 8 51 |
| LLANDRINDOD dp | 5 23 | 12 23 | 3 22 | | 8 47 |
| Builth Road dep | 6 30 | 12 50 | 4 6 | | 9 13 |
| Builth Wells arr | 6 33 | 12 53 | 4 9 | | |
| Builth Wells dep | 6 36 | 1 0 | 4 12 | | 9 50 |
| Llanfaredd | | 1 14 | 4 16 | | 9 54 |
| Aberedw | C | 1 19 | 4 21 | | 9 59 |
| Erwood | 6 49 | 1 25 | 4 27 | 9 30 | 10 5 |
| Llanstephan | | 1 31 | 4 33 | 9 36 | 1011 |
| Boughrood | 6 58 | 1 35 | 4 37 | 9 40 | 1015 |
| Three Cocks arr | 7 3 | 1 40 | 4 42 | 9 46 | 1021 |
| 81 HEREFORD arr | 8 31 | 2 56 | 7 31 | | 12 24 |

C—Calls to set down on informing guard.
a—Passengers can arrive Newbridge 12.30 on Mons.
b—Sats. only : to Sept. 14 only
d—Dep. 12.35 Mondays
J—Sats. excepted.
K—Calls when required.
M—Mondays only.
N—Calls Weds. and Sats.
S—Sats. only.

Two other routes to South Wales also closed. The Neath & Brecon had closed on 15 October 1962 and the passenger service between Brecon and Newport also ceased from New Year's Eve 1962.

### The Hay Railway

The HH & B was the least spectacular of the four because it climbed the wide and gentle Wye Valley while the South Wales lines approached in spectacular style up the valleys and over the hills and their flavour can still be captured by a ride on the Brecon Mountain Railway.

Its history is young compared with that of the HH & B whose ancestry dated back to the Hay Railway, a 3ft 6 inch horse drawn tramway opened in 1816, the year after Waterloo. Its history has been fully detailed in *The Hay Railway* by C.R. Clinker, one of the earliest railway books published by David & Charles.

As authorised in 1859, the HH & B was to stretch 34 miles, but this length was reduced to 27 miles by the truncation of two sections. That from Three Cocks Junction to Talyllyn Junction was transferred to the Mid Wales Railway and that between Talyllyn and Brecon to the Brecon & Merthyr.

The HH & B bought the Hay Railway in 1860 and adapted three miles for its own route. Construction was leisurely. The nine miles from Hereford to Moorhampton opened in October 1862 and a further five miles to Eardisley were completed in June 1863, followed by Eardisley to Hay (seven miles) in July 1864 and the remaining $5^1/_2$ miles to Three Cocks Junction on 19 September 1864 when a through service began.

The line did not attract the passenger and goods traffic for which its promoters had hoped and it was soon in financial

Another table from the *Hereford ABC Railway Guide* of summer 1935. Many tourists used the Hereford Hay & Brecon route to enjoy the scenery of the Wye Valley.

difficulties, from which it was rescued by the Midland Railway, which bought the company in 1874.

The value of the HH & B to the Midland was that it provided a through route to Swansea, although in passenger terms there was little to exploit and from 1874 until 1932 small 0-4-4 tanks valiantly performed trips of $79^1/_4$ miles in each direction on some of the longest tank locomotive diagrams in Britain.

Rather more important was the exploitation of the route by the LNWR, which it developed for freight between South Wales and Birmingham. In later years, the single line between Hereford (Moorfields Junction) and Three Cocks was worked by electric train token with crossing stations at Moorhampton (for a passenger and freight train, or two freight trains), and at Eardisley, Hay-on-Wye and Three Cocks.

Those trains and local passenger services were often in charge of Lancashire & Yorkshire 0-6-0s which seemed as far from home as did the Midland route from its Derby headquarters.

The 0-6-0s also worked passenger services, indeed the line became known for the variety of locomotives to be found on it. They included ex GWR 0-6-0 74XX tanks and 0-6-0's of class 2251. Their authorisation to work the line was subject to 'service and special speed restrictions'.

The passage of the SLS special did not quite mark the end of the HH & B for it continued to be a through route to South Wales until 4 May 1964 when it was cut back to Eardisley and to Hereford (Brecon Junction) four months later.

Much change subsequently took place at Hereford with track rationalisation and resignalling and the Midland shed at Moorfields, which had closed in the 1930s suddenly took on a new lease of life when, incorporated into Bulmer's Railway Centre it received a locomotive far bigger than before: *King George V*

Much of the trackbed has undergone far less spectacular development and modern OS maps show long breaks in the thin dotted lines marking the course of this, and neighbouring 'dismantled' railways. Intervening white spaces are evidence that the trackbed has gone. Despite the comparative remoteness of the area from towns, people began trespassing on what had been the trackbed. A Countryside Commission Report on *Disused Railways in the Countryside of England and Wales* published in 1970 discussed the problem of trespass along disused lines and on adjoining land.

It stated that it was acute not only in urban areas of South Lancashire and North Cheshire but had occurred in more rural areas and instanced parts of the HH & B. In some places where trackbed had been fenced off and reclaimed, people walking along unreclaimed parts had climbed or broke down fences when they found their way barred. One landowner had had to renew fencing more than once.

A place where the enthusiast can go to try to revive memories is on the south bank of the Wye at Hay, where the trackbed has been converted into a short footpath. It is not among the most beautiful parts of the banks of this lovely river for it is over-shadowed by the spindle legs of a modern bridge carrying the B4351 across the river.

The footpath is interesting as the most northerly of those in the Brecon Beacons National Park, which follows the bank for about three quarters of a mile as it embraces this town of history and bookshops within its boundaries.

The B4351 takes the tourist to the village of Clyro, where the poet Francis Kilvert arrived as curate in 1865, about a year after the railway opened. He wrote about local rail journeys in his Diaries, which so many people enjoy.

Railway enthusiasts are perhaps more likely to visit the area in search of Three Cocks, a junction spoken of with reverence whenever Britain's rural junctions are discussed. The station buildings and yard survive as a distribution centre for Calor Gas.

The Countryside Commission Report cited the HHB for an additional reason besides trespass, pointing out that a road bridge over the route at Kinnersley was the place to see an excellent example of how it was possible to reclaim minor cuttings by evening out its contours.

*Golden Valley Railway*

The Western Region's withdrawal on 9 June 1958 of local passenger services between Shrewsbury Hereford and Newport, already mentioned in the Shrewsbury & Hereford context, embraced Pontrilas, $11^1/_4$ miles south of Hereford. The loss of a stopping service was no novelty to this little station for it had suffered more than once before being the junction of the Golden Valley Railway to Hay, finally closed to passengers on 15 December 1941. The branch had an existence that was anything but golden, a fact realised even in Victorian times.

G Phillips Bevan noted in his *Tourists' Guide to the Wye*, 1892:

Taking into account the essentials of population, it would seem to have been an heroic proceeding on the part of those interested to construct a railway through such an unsophisticated valley, especially when the line stopped at Dorstone.

It was, in fact, as the guide suggested, destined to reach Hay. That was accomplished in 1889 - 13 years after the 18 mile route had been authorised.

It is hard to recall the line, which served some of the quietest parts of Herefordshire, because it is between three or four decades since it was closed and long sections have vanished beneath fields and its route no longer troubles the Ordnance Survey mapmakers. *Landranger* sheet 161 *Abergavenny and the Black Mountains* has a four mile gap in the trackbed north of the village of Abbeydore and another only about a mile shorter, north of Peterchurch. Both were long, straight stretches for which the branch was noted.

Yet despite partly vanishing off the face of the map, the line is assured of a place in memory through a full length history by an enthusiast, Professor Charles Mowat, published by the University of Wales Press in 1964. It carried an explicit sub-title: *Railway Enterprise on the Welsh Border in late Victorian times.*

Yet despite its minor stature in the railway world, the company was ever active in planning extensions and one to Monmouth of 12 miles was mooted three times.

The Company stated in *Bradshaw's Manual* for 1895:

The directors have agreed with the Severn & Wye for an interchange of traffic at Lydbrook for the facilitating of carriage to Sharpness Docks and across the Severn to Gloucester and Bristol.

More sensational, perhaps, was its conception of the line as part of a through route between Merseyside and Bristol as a rival to the Shrewsbury - Newport main line.

The directors' statement was made six years after the line had closed because of financial difficulties. That occurred in May 1889. The line remained silent until May 1901. By then it had been in GWR ownership for two years. It then settled down to a quiet existence, only becoming of some value when a Royal Ordnance Factory was opened about a mile north of Pontrilas and a connection made with an extensive system of lines worked by eight locomotives, including two transferred from the Ministry of Supply depot beside the Manchester - Crewe line at Chelford, within sight of my home as I write more than 40 years after the event.

Beside the loss of passenger services, the 1940s also saw complete closure of the northern eight miles between Dorstone and Hay, the economy taking place under British Railways auspices in December 1949. The branch wa further cut back from Dorstone to Abbeydore in 1953 and from Pontrilas (MOD) to Dorstone in 1957. The stub of the branch was closed when the ROF, which was subsequently reduced to a MOS Supply Depot, was shut down in December 1968.

Being GWR, branch traffic was routed via Pontrilas. At Hay, passenger trains reached the station from the Junction, a quarter of a mile away beside the Wye, over a double track section. After the Golden Valley became a dead-end branch, service timetable noted that: 'Side lights are not carried by the trains on this branch.' It was worked by a round, red o                                                    E 2069 R

# LMS

## Road and Rail Tour

### TO

# HEREFORD

### (FOR THE GOLDEN VALLEY)

## SUNDAY, AUGUST 16th, 1936.

| FROM | Departure Time | Third Class Rail and Motor Tour. | |
|---|---|---|---|
| | | Adults. | Children. |
| MANCHESTER (London Road) ......... | a.m.<br>9 50 | | |
| Hereford ..........................due | p.m.<br>1 16 | **9/6** | **5/3** |

(These Tickets can only be obtained at Manchester (London Road) Booking Office.)

### ITINERARY OF MOTOR TOUR.

**Upon arrival at Hereford** passengers proceed by Midland Red Motor Coaches for a tour of the Golden Valley.

The route from Hereford lies by way of the Wye Bridge to St. Devereux and Wormbridge, crossing the "Grey Valley" to Abbey Dore where the Golden Valley commences.

The Valley, which is narrow, is bounded on each side by low wooded hills.  Along its length are four villages : **Abbey Dore**, noted for its Cistercian Monastery founded in 1147, parts of which only now remain. **Vowchurch** with its 14th century chapel.  Between here and **Peterchurch** a good view of the Black Mountains may be obtained, the highest peak Waun Fach, 2,660 feet.  Peterchurch possesses a miniature cathedral of Norman origin.  Lastly **Dorstone**, where again the chief feature of interest is the church.

Soon the Golden Valley is left behind and the road runs through open country to Hay, where William the Conqueror raised a castle.  It is here that the River Wye  is again encountered and closely follows the road all the way back to Hereford, where the tower of the cathedral ahead proclaims the nearness of the city.

## The Return Train leaves Hereford at 7.45 p.m., due Manchester (Mayfield) at 11.15 p.m.

**TICKETS AND INFORMATION CAN** BE OBTAINED IN ADVANCE AT THE COMPANY'S STATIONS : ALSO THE TOWN AGENCIES.

**CONDITIONS OF ISSUE OF EXCURSION** TICKETS AND OTHER TICKETS AT LESS THAN ORDINARY FARES.
These Tickets are Issued subject to the Notices and Conditions shown in the Company's ...... Time Tables.

Despite the Golden Valley being a remote, little known tourist area, the LMS promoted it to encourage Sunday traffic. A coach tour from Hereford was necessary because the branch was closed on Sundays.

coloured staff carried by 'only one tank engine in steam at a time or tank engines coupled together'. Tender engines were not allowed.

In 1951, it was stated

Engine leaves shed 7.30 am and works trips with freight traffic to Elm Bridge Siding, Bacton, Vowchurch, Peterchurch or Dorstone as ordered by the Pontrilas Station Master, according to traffic requirements.

How many spotters recorded the numbers of those engines after glimpsing them through the window of a passing express? They were always worth looking out for : a momentary extra pleasure on a journey between Hereford and Abergavenny, two junctions of great interest.

### Bishop's Castle Railway

Far more exciting on a North to West express journey than the sight of a Golden Valley freight, must have been that of a train from the Bishop's Castle Railway on one of its short forays over the Shrewsbury & Hereford to reach Craven Arms station from Stretford Bridge Junction, three quarters of a mile to the north.

Reviewing a Shrewsbury-published paperback guide to the *South West Borderland of Shropshire* the *Railway Magazine* of January 1939 was pleased that the guide had not failed to refer at some length to the fate of the BCR, because, it was contended: 'This was a hard-up, shabby, leisurely line which floated waterlogged in the stormy seas of finance for 75 years, only to sink at the end.'

Beneath the review of a miniature pen and ink sketch of the *Coronation Scot* at full speed, and on the opposite page, a picture of Bassett-Scot at full speed, and on the opposite page, a picture of Bassett-Lowke's new 00 gauge locomotive, *Princess Elizabeth* seemed to emphasise the great antiquity of the BCR only four years after its death.

117

*In Memoriam* was the heading of T.R. Perkins' valediction in the October 1937 edition of the *Railway Magazine* issue. 'I seem almost to have lost an old friend'. Was it quite that bad?

The BCR was built by a company incorporated on 28 June 1861 to construct a line from the Oswestry & Newtown, (which became part of the Cambrian Railways three years later), near Newtown, to the S & H at Wistanstow: Stretford Bridge Junction, as it became. There was to be a branch from Lydham Heath to the ancient borough of Bishop's Castle, two and a quarter miles away.

The total distance was to be $19^{1}/_{4}$ miles, but all that was eventually built were $9^{1}/_{2}$ miles from Stretford Bridge to Bishop's Castle. It entailed an inconvenient reversal at Lydham Heath. Construction was slow and it was not until 24 October 1865 that an opening ceremony took place. And that was only formal for it was not until 1 February 1866 that regular passenger and goods service began along the route which the Victorian mapmakers symbolised as single by a spidery ladder. It snaked through the Onny valley under the southern slope of the Long Mynd. When John Piper and John Betjeman came to write *Shropshire*, which in 1951 became the first of the Shell Guides to be published after World War II they felt the romance of the valley was increased by the tragic remains of the railway, with little red-brick Gothic stations, overgrown and dead.

But some quickly came to life and one foggy morning when I ventured into the countryside before breakfast, I found the restored Plowden station building. It was about the time of day when, if the old railway operated faithful to the times in my 1908 *Bradshaw's*, the first train of the day might be calling. The 6.55 am from Bishop's Castle was due at 7.13 am, although it could be a minute or two later if there was a passenger waiting at Eaton. They were instructed in the timetable - which noted T.Cartwright as receiver and manager - to 'signal' trains to stop: a similar instruction applied to passengers using the earth mound that was Stretford Bridge Junction in the company's passenger timetable.

The Kington Branches – 2: *Plate 21 (above)* Kington, with Pannier No 7416
taking water before working a trip freight to Presteigne. 11 April 1956. *Plate
22 (below)* Presteigne station, was generously laid out. It was built when it was
found that the original station was too far from the town centre for both
passenger and goods traffic to be worked conveniently.

The Magic of Wye: *Plate 23 (above)* Three Cocks Junction where the Midland and Cambrian Railways met. BR 2–6–0 No 46515 on a Moat Lane – Brecon service, May 1959. The tail coach of a Brecon – Hereford train (right) is in front of the main station building, which included a refreshment room, one of the few on the remote lines of the Marches. *Plate 24 (below)* Hereford Hay & Brecon trains often seemed to have more than adequate accommodation for the generally sparse passenger traffic. Pannier No 9674 heads a train over an unmanned crossing near Whitney-on-Wye.

| BISHOP'S CASTLE and CRAVEN ARMS AND STOKESAY.—Bishop's Castle. | | | | | | |
|---|---|---|---|---|---|---|
| **Down.** | **Week Days only.** | | | | **Up.** | **Week Days only.** |

(timetable — Bishop's Castle)

*NOTES.*

Aa Stop when required.

| LLANBERIS and SNOWDON SUMMIT.—Snowdon Mountain. | | |
|---|---|---|
| **Week Days only.** | | **Week Days only.** |

**D** Runs when required.

No Trains will run with less than seven return Passengers, or the equivalent in Fares.   Trains will only run weather and other causes permitting.

The Bishop's Castle Railway's service was sandwiched between the Welsh Highland/Festiniog and the Snowdon Mountain in the miscellaneous section of the July 1927 *Bradshaw*.

But there was an important proviso about the 6.55 am: 'Runs on Bishop's Castle Fair Days only'.

Bishop's Castle was among the principal horse and cattle fairs in Britain and Ireland 'to and from which the LNWR carry. Either directly or inconjunction with other companies.'

Relations between the companies must have been friendly because the Bishop's Castle was listed among a handful of companies to which Euston gave concessions on the handling of sacks: 'Risk is to be calculated on both full and empty Sacks sent to Foreign Lines other than the Bishop's Castle . . .'

Despite its parlous state - or possibly because of it - the BCR was ever mindful of expansion and in 1865 it got Parliamentary powers for an extension from the village of Chirbury, roughly half way between Lydham Heath and Montgomery, to the S & H Joint Line branch at Minsterley. The distance was $9^1/_2$ miles and construction would have doubled its own length and again it would have been totally rural.

Nothing was done, yet the BCR did not easily forego its ambitions and after the GWR took over the Cambrian Railways in 1922, it suggested that it might like to build short cut between Craven Arms and the Cambrian coast by extending the BCR from Lydham Heath to Montgomery and buying it out! Neither prospect was attractive.

It is not for its territorial ambitions that the line is best

remembered, but rather for its highly individualistic character, reflected in its once decrepit assortment of locomotives
and rolling stock.

The most famous of the locomotives was an 0-6-0 which
Kitson's built for a Carlisle contractor in 1868 and was named
after the City. It was lavished with care and well polished and
continued to steam until 1937.

On Sunday 21 February of that year, T.R. Perkins recorded
that it arrived at Craven Arms yard with the last remains of
the track and was scrapped there soon afterwards. A splendidly
evocative history by Edward Griffith, published in 1948 and
subsequently revised, helps to keep memories alive and today
hoteliers, pubs, cafes and shops in Bishop's Castle enjoy the
legacy of a small tourist trade generated by enthusiasts who
go in search of its memorials.

# CHAPTER 7

# North of the Severn – 1

## *LNWR: Stafford – Wellington*

Of the two lines that served Wellington from north and east, the GWR secondary route to Nantwich was probably the most useful, not least because it enabled the company to reach Crewe. The LNWR accorded less importance to its own branch west from the West Coast main line, noting it in the second edition of its *Official Illustrated Guide* in 1861 as its 'Stafford and Shrewsbury branch.'

The author, George Measom, described it as 'a line of rail running through the iron district of Oaken Gates (sic) and Wellington, past the Wrekin.

> Oaken Gates is rather a district than a town, though we doubt not that eventually it will assume a more definite character. Wellington is a flourishing little town. The inhabitants are chiefly employed in coal and iron mines, limestone quarries, smelting furnaces, glassworks etc. The other places are unimportant to the traveller'.

But soon the Company thought more of the neighbourhood and Newport and other intermediate stations were mentioned.

The most interesting section of the route was at Stafford, where on 3 April 1878, Mr Bagnall, owner of Bagnall's Ironworks, reached agreement with the LNWR for it to maintain just six and three quarter yards of track on its land as part of a scheme to provide shunt-back access to a siding for the works from the branch. The junction was laid within feet of the LNWR Birmingham Division boundary.

Mr Bagnall had established the Castle Engineering Works three years earlier. It remained open until 1972 - six years after the Wellington branch closed completely west from Bagnall's Siding to Newport.

Bagnall's built nearly 2,000 locomotives and it is pleasant, if slightly futile, to reflect on how many different kinds, many for overseas, left the works through the siding. The junction was on what is now the short dead-end electrified stretch that curves away from the West Coast main line just north of Stafford No 5 box. The stub continues to serve the siding of the Universal Grinding Wheel company, and is occasionally used as a siding for merry-go-round trains.

The diagram for the 1878 agreement also shows the LNWR 'Engine Shed' just across a road on the London side of the works. Later, a second shed was built on the west side and became a substantial and important express locomotive depot.

Just before World War II, the LMS replaced the original shed with a brick and concrete structure, which closed 19 July 1965, a year after the withdrawal of Wellington and Shrewsbury passenger trains, often in charge of the shed's three Fowler 2-6-4 tanks, or class 5 4-6-0s. The shed, with prominent 'For Sale' notices facing the main line, fell into ruin until restoration began in 1987. The diagram also included what was perhaps the most highly individual feature of the Stafford rail scene, which although long neglected after death, was at least unobtrusive. It was the trackbed of the GNR's Stafford & Uttoxeter route *Forgotten Railways: The West Midlands* (volume 10). The branch joined the main line immediately opposite the Wellington branch.

The GNR had planned it as a route to North Wales, only to be thwarted by Euston reaching Wellington. It gained control of the route through is acquisition of the Shropshire Union

Railways and Canal company and the line was completed some 18 miles across the flat countryside on the borders of Staffordshire and Shropshire in 1849 and opened on the same day as the Shrewsbury & Birmingham between Shrewsbury and Oakengates.

This was jointly owned by the GWR and LNWR but the companies ran their own services between Wellington and Shrewsbury. Passengers wanting the timings of local trains faced reading a complicated table embracing Stafford, Wellington, Shrewsbury and Welshpool, although a change was necessary at Shrewsbury to cover those 49 miles. Despite the LNWR's ownership of the Coalport branch, there was never any suggestion of the local trains making connections at Wellington.

Passenger traffic between Wellington and Stafford had little growth potential and Haughton, just under four miles from Stafford, closed to passengers in 1949 and goods eight years later. Through passenger services ended in 1964, the post-Beeching year and the section between Stafford and Newport, which is being developed as a footpath, was closed completed from August 1966. But not all is lost, Wellington - Donnington being retained as a single line serving Ministry of Defence depot sidings just east of Trench Crossing.

The branch also served Granville Colliery near Donnington, the last in the Shropshire coalfield, which supplied Buildwas Power Station. The pit closed in 1979 after 115 years, many of them under the ownership of the Lilleshall Company. The last coal train ran on 2 October 1979.

The branch was also connected for many years to the Lilleshall works by a line almost two miles long.

Because it closely follows a main road, the A518, the route of the Stafford - Wellington trackbed is easy to follow. It is bisected by the north-south Newport A41 by-pass. This is one of the main roads used by visitors heading south to the Severn Valley Railway from northern towns. With the prospect of live steam, the sight of a long disused railway hardly excites the imagination of enthusiasts as they cross it.

## Wellington - Nantwich

Wellington - Nantwich or Nantwich - Wellington? In what direction do you consider a long forgotten line? The GWR Chester Division dealt with it as a 'Secondary Main Line' heading North and that is how it shall be recorded here. It had something of a reputation for crossing boundaries. Twice at Cox Bank, near Audlem (a pleasant village which remains very much on the canal map with a notable flight of locks), the railway crossed the Shropshire - Cheshire border. And in the final years of its existence, the line was controlled by the London Midland Region, as a result of boundary changes. Previously the Western Region had retained control as a 'penetrating line'. The LMR was to find it useful as a diversionary route during electrification of the West Coast main line south of Crewe.

Unlike the Severn Valley railway, closed to passengers on the same day, 9 September 1963, the Wellington - Nantwich line will never resound to resurrected steam for it has become a forgotten line as surely as any in Britain.

It owed its birth to two GWR supported companies: the Nantwich & Market Drayton of 1861, which completed $10^3/_4$ miles in two years, while the remainder was opened by the Wellington & Drayton Railway in 1867. Three years later, the North Staffordshire Railway arrived from Stoke-on-Trent with a line which served first industrial areas west of Stoke and then headed west into the Shropshire countryside.

The branch helped to stimulate traffic on the GWR line, although it was never heavy. In the early 1930's the GWR opened seven halts and the searcher of the old line today has to add six stations to the total of sites to be visited to get as complete a picture as possible.

The line was strategically important because it provided the GWR with access to Crewe and Stoke. The GWR had running powers from Market Drayton Junction on the western outskirts of Nantwich, to Crewe, where it developed a presence which, had it not been totally overshadowed by the LNWR and later the LMS, would have been far more in the railway limelight than ever it was.

But perhaps the GWR was guilty of a little exaggeration for what it called Gresty Lane marshalling yard was no more than five sidings, holding just over 200 wagons. Traffic in and out had to be carefully controlled and as far away as Peplow, only eight miles north of Wellington, a refuge siding was used occasionally 'putting a train from Oxley aside when the traffic cannot be accepted by Crewe'.

The sidings were close to Gresty Lane GWR shed, a two-road outpost of Wellington. It was used by a variety of locomotives, including two 2-6-2 tanks, allocated for Wellington workings. The shed closed in June 1963 and the site was incorporated into the *Mornflake* mills.

Immediately west of the shed was Crewe's least known passenger station. 'Gresty Motor Halt', as it was termed on LNWR track plans. It closed on 1 April 1918.

GWR freight working to Stoke and North Staffordshire goods workings through to Wellington yard demanded pages of complicated working instructions and the NSR issued a cloth-back *Appendix to the Working Time Book* for its 'servants' who worked over the GWR. It covered such points as the opening and closing times of signal boxes; engine whistles; catch points and codes for shunting horns.

NSR trains ran nearly six miles south to the village of Hodnet on market days. Hodnet has a hall which never had a locomotive named after it, yet perhaps it deserved one for it was the home of the early Victorian hymn writer, Bishop Heber, who is remembered for a number which include *From Greenland's Icy Mountains*

Nearer home, a GWR report noted: 'The country between Peplow and Hodnet is well stocked with game of all kinds, and is a favourite venue for the Meet of the Fox Hounds.'

Beside the hounds, the foxes were disturbed by goods

*J. Williams*

# North Staffordshire Railway.

# Appendix to Working Time Book.

## INFORMATION

AS TO

### Signal Boxes, and Times of Closing of Signal Boxes,

### Engine Whistles,

### Catch Points on Inclines, and

## INSTRUCTIONS

AFFECTING

### North Staffordshire Company's Servants

WHEN WORKING OVER THE

# Great Western Railway.

*Stoke Station, January, 1915.*

McCorquodale & Co., Limited, Printers to the Company.

trains and eight or nine passenger workings on weekdays, reduced to three on Sundays. They took up to 1hr 15mins between Wellington and Crewe, although in the 1930s, a 'Bournemouth and Portsmouth to Manchester Express,' accomplished the journey in 44 mins, including a minute's pause at Market Drayton. On Fridays it called additionally at Tern Hill 'to take up', while the southbound service called there 'to set down'.

During electrification, *The Pines Express* used the route. It was a heavy train and once I found an ageing *Royal Scot* locomotive a little out of condition, which allowed passengers extended time to view the countryside, although not on that occasion foxes.

Soon afterwards, Market Drayton lost its passenger service to Stoke, which ceased on 7 May 1956, goods surviving for another decade. The Wellington - Nantwich section closed to passengers in September 1963. Freight trains used the route for another four years and then the scene was set for the development of Market Drayton station area and the entire trackbed for other use.

Most useful was a stretch on the western outskirts of the town and it was quickly exploited for part of a by-pass carrying the A53 Potteries - Shrewsbury road clear of the congested town centre.

When Cheshire County Council considered turning a number of disused lines into footpaths, the Wellington - Nantwich trackbed was not thought to be 'particularly attractive for walkers'.

But to the planners of The Silkin Way (page 68) it was more useful and they exploited the trackbed to provide 'the last mile home' between Admaston and Bratton, where the

Operating instructions between Wellington and Market Drayton, not for the staff of the GWR, owners of the line, but 'North Staffordshire Company's Servants when working over the GWR'. Issued in January 1915, the 13 page booklet did not mention any war traffic.

northern end of the Walk was established beside the B5063. It is by the Gate Inn, three quarters of a mile south of the site of Longdon Halt.

The guide to the Silkin Way recalls the 150 year history of Admaston Spa. A GWR Report noted:

About a mile from Market Drayton Junction on the Up side of the line 'The Old Clock House' at Admaston can be seen. This house was at one time well known for its Spa water and baths.

Today, not only does the Silkin Way begin and end on former railway land. It also provides a link between the LNWR and GWR which was not in being during the existence of the companies.

Although the single Hooton – West Kirby branch never had a service of the intensity of those on the Mersey underground system, it did have one that was good for an area where the pre-war population was relatively small.

## LIVERPOOL (CENTRAL, LOW LEVEL) and BIRKENHEAD to NEW BRIGHTON and WEST KIRBY

| Miles | | Week Days mrn | mrn | mrn | mrn | | aft | aft | | Sundays mrn | mrn | | mrn | mrn | mrn | | aft | aft |
|---|---|---|---|---|---|---|---|---|---|---|---|---|---|---|---|---|---|---|
| | Liverpool (Central, L.L.)......dep. | 6 8 | 6 17 | 6 23 | 6 32 | And at frequent intervals until:— | 1123 | 1132 | .. | 8 55 | 9 10 | And every 30 minutes until:— | 1040 | 1055 | 11 0 | then every 15 minutes afterwards until:— | 1110 | 1115 |
| ½ | ,, (James St.)........ | 6 10 | 6 19 | 6 25 | 6 34 | | 1125 | 1134 | .. | 8 57 | 9 12 | | 1042 | 1057 | 11 2 | | 1112 | 1117 |
| 1½ | Birkenhead (Hamilton Square).... | 6 13 | 6 22 | 6 28 | 6 37 | | 1128 | 1137 | .. | 9 0 | 9 15 | | 1045 | 11 0 | 11 5 | | 1115 | 1120 |
| 3 | ,, Park ........ | 6 17 | 6 26 | 6 32 | 6 41 | | 1132 | 1141 | .. | 9 4 | 9 19 | | 1049 | 11 4 | 11 9 | | 1119 | 1124 |
| 4 | ,, North........ | 6 19 | 6 28 | 6 34 | 6 43 | | 1134 | 1143 | .. | 9 6 | 9 21 | | 1051 | 11 6 | 1111 | | 1121 | 1126 |
| 5½ | Wallasey Village ........ | 6 23 | .. | 6 38 | .. | | 1138 | .. | .. | 9 10 | .. | | .. | 1110 | .. | | 1125 | .. |
| 6 | Wallasey ........ | 6 25 | .. | 6 40 | .. | | 1140 | .. | .. | 9 12 | .. | | .. | 1112 | .. | | 1127 | .. |
| 7 | New Brighton........arr. | 6 29 | .. | 6 44 | .. | | 1144 | .. | .. | 9 16 | .. | | .. | 1116 | .. | | 1131 | .. |
| 4½ | Bidston........ | .. | 6 31 | .. | 6 46 | | .. | 1146 | .. | .. | 9 24 | | 1054 | .. | 1114 | | .. | 1129 |
| 5¾ | Leasowe........ | .. | 6 33 | .. | 6 48 | | .. | 1148 | .. | .. | 9 26 | | 1056 | .. | 1116 | | .. | 1131 |
| 6½ | Moreton........ | .. | 6 35 | .. | 6 50 | | .. | 1150 | .. | .. | 9 28 | | 1058 | .. | 1118 | | .. | 1133 |
| 8 | Meols........ | .. | 6 39 | .. | 6 54 | | .. | 1154 | .. | .. | 9 32 | | 11 2 | .. | 1122 | | .. | 1137 |
| 9¼ | Hoylake........ | .. | 6 42 | .. | 6 57 | | .. | 1157 | .. | .. | 9 35 | | 11 5 | .. | 1125 | | .. | 1140 |
| 10½ | West Kirby *(below)*........arr. | .. | 6 46 | .. | 7 1 | | .. | 12 1 | .. | .. | 9 39 | | 11 9 | .. | 1129 | | .. | 1144 |

| | Week Days mrn | mrn | mrn | mrn | | aft | aft | aft | aft | aft | Sundays mn | mrn | | mrn | mrn | mrn | mrn | mrn | mrn | | aft | aft | aft |
|---|---|---|---|---|---|---|---|---|---|---|---|---|---|---|---|---|---|---|---|---|---|---|---|
| West Kirby........dep. | .. | 5 56 | .. | 6 11 | And at frequent intervals until:— | 1056 | .. | 11 8 | .. | 1123 | .. | 8 44 | And every 30 minutes until 10 44 mrn. and at:— | .. | .. | 1039 | .. | .. | 1010 | then every 15 minutes afterwards until:— | 1055 | .. | .. |
| Hoylake........ | .. | 5 58 | .. | 6 13 | | 1058 | .. | 1110 | .. | 1125 | .. | 8 46 | | .. | .. | 1041 | .. | .. | 1112 | | 1057 | .. | .. |
| Meols........ | .. | 6 1 | .. | 6 16 | | 11 1 | .. | 1113 | .. | 1128 | .. | 8 49 | | .. | .. | 1044 | .. | .. | 1115 | | 11 0 | .. | .. |
| Moreton........ | .. | 6 6 | .. | 6 21 | | 11 6 | .. | 1118 | .. | 1133 | .. | 8 54 | | .. | .. | 1049 | .. | .. | 1120 | | 11 5 | .. | .. |
| Leasowe........ | .. | 6 8 | .. | 6 23 | | 11 8 | .. | 1120 | .. | 1135 | .. | 8 56 | | .. | .. | 1051 | .. | .. | 1122 | | 11 7 | .. | .. |
| Bidston........ | .. | 6 10 | .. | 6 25 | | 1110 | .. | 1123 | .. | 1138 | .. | 8 58 | | .. | .. | 1053 | .. | .. | 1124 | | 11 9 | .. | .. |
| New Brighton.....dep. | 5 56 | .. | 6 11 | .. | | .. | 1111 | Saturdays excepted | 1121 | Saturdays only | 838 | .. | | 10 8 | 1033 | .. | 1057 | 11 8 | .. | | .. | 11 8 | 1135 |
| Wallasey........ | 5 58 | .. | 6 13 | .. | | .. | 1113 | | 1123 | | 840 | .. | | 1010 | 1035 | .. | 1059 | 1110 | .. | | .. | 1110 | 1137 |
| Wallasey Village........ | 6 0 | .. | 6 15 | .. | | .. | 1115 | | 1125 | | 842 | .. | | 1012 | 1037 | .. | 11 1 | 1112 | .. | | .. | 1112 | 1139 |
| Birkenhead North ...... | 6 3 | 6 13 | 6 18 | 6 28 | | 1113 | 1118 | | 1128 | | 845 | 9 1 | | 1015 | 1040 | 1056 | 11 4 | 1115 | 1127 | | 1112 | 1115 | 1142 |
| ,, Park ...... | 6 7 | 6 16 | 6 22 | 6 31 | | 1116 | 1122 | | 1132 | | 849 | 9 4 | | 1019 | 1044 | 1059 | 11 8 | 1119 | 1130 | | 1115 | 1119 | 1146 |
| ,, (Ham. Square) | 6 11 | 6 20 | 6 26 | 6 35 | | 1120 | 1126 | | .. | | 853 | 9 8 | | 1023 | 1048 | 11 3 | 1112 | 1123 | 1134 | | 1119 | 1123 | .. |
| Liverpool (James St.).... | 6 14 | 6 23 | 6 29 | 6 38 | | 1123 | 1129 | | .. | | 856 | 9 11 | | 1026 | 1051 | 11 6 | 1115 | 1126 | 1137 | | 1122 | 1126 | .. |
| ,, (Central, L.L.)arr. | 6 16 | 6 25 | 6 31 | 6 40 | | 1125 | 1131 | | .. | | 858 | 9 13 | | 1028 | 1053 | 11 8 | 1117 | 1128 | 1139 | | 1124 | 1128 | .. |

On WEEK DAYS a Thro' Carriage to London (Euston), (see below) is conveyed on Train departing New Brighton 9 58, Wallasey 10 1, Wallasey Village 10 3, Moreton 10 11, Meols 10 15, Hoylake 10 20, West Kirby Joint Sta 10 26 mrn

RETURNING to West Kirby Joint Sta. 10 4, Hoylake 10 8, Meols 10 11, Moreton 10 15, Wallasey Village 10 21, Wallasey 10 24, and New Brighton 10 28 aft

For **OTHER TRAINS** between Liverpool and Birkenhead, page 1089

## HOOTON and WEST KIRBY—L M S & G W

| Miles | Up | Week Days mrn | | | | | | | aft | | | | | | | | | | | | | | | | | | | | | | Sundays mrn | | | aft | | | | | | | |
|---|---|---|---|---|---|---|---|---|---|---|---|---|---|---|---|---|---|---|---|---|---|---|---|---|---|---|---|---|---|---|---|---|---|---|---|---|---|---|---|---|---|
| | HOUR | 6 | 7 | 7 | 8 | 10 | 11 | | S 12 | 1 | S 1 | 2 | S 3 | 3 | 4 | 4 | | E 5 | 5 | E 5 | 6 | | 7 | 7 | 8 | Z 9 | 10 | 10 | 11 | | 8 | 11 | | 12 | 2 | 3 | 6 | 6 | 7 | 8 | 9 |
| — | Hooton..........dep. | 35 | 25 | 56 | 18 | 31 | 40 | . | 52 | 4 | 58 | 42 | 8 | 30 | 0 | 40 | . | V | 37 | 57 | 20 | . | 10 | 48 | 36 | 30 | 2 | 45 | 41 | . | 38 | 26 | . | 44 | 50 | 47 | 14 | 42 | 47 | 33 | 50 |
| 1½ | Hadlow Road.......... | 39 | 29 | 0 | 22 | 35 | 45 | . | 56 | 8 | 2 | 46 | 15 | 34 | 4 | 44 | . | 27 | 41 | 1 | 24 | . | 14 | 53 | 41 | 34 | 6 | 49 | 45 | . | 42 | 30 | . | 48 | 54 | 51 | 18 | 46 | 51 | 39 | 54 |
| 3¼ | Neston.......... | 45 | 35 | 6 | 28 | 41 | 51 | . | 2 | 14 | 8 | 52 | 22 | 40 | 10 | 50 | . | 33 | 47 | 7 | 30 | . | 20 | 0 | 49 | 40 | 12 | 55 | 51 | . | 48 | 36 | . | 54 | 0 | 57 | 24 | 52 | 57 | 45 | 2 |
| 4¾ | Parkgate.......... | 48 | 38 | 9 | 32 | 45 | 54 | . | 5 | 17 | 11 | 55 | 25 | 43 | 13 | 53 | . | 36 | 50 | 10 | 33 | . | 23 | 3 | 52 | 43 | 15 | 58 | 54 | . | 51 | 39 | . | 57 | 3 | 0 | 27 | 55 | 0 | 48 | 5 |
| 7 | Heswall.......... | 55 | 45 | 14 | 40 | 51 | 59 | . | 10 | 22 | 16 | 0 | 30 | 50 | 18 | 58 | . | 41 | 55 | 15 | 40 | . | 28 | 8 | 57 | 48 | 20 | 3 | 59 | . | 56 | 44 | . | 2 | 8 | 5 | 32 | 0 | 5 | 53 | 10 |
| 9¼ | Thurstaston.......... | 0 | 50 | 20 | 49 | 57 | 5 | . | 15 | 27 | 21 | 5 | 35 | . | 23 | 4 | . | 46 | 1 | . | 45 | . | 33 | 14 | 2 | 53 | 25 | 11 | . | . | 1 | 49 | . | 7 | 13 | 10 | 37 | 7 | 10 | 0 | 15 |
| 10½ | Caldy.......... | 4 | 54 | 25 | 54 | 1 | 9 | . | 19 | 31 | 25 | 9 | 39 | . | 27 | 8 | . | 50 | 5 | . | 49 | . | 39 | 20 | 6 | 57 | 29 | 15 | . | . | 5 | 53 | . | 11 | 18 | 14 | 41 | 12 | 14 | 6 | 19 |
| 11¼ | Kirby Park.......... | 7 | 57 | 28 | 57 | 4 | 12 | . | 23 | 35 | 29 | 12 | 42 | . | 30 | 12 | . | 53 | 8 | . | 52 | . | 42 | 23 | 9 | 0 | 32 | . | . | . | . | . | . | . | . | . | . | . | . | . | . |
| 12 | West Kirby *(above)*..arr. | 10 | 0 | 31 | 0 | 7 | 15 | . | 26 | 38 | 32 | 15 | 45 | . | 33 | 15 | . | 56 | 11 | . | 55 | . | 45 | 26 | 12 | 3 | 35 | 20 | . | . | 10 | 58 | . | 16 | 23 | 19 | 46 | 17 | 19 | 11 | 24 |

| Miles | Down | Week Days mrn | | | | | | | | | aft | | | | | | | | | | | | | | | | | | | | Sundays mrn | | | | | | | | aft | | |
|---|---|---|---|---|---|---|---|---|---|---|---|---|---|---|---|---|---|---|---|---|---|---|---|---|---|---|---|---|---|---|---|---|---|---|---|---|---|---|---|---|---|
| | HOUR | 6 | 7 | C 8 | 8 | 8 | 9 | Y 10 | 11 | | S 12 | E 12 | E 1 | S 1 | S 2 | S 2 | 3 | E 4 | S 3 | 4 | 5 | 6 | E 6 | E 7 | 7 | 8 | 9 | 10 | 10 | | 9 | | 12 | 1 | 3 | 4 | 7 | 7 | | 8 | 9 |
| — | West Kirby........dep. | 40 | 30 | 11 | . | 40 | 15 | 26 | 17 | . | 27 | 30 | 48 | 50 | 10 | 45 | 25 | . | 54 | 43 | 25 | 25 | . | 0 | 25 | 40 | 22 | 15 | 50 | . | 22 | . | 10 | 55 | 45 | 28 | 0 | 50 | . | 42 | 28 |
| ¾ | Kirby Park.......... | . | 32 | 13 | . | 42 | 17 | 28 | 19 | . | 29 | 32 | 50 | 52 | 12 | 47 | 27 | . | 55 | 45 | 27 | 27 | . | 4 | 27 | 42 | 24 | 17 | 52 | . | . | . | . | . | . | . | . | . | . | . | . |
| 1½ | Caldy.......... | 43 | 35 | 16 | . | 45 | 20 | 31 | 22 | . | 32 | 35 | 53 | 55 | 15 | 50 | 30 | . | 58 | 48 | 30 | 30 | . | 7 | 30 | 45 | 27 | 20 | 55 | . | 25 | . | 13 | 58 | 48 | 31 | 3 | 53 | . | 45 | 31 |
| 2¾ | Thurstaston.......... | 48 | 39 | 20 | . | 49 | 24 | 35 | 26 | . | 36 | 39 | 57 | 59 | 20 | 54 | 34 | . | 2 | 52 | 34 | 34 | . | 11 | 34 | 49 | 31 | 25 | 59 | . | 29 | . | 17 | 2 | 52 | 35 | 7 | 58 | . | 49 | 35 |
| 5 | Heswall.......... | 54 | 44 | 27 | 40 | 54 | 29 | 40 | 31 | . | 41 | 44 | 2 | 4 | 27 | 0 | 39 | 7 | 7 | 58 | 41 | 39 | 52 | 16 | 39 | 55 | 36 | 31 | 4 | . | 34 | . | 22 | 7 | 3 | 40 | 12 | 4 | . | 54 | 40 |
| 7¼ | Parkgate.......... | 59 | 49 | 32 | 44 | 59 | 34 | 45 | 36 | . | 46 | 49 | 7 | 10 | 33 | 6 | 44 | 12 | 12 | 3 | 47 | 44 | 56 | 21 | 44 | 3 | 42 | 36 | 9 | . | 39 | . | 27 | 12 | 11 | 45 | 17 | 11 | . | 0 | 45 |
| 8¾ | Neston.......... | 3 | [illegible] | 36 | 48 | 3 | 38 | 49 | 40 | . | 50 | 53 | 11 | 16 | 39 | 10 | 48 | 18 | 18 | 7 | 55 | 48 | 0 | 28 | 48 | 7 | 48 | 40 | 13 | . | 43 | . | 31 | 16 | 15 | 49 | 21 | 15 | . | 4 | 49 |
| 10½ | Hadlow Road.......... | 8 | 0 | 41 | 53 | 8 | 43 | 54 | 45 | . | 55 | 58 | 16 | 21 | 46 | 15 | 53 | 23 | 23 | 12 | 0 | 53 | 5 | 33 | 53 | 12 | 53 | 48 | 18 | . | 49 | . | 37 | 22 | 21 | 55 | 27 | 21 | . | 10 | 55 |
| 12 | Hooton 495, 498, 500 arr. | 12 | 6 | . | 58 | 13 | 47 | 59 | 50 | . | 1 | 2 | 21 | 26 | 52 | 21 | 58 | 28 | 28 | 17 | 6 | 57 | 9 | 38 | 57 | 17 | 58 | 55 | 22 | . | 54 | . | 44 | 27 | 26 | 0 | 32 | 26 | . | 15 | 0 |

**C** To Birkenhead (arr 8 57 mrn) p 498 **E** Except Sats **S** Sats only **V** From Birkenhead (dep 5 3 aft) p 501
**Y** Thro Carr, New Brighton (dep. 9 58 mrn.) to London (E) pp above and 500 **Z** Thro Carr from London (E.) to New Brighton (arr. 10 28 aft.), pages 498 and above.

# CHAPTER 8

# North of the Severn - 2

## *Chester: Variety and Change*

To write about the Chester railway scene I covered my desks with public and working timetables, brown, well thumbed *Railway Clearing House* and Ordnance Survey maps, ancient and modern, the weighty tome of the first volume of Macdermot's *History of the Great Western Railway* and guide books of several eras. But the exercise was unnecessary because I have known all the lines radiating into Chester for more than half a century and my desk display was simply an excuse to wallow in nostalgia.

As at Shrewsbury, changes at Chester have been far more sweeping than a casual observer could be aware of - not least the loss of an operating situation in which London bound expresses ran over the same stretch of line in opposite directions, as at Exeter.

There were three distinctive flavours at Chester: the Joint Lines of the LMS and GWR; others solely owned by those companies, and the system of the Cheshire Lines Committee. It was independent of the other lines until a wartime junction opened at Mickle Trafford in 1942. It was modified in 1969 when Northgate Station closed and Chester General station, which was built 1847-8 by Francis Thompson, was renamed Chester.

Having survived into an age in which the pleasures and values of railway architecture are appreciated, it is recognised as one of the City's finest Victorian buildings.

This is partly due to the West Wing having been 'magnificently restored as an architect's office with the assistance of grant aid', to quote from *Heritage and the Environment*, published by BR Property Board in 1986. It dealt with the project under the heading 'Risen from the ashes'. The phrase was apposite as there would have been more ashes had BR been successful in an attempt to demolish the adjoining Mold Wing in 1970 to provide more car parking. Conservationists won the day, unlike passengers who a decade earlier had protested against the withdrawal of local trains to Mold, Denbigh and Corwen - the service from which the Wing had taken its name. For years, the roof of the Wing was impregnated by smoke from veteran Webb 2-4-2 tanks, and also Class 2 4-4-0s which I watched run in and out of the bay platforms.

There were no public objections to resignalling and track re-modelling, completed in 1984 at a cost of £6.7 million. The scheme involved demolition of notable signal gantries at the north and south of the station and several LNWR signal boxes of varied designs. They included Chester No 6 above the Holyhead tracks beside the north end triangle and close to the eastern mouth of Windmill Lane Tunnel (111 yds), over which ran the lines to Northgate station.

It was the closest of the Chester & Holyhead boxes to the City's heart and Cathedral and the House of the Bishop, the Right Reverend Michael Baughan, a railway enthusiast, who often refers to them in his Diocesan newsletters. When he opened the new signalling centre, he was presented with the No 6 box nameplate.

The General station of 1848 replaced two primitive ones which lay on both sides of a long, low hump-back road bridge between the City Centre and what used to be the urban district of Hoole. The Chester & Birkenhead Railway opened a terminus on the north side of the bridge on 23 September 1840, just ahead of the arrival of the Chester & Crewe, which by then had been absorbed by the Grand Junction.

It built its terminus just south of the bridge and a small works, centred on a stout, squarish building, fed by two short sidings. It is not known when the works closed, though it seems they became redundant when the Grand Junction was absorbed by the LNWR. The building survives as the offices of a national vehicle hire company.

The Birkenhead and Crewe lines were joined by a single track which ran under the Hoole Road bridge. The General station was built on the initiative of the Chester & Holyhead and Shrewsbury & Chester companies, rather than the Birkenhead and Crewe ones, which showed little interest in improvements during their short lives before absorption.

### The Penny Bridge

Major improvements and extensions to the Joint station in 1890 included constructed of a long footbridge from the Hoole (eastern) side to a large new central platform. The bridge became highly popular, being used not only by passengers, but people walking to and from work. In the 1950s, I mused in the *Liverpool Daily Post* about why an average of 800 people a day went to the station without ever thinking of catching a train. Being fully covered, the bridge gave bad weather cosiness not available on a tramp across the long road bridge, still as unpleasant today in bad weather as ever it was.

Some 'penny platformers', as the migrating masses were known, were simply in search of a good cuppa in the station refreshment room. I knew it well. Under its ornate and lofty ceiling and in front of a roaring fire, I waited for many a train home to Wallasey, via Birkenhead but sometimes I wandered in to assuage the disappointment I felt when I had just missed a locomotive that I wanted to cop.

Sadly I cannot tell you the last time I - or anyone - walked the bridge's echoing planks for I have no date of its closure, but I recently found an appropriate memorial: a half-moon iron bracket which supported a gas lamp over the Hoole entrance. It rested on brick posts which still form part of a gateway to memory.

The GWR main goods depot was among sidings fed

from the Chester & Birkenhead line. Some GWR trains from Manchester and Warrington, which the company reached from Chester with running powers, terminated at Brook Lane while others started from there until 21 September 1925.

Most of the staff and work were transferred to Saltney Yard, only eight guards remaining at Brook Lane to work Joint freight trains, which picked up or detached wagons there.

'By these new arrangements', stated a report, 'considerable economies have been effected in the Joint personnel which dealt with the GWR trains at Chester.'

The GWR's 13 passenger guards worked from the Joint Station which was under the supervision of the Joint Line Superintendent at Shrewsbury. At Chester, the GWR Divisional Superintendent had a personal staff of 35 for a district which stretched from Leaton, near Shrewbsury, to Birkenhead and Liverpool (James Street) and included GWR branches in the Wrexham area. The Liverpool office, long demolished, was opposite the entrance to the Mersey underground and included passenger enquiry and parcels offices.

Next door was the Gregg School which taught a system of shorthand invented in Liverpool by an unemployed man, which I have used all my life and years ago used to copy minutes of the Cambrian Railways board meetings at BRB Records.

In the same building as the school were the offices and presses of *The Journal of Commerce*, a daily paper which gave details of the world wide movement of ships, among them ships docking at Birkenhead to load and unload cargoes handled by the GWR and routed via Chester.

At Chester, the GWR had a useful parcels traffic, transported by two horse 'vehicles'. They were two 'horse parcels vanmen' and there was also a 'van guard'. Among ten other staff were three station lampmen who 'lamped' trains of GWR stock.

*GWR Engine Shed*

It is the content rather than the structure of the former GWR engine shed that has changed. The main buildings of what is now a diesel maintenance depot can still be viewed from the station, even though the northern tip of the old platform 4 was removed for a colour light signal gantry and although the buildings have been modified, they are recognizable enough to keep long memories green.

The Great Western gave the shed a rating of five 'Saints' the glorious 4-6-0s, which looked venerable even in youth, representing a tenth of the depot's allocation. Another veteran was a 'Bulldog' 4-4-0 (3366) and an 'Aberdare' (2662) was among ten 2-6-0s of several classes.

Heavy freight for Merseyside docks brought occasional visitors to Chester from far away and sometimes small and remote sheds. Chester shed was virtually spotter-proof, even at weekends: there was too much activity inside for the smallest of visitors not to be seen. But because of the heavy traffic, few locomotives stayed inside long so there was often a chance of making a cop.

The shed dated from 1856 and there is a passing reference to it in *Black's Picturesque Guide to North wales* in 1869:

The General Railway Station is extensive and commodious, and in every respect adapted to its purpose . . . The goods-station, the warehouses, the sheds for spare carriages and engines, and all other required buildings, are, in like manner, spacious and well arranged.

Officials did not always regard the shed as spacious because in the early 1920s they bought land near Green Lane Crossing at the southern end of Saltney yard to build a bigger one. But there was a snag:

It is not anticipated that the work will be proceeded with for some years to come, in consequence of difficulty with

*Photo:*

*W. A. Camwell*

G.W.R. 896, ex Cambrian Railways, on the 2–40 p.m. Moat Lane—Brecon, entering Newbridge on Wye on 15th September, 1949.

### Photographic Souvenir

in connection with the

## LAST PASSENGER TRAIN

on the

Moat Lane to Brecon and Brecon to Hereford lines

SUNDAY, 30th DECEMBER, 1962.

*Organised by the*

STEPHENSON LOCOMOTIVE SOCIETY

(Midland Area)

Death in the Borders: *Plate 25* Baldwin 4–6–0 tank No 3 outside Snailbeach engine shed 21 April 1950, nearly four years after it ceased work and only days before being cut up on site. *Plate 26* 'Cam' Camwell's railtours were always memorable and their black-edged Photographic Souvenirs are now collectors' items. The last passenger train from Moat Lane to Brecon and Brecon to Hereford ran on a snowy Sunday.

Wye & Golden Valleys: *Plate 27 (above)* Hay-on-Wye station with its distinctive Midland Railway style buildings, signal box and footbridge, added variety to the architectural styles of the Great Western and Cambrian Railways. *Plate 28 (below)* The Golden Valley Railway which joined the Hereford Hay & Brecon at Hay, led an ailing life for many years under private ownership and later that of the Great Western. The scene at Westbrook in 1932.

the Cestrian Brick Company, who have a lease of 14 years to run for working the clay under a portion of the land.

Had it been built, few GWR freight engines would have been seen at Chester station and certainly my spotter's log, with brown cardboard covers because of wartime economy, would have been a little emptier.

And I would not have watched locomotives turned on a table in the spacious triangle at Holyhead, Birkenhead and Crewe lines opposite the shed. After the turntable's removal, the area was landscaped in spring 1987.

There are better legacies to the GWR presence at Chester and in North Wales. They include the Llangollen Railway and a locomotive that began running on it in 1987: *Foxcote Manor*. It owes its presence there to a group of enthusiasts based in Chester, who bought it in 1974 and began restoration at the Cambrian Railways Society depot at Oswestry and completed it at Llangollen.

### *Chester LNWR Shed*

The first LNWR shed was close to that of the GWR and it is conceivable that it was among buildings referred to in *Black's* guide for it was also within sight of the station beside the line curving away towards Birkenhead.

After it closed it was used by the GWR as an extension of its own shed facilities. The site has proved valuable and convenient for there is a modern building on it today.

The LNWR shed that survived LMS days until closure on 5 June 1967, was smaller than the GWR's yet larger than the City's other one, established at Northgate.

The LNWR allocation was of some 40 locomotives of standard classes, to which were temporarily added some GWR passenger types after that shed closed to steam in April 1960. Freight locomotives went to spend their last days at Mold Junction.

When the 'Saints' were marching into the north end of

Chester station with the Paddington - Birkenhead and other through expresses, 'Royal Scots' ran into the adjoining platforms with Holyhead expresses. Other main line passenger services were generally the prerogative of class five 4-6-0s and secondary services were often worked in the 1940s by the last four 4-4-0s of the 'Precursor' and 'George V' classes. They had dignity - and pace - in old age, but to schoolboy eyes they were no match for the 'Castles' which began to appear at Chester in increasing numbers until the advent of the 'County' class 4-6-0s.

The shed was demolished soon after closure and has remained a waste-land much favoured by dog walkers, for some 20 years. The levelled site, on which the concrete basis of a few buildings remain, is a barren place at which to try to revive memories - especially when Chester has so many interesting buildings to offer the occasional visitor.

### LNWR Goods Traffic

The LNWR handled most of its goods traffic at Chester from a large depot at Hoole on the east side of the Joint station. It had a 10-ton crane and other facilities, noted in a standard, yet now vaguely quaint entry in the *RCH Hand Book of Railway Stations*, were shown as being for 'Furniture Vans, Carriages, Portable Engines and Machines on Wheels'. Such traffic arrived and departed at the yard which had a 245 wagon capacity.

After the depot closed, its large goods shed became a National Carriers depot, but it is now Chester Enterprise Centre for small businesses, officially opened 17 September 1984. This development has ensure the future of a building immediately recognisable as an interesting, if not particularly distinguished example of LNWR architecture.

### Chester - Whitchurch

Although the Chester - Whitchurch route was totally English, mostly running through Cheshire, you could see the hills of North Wales from the carriage window on clear days. The

LNWR ran passenger trains from the opening of the line in 1872 and they continued until September 1957 when the last regular one was manned by Guard Fred Evans, then aged 64, who had worked on the route for 37 years. Goods trains ran for another six years and also occasionally diverted Chester and Crewe passenger services.

Yet the line's concept had been grander as George P Neele, for many years the LNWR's Superintendent of the Line, revealed in *Railway Reminiscences* 1904. He described it as 'a direct line of our own from Ireland to Hereford and South Wales and a competing route between Shrewsbury and Chester, unsatisfactory, probably, to the Great Western Company, who had hitherto possessed a monopoly of the traffic.'

Although it was double tracked, there is no evidence that the branch was heavily used as a through route. The pattern of local passenger train services changed little over the years and after leaving the south end of General station, they ran the three miles to Waverton and another one and a half miles to Tattenhall Junction with the Chester & Crewe main line.

The small village of Tattenhall was well served by Euston for although there was Tattenhall Road on the main line, a station called simply Tattenhall was opened on the branch. It was much closer to the village. This station and Broxton, to the south, were starting points recommended in *Ramblers' Outings from Merseyside* published during World War II to encourage factory and other workers to get the most enjoyment from a day in the country.

Although is now nearly a quarter of a century since the branch closed, enthusiasts still go to Malpas to view its station, a notable example of private restoration. But beware, the station is well over a mile from the village. When there were suggestions in 1974 that an attempt might be made to reopen the branch, the *Chester Chronicle* pointed out that none of its stations had been well sited or used. The paper stated that revival rumours were without foundation because the cost would be prohibitive.

Today, Grindley Brook, on the outskirts of Whitchurch

and site of the only halt, features in another walkers' guide, which Cheshire County Council publishes for its Sandstone Trail, winding 30 miles across the county's gently undulating countryside to Beacon Hill at Frodsham, which overlooks a Chester railway that survives - the main line to Warrington.

The Sandstone Trail ends at Grindley Brook, close to where the Welsh branch of the Shropshire Union Canal - the Llangollen Canal - is bridged by the trackbed. Walkers are then beside the A41 Midlands - Birkenhead road and the Guide points out that this junction of road, rail and canal is a fitting place to end 'a new journey through Cheshire'.

Another 'new journey' considered by the County Council was along the trackbed itself, but the idea was quickly rejected because, unlike the countryside to the east, it was unlikely to attract many ramblers.

The County Council did, however, create a picnic site at Broxton, junction of two major roads, the A41 and A534 from Nantwich and South Cheshire to Wrexham. It is well used by drivers stretching their legs, if only briefly.

The branch left the Shrewsbury & Crewe main line within sight of Whitchurch station. Chester Junction signal box closed on 15 June 1959, but a splendid pedestrian suspension bridge still spans the main line. Canon Roger Lloyd wrote in *The Fascination of Railways* (Allen & Unwin, 1951) about the joys of Whitchurch, noting the Chester trains as travelling rather after the manner of an elderly tortoise, pulled by Cauliflower 0-6-0s.

He thought Whitchurch station was incredibly ugly. Much of it has been pulled down in recent years, but the description still applies. Yet Whitchurch still has the power, for those who remember, to stir the memories, as it did for Robert Hughes when he wrote in the *Chester Chronicle* a decade ago, albeit in a somewhat critical vein. He found the Chester bay platform akin to 'a toothless hag', while that of the Oswestry line was 'a meaningless sweep of stone'.

Yet that platform edge was once a frontier, between the mighty LNWR and the small, yet lively, Cambrian Railways.

After the Oswestry Ellesmere & Whitchurch Railway closed in 1965, the LNWR shed turntable just beyond the platform end was dismantled and you can now find it at Bridgnorth.

### Waverton Station

Waverton station, which the branch trains used, closed on 15 June 1959 at the age of 68 years and one week. The main building on the Up side is still there and much admired. It belonged to the village's second station, opened on 6 June 1898, to replace one half a mile further south dating from completion of the Chester & Crewe in 1840 and known before opening as Black Dog because the area was sparsely populated. Its platforms lay on either side of an overbridge carrying what became the A41. In 1971 the spot was the scene of a fatal crash involving a school special returning to Birmingham from Rhyl. Two children died when the two rear coaches left rails buckled in a heatwave and overturned.

The second Waverton station was built for the Duke of Westminster and no expense was spared. It was designed in keeping with local houses and beside ornate chimney stacks, had pine-panelled 1st and 3rd class waiting rooms, a ladies' room and verandah. In late LMS days it was staffed by a station master, two porters and three signalmen.

Forty chains separated old and new stations and over that distance in 1897 was carried Waverton's Lost Property Register (LNWR form no 337). It had been opened on Tuesday 2 July 1872 to record the finding of a black silk hat. Using nib-pens, staff maintained a flow of entries in spidery handwriting until 28 October 1939 when a child's red leather handbag was noted.

Lost umbrellas and hats were the most frequently logged items, although few were recorded as having been reclaimed. In October 1895, a soldier's helmet was found on the main line between the station and Tattenhall Junction.

It had 'East York badge on Brass on front. Numbered 10693'. Nine days later it was 'sent depot', the customary cryptic entry. A soldier's uniform cap (no badge) was among only six articles

# EASTER EXCURSIONS, 1933.

# A DAY IN NORTH WALES.

## EASTER MONDAY, APRIL 17th,

### EXCURSION TICKETS TO

# Prestatyn, Rhyl, Colwyn Bay and Llandudno

| FROM | Times of Starting. | | | RETURN FARES—THIRD CLASS. | | | |
|---|---|---|---|---|---|---|---|
| | A | B | C | To Prestatyn. | To Rhyl. | To Colwyn Bay | To Llandudno. |
| | a.m. | a.m. | a.m. | s. d. | s. d. | s. d. | s. d. |
| Worleston | 8 16 | ... | 11 16 | 4 6 | 5 0 | 6 0 | 7 0 |
| Calveley | 8 23 | ... | 11 23 | 4 0 | 4 6 | 5 6 | 6 6 |
| Beeston Castle & Tarporley | 8 29 | ... | 11 29 | 4 0 | 4 6 | 5 6 | 6 6 |
| Tattenhall Road | 8 37 | ... | 11 36 | 3 6 | 4 6 | 5 0 | 6 6 |
| Waverton | 8 43 | 9 29 | 11† 0 | 3 0 | 3 6 | 4 6 | 5 6 |
| Whitchurch | ... | 8 53 | 10†30 | 5 0 | 5 6 | 6 0 | 7 0 |
| Malpas | ... | 9 4 | 10†41 | 4 0 | 4 6 | 5 6 | 6 6 |
| Broxton | ... | 9 13 | 10†47 | 4 0 | 4 0 | 5 0 | 6 0 |
| Tattenhall | ... | 9 19 | 10†52 | 3 6 | 4 0 | 5 0 | 5 6 |

**A**—Passengers change at Chester into train leaving at 9.2 a.m.

**B**—Change at Chester and proceed by special train at 9.45 a.m.

**C**—Change at Chester and proceed by special train at 12.5 p.m.

†—Passengers change at Chester into train leaving at 11.45 a.m.

**RETURN ARRANGEMENTS**—Passengers return the same day as under :—

**For Stations Waverton to Worleston**—Llandudno **5.40** or **7.30** p.m., Colwyn Bay **6.5** or **7.55** p.m., Rhyl **6.25** or **8.15** p.m., Prestatyn **6.34** or **8.24** p.m.

**D—For stations Tattenhall to Whitchurch**—Llandudno **6.55** p.m., Colwyn Bay **7.17** p.m.; Rhyl **7.39** p.m., Prestatyn **7.52** p.m.

**D—9.10 p.m.** Chester to Whitchurch, will run specially on this date.

Children under 3 years of age free ; 3 and under 14 half fares.

### LUGGAGE ALLOWANCE.

Passengers holding Day or Half-Day Excursion Tickets are not allowed to take any luggage except small handbags, luncheon baskets, or other small articles intended for the passenger's use during the day. On the return journey only, passengers may take with them, free of charge, at Owner's Risk, goods for their own use, not exceeding 60 lbs.

### Conditions of Issue of Excursion and other Reduced Fare Tickets.

Excursion Tickets, and Tickets issued at Fares less than the Ordinary Fares, are issued subject to the Notices and Conditions shewn in the Company's current Time Tables.

Further information can be obtained on application to F. P. KINSMAN, District Goods and Passenger Manager, CHESTER. 'Phone Chester 1090—Extension 17.

March, 1933. (Ex/Easter/G) **ASHTON DAVIES, Chief Commercial Manager.**

(E.R.O. 53302.)

(2,500)     McCorquodale & Co., Ltd., Printers, London and Newton.—651     K 115

Easter seaside 1933: Excursions from eight now long closed stations, including the five intermediate ones on the Chester & Crewe main line. A special train ran from Chester to Whitchurch to get trippers home. Luggage was restricted - but 'luncheon baskets' were permitted.

handed to staff in 1937. Over the years a number of military items were found, possibly due to Waverton being about three miles from Saighton army camp on the southern outskirts of Chester. Most troops will have used Chester General station for, although being about the same distance from the camp, it was at the terminus of a city bus route.

Country stations seemed to suffer at the hand of guide book writers. The *LNWR Official Guide* (1876) noted that after leaving Chester for Crewe 'the train passes the unimportant stations of Waverton and Tattenhall'. It made no mention of the Whitchurch branch which, by then had been open four years and for which the LNWR was presumably seeking traffic.

On the eve of Nationalisation, the LMS published a series of five route books, collector's items today. No 1, *The Track of the Irish Mail* told passengers about marl pits between Tattenhall Road and Waverton and stated that after Waverton station 'if it is clear', the bold square tower of Chester Cathedral could been seen ahead. It did not mention that it could also be seen from the Up platform at Waverton. But then, it must be agreed route books were for long distance rather than local travellers.

### Chester: GWR Presence

While Paddington's dream of broad gauge to the Mersey ended at Wolverhampton, it did reach the Mersey via Chester and handled heavy traffic from the docks via the Chester & Birkenhead Joint Line.

Saltney was important in Chester's early railway history for it was the northern end for a time of the North Wales Mineral Railway, forerunner of the Shrewsbury & Chester. Saltney became an important locomotive and carriage works of that company and when, as the GWR system developed, the Wolverhampton locomotive works were constructed, Saltney remained the carriage and wagon centre and later became the main carriage works of the GWR North Division.

## Saltney Quay Branch

The railways soon developed what became the port of Chester, a rather pretentious name for short tidal wharves straggling the border between England and Wales at Saltney on the western edge of the City. They were within sight of the Chester & Holyhead main line, but never connected to it. Saltney's growth in mid-Victorian days was reflected in *Black's Guide of 1869*.

> The railway company having laid out an extensive wharf and obtained power to construct docks, it rose rapidly into importance as a port for the coasting trade. It is the nearest and most convenient outlet for the whole of the central district of North Wales, and for the mining fields of Shropshire. Here also are extensive ironworks for the manufacture of anchors, chain-cables etc.

Fifty-six years later, Saltney still featured in GWR guides. *Through the Window* routebook number two: *Paddington to Birkenhead* told passengers: '. . . we must notice on the left Saltney which serves as the port of Chester on the broad straight cut through which the Dee flows before opening out into its estuary.'

The owner of a copy, which I bought in a Chester secondhand bookshop, never took notice of the command for after 60 years, I found the binding crackled because most of the pages had never been opened.

Saltney's main industry remained maritime based until recent years. *Flintshire's Industrial Handbook*, published shortly before Nationalisation stated that the very considerable output of ships cables and anchors and crane and hoist chains, was absorbed principally by the Admiralty, government railways overseas, and home and foreign dock and harbour authorities.

> The manufacture of superphosphate fertilizers is also carried out at Saltney and constitutes another important local industry of considerable magnitude.

A GWR Divisional Report noted that the Saltney Quay branch served two manure works - those of Webb and Sons and Dobbins - and the wire making works of Wompees Ltd and Crichton's shipbuilding yard.

A fair amount of business is done by Messrs Crichtons who build barges, river and lake steamers and launches, which are sent to various parts of the world.

The Report also stated that there was some dispute as to the ownership of the land on which the branch was built, but gave no details.

After World War II, the industries changed and the branch was extended a short distance westwards along the river bank to the Dee Oil Works, which later changed in character and became No Nail Boxes Ltd. A concrete bridge which carried the extension over a stream is now used as a road bridge to a supermarket.

The branch was known by several titles: Saltney Quay . . . the Dee Branch . . . the Riverside Branch.

There were road as well as rail operating problems for it had a level crossing 'very extensively used by the public' beside the Anchor Inn on what was a main road from Chester to North Wales, the A55 (now A549).

That was in an era when the Dee sometimes flooded sidings in Saltney Lower Yard, making it the most northerly place where the GWR got its feet wet. The service time tables stated that only light shunting engines were to run on the Dee branch 'Beyond Flood Gates'.

The area around the branch route has changed greatly in recent years and the trackbed has been virtually obliterated. The level crossing was removed to allow widening of the main road (High Street) and River Lane. Electrical and carpet stores were built across the trackbed between High street and the Chester & Holyhead main line, where the four tracks have been reduced to two and the two southern spans over the trackbed removed. The abutments remain. The wharf was closed some years ago and banked by grassy mounds as part of a flood protection scheme.

*Saltney Marshalling Yard*

The year 1967 not only saw an end of the Paddington - Birkenhead expresses, which ran through Saltney Junction in the opposite direction to those from Euston to Holyhead, but also trip working between marshalling yards which the LNWR and GWR created just over the Welsh border because there was no land available nearer the city.

Mold junction was Euston's choice while Paddington constructed Saltney Yard almost within sight of it.

Traffic was exchanged between them for years. A decade or so before closure of Saltney yard on 3 April 1967, the Western Region allowed 28XX class 2-8-0s and 51XX and 61XX 2-6-2 tanks to work between them 'without the ATC shoes clipped up'. The weekday only trains were limited to two brake vans and 38 wagons - 15 more than pre-Grouping days when exchanges were carried out at a siding at Saltney Junction - except when it was foggy or snow was falling.

Singling of the Shrewsbury & Chester main line between Saltney and Wrexham in the mid 1980s caused far more local concern among railwaymen than the yard economy had done. Enthusiasts never took much interest in the Yard, possibly because it was so isolated from the Chester railway scene. It stretched south on a flattish site not overlooked by roads or crossed by bridges. It was almost a secretive place.

The crash of buffers; the sudden exertions of yard shunters, the slow, measured beat of 2-8-0s and *moguls* leaving with heavy trains, disturbed only a few people living in the area. The yard was shown in working timetables as being, in rounded figures, 193 miles from London, via Bicester; 212 via Oxford and 70 miles from Wolverhampton. The main building included the offices of the yardmaster, his clerk, four inspectors and 38 goods guards. There was also an office used by 'the special police department'.

The yard capacity of 2,000 wagons was rarely reached, the average daily turn-over being about 1,200, formed from 90 arriving and departing trains, dealt with by three shunting locomotives.

Staff, high and low ranking, who were based far and wide on the GWR system were involved with running the yard. The nearest 'outsider' was the porter at Balderton, a mile up the line towards Wrexham. Besides looking after the station's oil lamps, he attended to those in the yard signals.

The lower yard goods depot was the responsibility of the Chester Goods Agent, who worked to the district goods manager at James Street, Liverpool. The same chain of authority embraced the GWR goods depot in Brook Lane, Chester.

Also in the lower yard was a repair depot of the GWR Sheet Department. That was controlled by the sheet superintendent, based at Worcester. Saltney carriage & wagon shops, adjoining the sheet depot, was the responsibility of the locomotive superintendent at Wolverhampton.

Today, the shell of a building in Boundary Lane, Saltney, close to High Street, is the best relic of railway presence for the rest of the site lay undeveloped up to 1988. The building is fenced, awaiting restoration and looking rather like an unadorned Roman temple, appropriate perhaps for Chester.

### Saltney Station

How history can slip from beneath your feet! For 18 months I lived within a quarter of a mile of Saltney station, yet never used it. I should have done on purely historic grounds for it was a station with the distinction of having once been closed for 15 years. The situation in 1922, five years into closure, was, in GWR terms:

'Up to 1916 there was a passenger station at Saltney, but owing to the War it was closed and ultimately dismantled. The passenger traffic was very small and did not pay the expenses of the staff employed to look after the station.

The platforms were situated where the line crosses the Queensferry road by a bridge, the Booking Office and waiting Rooms being on the street level.

In the 1930s, Saltney was growing sufficiently to be considered worthy of a station and in 1932 it re-opened, the entrance path being on the Down (Chester) side. Wrexham passengers had to use a foot crossing over the main line tracks.

The second station was smaller than the first with platforms only 100 ft long and that created problems. The *Appendix* to No 14 section of the service timetables (from Saltney Junction to Oxley North, $67^1/_2$ miles), stated:

Enginemen must approach carefully, and bring the vehicle in which the Guard is riding, together with the adjoining coach, to a stand at the platform . . . The Guard is responsible for seeing that passengers do not alight from, or join, the train except at the platform.

Despite the operating complications, the GWR and Western Region served Saltney well, not only with Chester - Wrexham local services, but with those from further afield. The second Down service of the morning was the 7.35 am from Oswestry; the second, the 7.10 am from Wellington, which did not reach Saltney until almost $2^1/_2$ hrs later. Those services were in the Winter 1958-59 Timetable. But in *Bradshaw's* from 12 September 1960 Saltney had a capital 'M' beside its name and a footnote: 'Rail Service Withdrawn'. It was an economy enginemen must hardly have regretted.

### Chester: Cheshire Lines Committee

Few things have changed more than the Chester rail scene with which I grew up as a boy during World War II and I know of no better way to reflect upon the thought than to remember the barn-like wind tunnel that was Northgate station on nights when the stars above the open platform ends were brighter than the dimmed black-out lights under the roof.

Wartime was grim, if memorable. Today, Northgate is ablaze with lights in and around the £5 million pound Northgate Leisure Centre which straggles the station site. How much more cheery it is to view the leisure pool, especially when it entices visitors by offering 'tropical magic with special lighting effects'.

Trains occasionally use Northgate still; I have spotted Hornby Gauge 0 tinplate models working during swapmeets held in the lofty sports hall.

Sometimes railway enthusiasts have to admit that closing lines and knocking down stations and redeveloping their sites lead to major improvement in local amenities. Planners charged with protecting historic Chester are careful about any change likely to alter its character. Yet it is unlikely that they hesitated in allowing the demolition of Northgate station, not least because it was an eyesore close to the City's heart and within sight of its Wells.

The station has vanished almost without trace: twelve brick arches forming a retaining wall between two car park levels, close to where the Chester & Holyhead main line plunges into Windmill Lane tunnel beneath the station site, are the most evocative remains. The car parks are part of the Northgate Leisure Centre, opened in 1977.

When Northgate came into my life I was party to defying, possibly with a slight guilt which nearly fifty years have erased, of ignoring platform posters which pleaded: 'Is Your Journey Really Necessary?' That was when the Christiansen family - father, mother and son - made pleasure sorties from its blitzed home in Wallasey, to Chester - a City on the outskirts of which mother was born, father loved and I came to love when I worked in it for a time after demobilisation from national service.

We travelled from Liscard & Poulton on a 'Wrexham Rattler', changing at Hawarden Bridge (sometimes called a station and sometimes a halt), to a Wrexham - Chester train which, if it had an N5 0-6-2 tank at its head, announced its

**WREXHAM, SHOTTON, CHESTER AND NEW BRIGHTON**

**WEEKDAYS**

| WREXHAM CENTRAL | Z | dep |
| Wrexham Exchange | | |
| Gwersyllt | | |
| Cefn-y-bedd | | |
| Caergwrle Castle and Wells | | |
| Hope Village | | |
| Penyffordd for Leeswood | | |
| Buckley Junction | | |
| Hawarden | | |
| Shotton High Level | L | |
| Hawarden Bridge | | |
| Sealand | | |
| Blacon | | |
| CHESTER Northgate | A | arr |
| CHESTER Northgate | A | dep |
| Blacon | | |
| Sealand | | |
| Neston North | | |
| Heswall Hills | | |
| Upton | | |
| Bidston | | |
| WEST KIRBY | | arr |
| BIRKENHEAD Hamilton Square | | arr |
| LIVERPOOL Central Low Level | | arr |
| Wallasey Village | | |
| Wallasey Grove Road | | |
| NEW BRIGHTON | | arr |

**WEEKDAYS—continued**

| WREXHAM CENTRAL | Z | dep |
| Wrexham Exchange | | |
| Gwersyllt | | |
| Cefn-y-bedd | | |
| Caergwrle Castle and Wells | | |
| Hope Village | | |
| Penyffordd for Leeswood | | |
| Buckley Junction | | |
| Hawarden | | |
| Shotton High Level | L | |
| Hawarden Bridge | | |
| Sealand | | |
| Blacon | | |
| CHESTER Northgate | A | arr |
| CHESTER Northgate | A | dep |
| Blacon | | |
| Sealand | | |
| Neston North | | |
| Heswall Hills | | |
| Upton | | |
| Bidston | | |
| WEST KIRBY | | arr |
| BIRKENHEAD Hamilton Square | | arr |
| LIVERPOOL Central Low Level | | arr |
| Wallasey Village | | |
| Wallasey Grove Road | | |
| NEW BRIGHTON | | arr |

**NOTES**

A—At Chester Northgate connections are available to and from Northwich, Manchester Central, etc. Particulars may be obtained on application at stations.

B—6 minutes later on Saturdays.

C—On Saturdays arrive West Kirby 5.10 p.m.

H—By Chester to Shotton or Wrexham service, changing at Hawarden Bridge.

L—Particulars of connecting services via the adjacent Shotton Low Level Station to and from Rhyl, Llandudno, Bangor, etc., may be obtained on application at stations.

SO—Saturdays only.

SX—Saturdays excepted.

Z—Particulars of connecting services to and from Western Region stations (Gobowen for Oswestry), Shrewsbury, Wolverhampton Low Level, Birmingham Snow Hill, etc.) via Wrexham Exchange.

THESE SERVICES ARE SUBJECT TO ALTERATION.

arrival in Chester by squealling round the curve into Northgate. This fact was first noted for posterity by J.E. Feild in an itinerary for the Wrexham Mold & Connah's Quay Railtour of 29 April 1967, organised by the Railway Correspondence & Travel Society. He noted that the 1 in 39 curve 'was always a difficult task for the small G.C. locomotives'. When they shunted empty trains out of the platform they had to restart on the steep gradient with trains locked on the curve.

Now builders are locked on the curve for in summer 1985 work began on the second development on the site. Northgate Village is being developed by a company which won a design competition.

Its prospectus stated: 'You can say goodbye to costly and time-wasting commuting for good. 'When the village is complete, it is possible that more commuters will arrive and depart from houses and flats than ever used the station.

Yet never again will I be able to enjoy what became almost a ritual on reaching Northgate when walking - and sometimes running past the engine at the buffers, turned right behind them to get to the ticket barrier, and then headed for the bookshop of Phillipson and Golder in Eastgate Row. It was dark, dignified and heavy with wood panelling almost the library of a stately home. And it was also a publishing house for the company produced a monthly *Railway Guide*, a collector's item today because it also included bus services within the City and to North Wales.

A study of its tables revealed a microcosm of road - rail competition. There were rarely major changes in the two routes from Northgate station, possibly because they were duplicated by ones from Chester General, from where the GWR ran direct to Wrexham - a route on which local travellers often

Chester Northgate was included in Merseyside's first completely dieselised passenger service, which revived direct trains to Wallasey: They were switched, with the Wrexham Central service, to New Brighton from the Bidston - Seacombe branch, which was closed. The DMUs never attracted the passenger traffic hoped for, but they helped to extend the life of Northgate Station.

## CHESTER (General) & WHITCHURCH (Week-days Only).

S Sats. only.   SX Sats. excepted.
W Wednesdays only.   WSX Wednesdays and Saturdays excepted

| depart | a m | | | | WSX | S | W | S | S X | | p m | SX | SX | | | | S | |
|---|---|---|---|---|---|---|---|---|---|---|---|---|---|---|---|---|---|---|
| Chester ... „ | 8 2 | | | | 11 4² | 12 40 | 1 10 | 2 14 | 4 10 | | 5 20 | 6 10 | 8 20 | | | | 10 5 | |
| Waverton „ | 8 8 | | | | 11 48 | 12 46 | 1 16 | | 4 16 | | 5 27 | 6 21 | 5 26 | | | | 10 11 | |
| Tattenhall „ | 8 17 | | | | 11 57 | 12 55 | 1 25 | 2 27 | 4 35 | | 5 36 | 6 30 | 8 35 | | | | 10 20 | |
| Broxton ... „ | 8 2³ | | | | 12 3 | 1 1 | 1 31 | 2 33 | 4 31 | | 5 42 | 6 36 | 8 41 | | | | 10 27 | |
| Malpas „ | 8 32 | | | | 12 12 | 1 10 | 1 40 | 2 42 | 4 41 | | 5 52 | 6 46 | 8 50 | | | | 10 36 | |
| Grindley Brook | 8 39 | | | | 12 19 | 1 17 | 1 47 | | 4 48 | | 5 59 | 6 53 | 8 57 | | | | 10 43 | |
| Whitchurch arr. | 8 47 | | | | 12 27 | 1 25 | 1 55 | 2 55 | 4 55 | | 6 8 | 7 1 | 9 5 | | | | 10 53 | |

| depart | a m | a m | a m | S | | | SX | | SX | S |
|---|---|---|---|---|---|---|---|---|---|---|
| Whitchurch dep. | 7 5 | 8 11 | 9 3? | 1 10 | | | 4 12 | | 5 20 | 6 4? |
| Grindley Brook | 7 10 | 8 16 | 9 43 | 1 15 | | | 4 17 | | 5 25 | 6 50 |
| Malpas „ | 7 18 | 8 24 | 9 51 | 1 23 | | | 4 25 | | 5 33 | 6 59 |
| Broxton ... „ | 7 25 | 8 3? | 9 58 | 1 30 | | | 4 32 | | 5 40 | 7 6 |
| Tattenhall „ | 7 31 | 8 39 | 10 4 | 1 36 | | | 4 40 | | 5 50 | 7 12 |
| Waverton „ | 7 38 | 8 46 | 1011 | 1 43 | | | 4 48 | | 6 0 | 7 19 |
| Chester ... arr. | 7 46 | 8 54 | 1019 | 1 51 | | | 4 59 | | 6 8 | 7 27 |

## MANCHESTER (London Rd.), CREWE & WELLINGTON | Suns.

‡ Saturday nights.   Z Except Weds & Sats.   W Weds. & Sats.

| depart | a m | a m | a .. | a m | W | Z | p m | p m | a m | p m | |
|---|---|---|---|---|---|---|---|---|---|---|---|
| MANCHESTER (L. Rd ) | 12 50 | | 8 5 | 1 10 | 1 18 | | 3§20 | 7 10 | 11‡55 | 7 5 | |
| CREWE ... dep | 6 5 | | 9 30 | 12 5? | 3 15 | | 5 10 | 8 50 | 6 40 | 8 35 | |
| Nantwich „ | 6 13 | | 9 38 | 1 2? | 3 23 | | 5 20 | 8 58 | 6 48 | 43 | |
| Audlem .. „ | 6 23 | | 9 48 | 1 13 | 3 33 | | 5 31 | 9 | 7 0 | 8 52 | |
| Adderley „ | 6 30 | | 9 54 | 1 20 | 3 39 | | 5 37 | 9 16 | 7 8 | 8 57 | |
| Market Drayton „ | 6 41 | 8 0 | 10 3 | 1 29 | 3 50 | 3 50 5 | 5 49 | 9 25 | 7 2 | 9 5 | § Mayfield Station |
| Tern Hill „ | 6 48 | 8 6 | 10 9 | 1 35 | 3 55 | 3 55 5 | 5 55 | 9 3? | 7 25 | 9 10 | S Sats. only † a.m. |
| Hodnet .. „ | 6 57 | 8 14 | 1016 | 1 4? | 4 ? | 4 ? 6 | 2 9 | 3? | 7 32 | 9 15 | |
| Peplow .. „ | 7 3 | 8 19 | 1021 | 1 48 | 4 7 | 4 7 6 | 7 9 | 44 | 7 37 | 9 20 | |
| Crudgington .. „ | 7 15 | 8 32 | 1032 | 2 0 | 4 18 | 4 18 6 15 | 9 53 | | 7 50 | 9 30 | |
| WELLINGTON ...arr. | 7 28 | 8 45 | 1043 | 2 13 | 4 35 | 4 35 6 31 | 10 4 | | 8 1 | 9 39 | |

| depart | a m | a m | n'n | Z | W | p m | | a m | p m | |
|---|---|---|---|---|---|---|---|---|---|---|
| WELLINGTON .. „ | 7 30 | 10 0 | 1215 | 1 0 2 45 | 2 45 5 55 | 9 25 | | 9 15 | 10 55 | † On Sats. arrive Manchester 10·51 |
| Crudgington .. „ | 7 37 | 10 9 | 1225 | 1 9 2 54 | 2 54 6 5 | 9 35 | | 9 25 | 11 7 | |
| Peplow .. „ | 7 47 | 1022 | 1238 | 1 21 3 6 | 3 6 17 | 9 48 | | 9 37 | 11 17 | |
| Hodnet .. „ | 7 53 | 027 | 1243 | 1 26 3 11 | 3 11 6 22 | 9 53 | | 9 42 | 11 24 | |
| Tern Hill „ | 8 2 | 1035 | 1251 | 1 35 3 19 | 3 19 6 30 | 9 58 | | 9 50 | 11 33 | |
| Market Drayton „ | 8 12 | 1045 | 1 2 | 1 42 3 26 | 3 26 6 41 | 10 9 | | 10 0 | 11 44 | |
| Adderley „ | 8 20 | 1050 | 1 8 | 3 34 6 47 | | 10 16 | | 10 5 | 11 52 | |
| Audlem .. „ | 8 26 | 1057 | 1 15 | 3 40 6 55 | | 10 23 | | 10 11 | 11 59 | |
| Nantwich „ | 8 38 | 11 9 | 1 27 | 3 51 7 8 | | 10 33 | | 1 22 | 12 17 | |
| CREWE .. arr. | 8 49 | 1121 | 1 38 | 4 0 7 18 | | 10 42 | | 1033 | 12 30 | |
| MANCHESTER „ | 9f49 | 1 55 | 2 3? | 5 20 8 45 | | 1‡32 | | 1136 | 1 32 | |

## CREWE and STAFFORD (Local Service).

a 3 minutes later on Fridays

| | | am | SX | S | pm | | | am | SX | S | pm | pm |
|---|---|---|---|---|---|---|---|---|---|---|---|---|
| Crewe | dep. | 650 | 1145 | 1228 | 555 | Stafford | dep. | 8 3 | 11 48 | 125 | 527 | 9 31 | — |
| Madeley | „ | 7 3 | 1158 | 1241 | 6 8 | Norton Bge | „ | 811 | 11 57 | 134 | 535 | — | — |
| Whitmore | „ | 7 9 | 12 3 | 1246 | 613 | Standon Bge | „ | 819 | 12 5 | 142 | 543 | 9 46 | — |
| Standon Bge | „ | 718 | 1210 | 1253 | 620 | Whitmore | „ | 827 | 12 13 | 150 | 551 | — | — |
| Norton Bge | „ | 726 | 1217 | 1 1 | 628 | Madeley | „ | 832 | 12 18 | 155 | 556 | — | — |
| Stafford | arr. | 738 | 1226 | 1 11 | 638 | Crewe | arr. | 844 | 12a30 | 2 9 | 611 | 10 6 | — |

Besides being linked with Craven Arms, Wellington also had services to Crewe and Manchester (London Road), shown on page 49 of another local timetable: *Phillipson & Golder's Railway Guide* which the Chester company produced monthly. In the January 1951 edition, page 49 was completed by another long forgotten service, that of stopping trains over the West Coast main line between Crewe and Stafford. Norton Bridge is the only intermediate station still open and it has a very restricted service.

North of the Severn – 1: *Plate 29 (above)* The Stafford–Wellington branch gave the LNWR access to Shrewsbury and Welshpool. Newport, the main intermediate town between Stafford and Wellington, had a substantial station, incorporating a large water tower. *Plate 30 (below)* The main routes to Chester Northgate – the Cheshire Lines Committee terminus – were from Wrexham and Manchester (Central). Both were duplicated by quicker routes. Ex GCR class C 13 4–4–2 tank (auto fitted) on the 4.15 pm to Manchester (Central). 29 September 1949.

North of the Severn – 2: *Plate 31 (above)* Blacon, on Chester's outskirts, had a station designed in the style of Victorian merchants' large houses built close to Chester Northgate station. *Plate 32 (below)* The Hooton–West Kirby branch ran for several miles along the low cliffs of the Dee Estuary and there were fine views of North Wales from the carriage window. An RCTS Cheshire Railtour pauses at Thurstaston. 26 March 1960.

caught Paddington - Birkenhead expresses; and the LMS ran expresses to Manchester Victoria, via Warrington, an industrial town far bigger than any on the route from Northgate to Manchester (Central), via Altrincham.

The January 1951 copy of the P & G *Guide* shows a weekday service of 11 through trains on the route, with one the 4.15 pm from Chester, being the only one to call at Mickle Trafford. On Sundays, Northgate dispatched and received three Manchester trains, but Wrexham was better served, six of the ten departures being extended from Connah's Quay & Shotton. Three trains gave connections to Seacombe.

Northgate's demise was slow, partly because of public opposition and fifty weeks elapsed between the Minister of Transport consenting to its closure and the actual event itself.

The event took place in autumn 1969 when the Manchester service was diverted to General station which since then has services to Manchester Victoria and Oxford Road. School buses between Northgate and the King's and Queen's Schools were also switched to and from General station.

The Wrexham service died, but the route remained, used by through freight trains between the Manchester area and North Wales. But that steadily dwindled, not least when production ceased at Shotton steelworks.

### Chester - Dee Marsh Junction

The London & North Western and the Great Western were established in Chester long before rival companies began advancing west across Cheshire from Stockport, and it was not until 1869 that they reached the Chester - Warrington route at Helsby. Four years earlier, the Chester & West Cheshire Junction was authorised for $7^1/_2$ miles from Mouldsworth, its nearest point to Chester, to Northgate. Construction was slow and the line was not used by goods until November 1874 and passengers until six months later.

A junction with the Chester - Warrington line at Mickle Trafford was never opened because of a dispute between the

Cheshire Lines and Birkenhead Joint (GW & LNW) and it was removed in 1903, only to be re-opened for wartime traffic in 1942. But that junction faced the opposite direction to the one originally planned.

In 1969, in preparation for the Northgate closure, the junction was reversed to its original pattern. Subsequently it became a scissors-crossing.

The route west from Chester East junction was built by the Manchester Sheffield & Lincolnshire Railway under the title of Chester & Connah's Quay Railway. The MS & L financed the only railway crossing of the canalised Dee north of Chester when the Wrexham Mold & Connah's Quay could not afford to do so, being able only to manage construction of the $4^1/_2$ mile Hawarden Loop, as another part of the link between Chester and Wrexham, which opened in March 1890, contemporary guide books very much over-eulogising the virtues of the Hawarden swing bridge, a rather modest structure still in use today.

Four stations were built between Northgate and Hawarden Bridge. Just beyond the end of the Northgate curve was Chester (Liverpool Road), a four platform station built to serve an area of the City where prosperous Victorian merchants built large houses.

It was an oppulence quietly reflected in the village stations at Blacon and Saughall, built in the pseudo half-timbered style of Chester's old houses. It is a pity that both stations were demolished soon after the end of passenger services for had they survived they would be pleasing architectural features in expanding areas, especially in Blacon, which has become one of the city's largest suburbs.

The line crossed the Welsh border half way between Blacon and Saughall and left the Cheshire village of Saughall with its station in Wales, and the County of Flintshire, which became Clwyd 20 years after Saughall closed to passengers and goods in February 1954. That was three years after a similar economy had taken place at Liverpool Road station, Chester.

When searching for the remains of Saughall station, I

walked over a sharply humped-back road bridge and looked towards the Welsh hills, only a mile or two to the west. I pondered how they might have looked to passengers on Cheshire Lines expresses between Manchester Central and Aberystwyth, begun in 1896 to exploit the newly completed Wrexham & Ellesmere Railway, over which they reached the Cambrian. It was a long way round.

Yet in 1903 the service was extended south to Leicester, only to be cut back to Sheffield in 1912. By the time the expresses had reached the Chester area, passengers must have felt that they had embarked on an interminable journey. Not even the spirit of the golden age of railways could sustain such a service.

Sealand station, beside the main road from Merseyside to North Wales via Queensferry road bridge, expanded to serve an RAF aerodrome built on both sides of the line west towards Dee Marsh Junction during World War I. The aerodrome, which for many years has been a maintenance depot, had sidings worked by its own locomotives.

Dee Marsh became a triangular junction when the North Wales & Liverpool Railway opened through central Wirral to Bidston, on the outskirts of Birkenhead in 1896. This completed lines used by passenger trains from Chester Northgate.

Reclaimed marshes near the junction became popular with golfers and in 1891 a platform was built for the Chester club close to it. It was replaced when John Summers of Stalybridge built a large steelworks. The new platform was shown on RCH maps of the 1930s as being 44 chains west of Sealand station and only 2 chains from Dee Marsh East junction. Golfers also used 'Birkenhead Junction Golf Club platform', just north of the triangle. Later that was swallowed by steelworks extensions.

Steelmaking stopped at Shotton some years ago and the nine miles between Dee Marsh and Mickle Trafford closed in September 1968. But new plant was built on the site and the line reopened on 1 September 1986 for trains carrying steel coils for processing and pulp and paper trains to and from a new mill.

There was uncertainty over its use after closure for local

Discovering Wirral's Heritage

Wirral Country Park

# In Days of Steam

Metropolitan Borough of Wirral
Department of Leisure Services & Tourism

*In Days of Steam* - among the latest in a line of informative leaflets about the Wirral Country Park. Obtained from the Visitor Centre at Thurstaston.

councils wanted to develop the trackbed for recreation while enthusiasts of the Cheshire Lines Steam Railway Group had well publicised plans for a steam operated route to supplement Chester's many tourist attractions.

Neither plan was likely to rob the route of the air of mysticism the route holds for many enthusiasts as a Great Central outpost on the Welsh border.

### Hooton - West Kirby

It is possible to ridicule any claim to the Hooton - West Kirby, which was entirely in Cheshire, having any connection with railways of the Welsh border, except perhaps that the views across the Dee estuary from its carriage windows beckoned generations to go and explore the rolling green hills they saw stretching away from the far shore.

It was not even a good line to use to get from Merseyside to North Wales. The best Welsh connection I can find is that Hooton was one of the stations served by trains from Birkenhead Woodside - a long closed terminus - to Llangollen and Barmouth.

The Ruabon - Morfa Mawddach trackbed supports two revived railways and the five miles west from Penmaenpool have been converted into a footpath with fine mountain and river views.

Something of a similar fate befell the West Kirby branch after closure when it was converted into the Wirral Country Park, one of the first created under the Countryside Act of 1968. It has been hugely successful ever since, being enjoyed by some 500,000 visitors a year.

It is very much a 'manicured' trackbed, where walkers and horse riders are segregated. There is no scrambling down overgrown embankments to try to trace a route heavily overgrown. All is well defined and sign-posted and Hadlow Road, near Hooton, is a delightfully restored station.

Like a number of other border lines the branch had extra character that twin company ownership often bestowed.

161

When the Wirral Country Park was being developed, people living in houses backing on to it feared loss of privacy, but once the Park was established and managed by rangers, they began building gates to get direct access and close proximity to the Park is now regarded as an attractive selling point for houses.

The branch lasted under a century after its creation by the LNWR/GWR jointly under an Act of 1862 for four miles between the Chester & Birkenhead at Hooton, eight and a quarter miles north of Chester, to the village of Parkgate on the Dee. Its prosperity had declined because it was no longer a port for the Irish packets due to the silting up of the Estuary. But there was a large colliery called Denhall or Wirral, which ran two miles under the river and was much better placed to serve the growing Merseyside area, and especially the industries of Birkenhead, than those of the North Wales coalfield.

The main engineering feature was Neston rock cutting, into which the Park planners incorporated a nature trail of such interest that it has its own guide to supplement one for the whole Park, also published by Cheshire County Council.

Parkgate was rail served from 1 October 1866, but it was another 20 years before the branch was extended along the low cliffs to the small and attractive town of West Kirby, at the mouth of the Estuary. Few, if any, passengers travelled to Birkenhead via Hooton because West Kirby was linked directly to Liverpool by the Mersey underground and Wirral Railways, which met at Birkenhead Park. Passengers had to change trains until the LMS Wirral electrification was opened in 1938.

Two aspects of branch passenger services are worthy of memory. A morning train from Heswall which had a club carriage for wealthy businessmen who went to live on the hillside overlooking Wales after the branch opened; and a through coach service between Euston and New Brighton, run by the LMS until the start of World War II.

The war brought the branch trains of a different kind. They ran to West Kirby carrying thousands of men to an RAF personnel dispatch and training camp and their journey was often the last long one before being posted overseas and sailing from the Mersey.

Branch decline began soon after the war ended and Thurstaston and Caldy stations closed in February 1954, with Kirby Park following five months later. A sustained fight against passenger closure was taken to the Central TUCC for Great Britain, but its members felt that the line could not be revived by diesel trains and passenger services were withdrawn from September 1956, freight continuing until May 1962.

As a Country Park of outstanding merit, the branch has achieved national fame, something it never did during its life.

The ever changing skies and sunsets over the Dee Estuary helped to place it among the most pleasant of Britain's coastal railways. It never received much attention from enthusiasts, although a writer recalling memories of the Bristol - Birmingham main line of 60 years ago, in the *Railway World* in 1964, mused on nostalgic memories. He felt that one might be 'a dead-still winter's day on the Wirral shore; over the river at the foot of the Welsh hills a pencil streak of steam spreads rapidly towards the open sea as there rolls across the sands of Dee the roar and rumble of the *'Irish Mail'*.

To have known railways on both sides of the Border in steam days is to have been privileged, as I remind myself every time I walk a trackbed which thousands have only ever known as the Wirral Way.

# Gazetteer

There are few greater pleasures than recalling railway memories, and especially going in search of old branch lines - either by simply sitting down for five minutes (or hours), or by spending days deep in remote and lovely countryside, perhaps guided by Ordnance Survey maps which feature so prominently in this Gazetteer.

Some entries detail the remains of long-forgotten lines and often they reflect changing patterns in the countryside where farms may have swallowed trackbeds, or where stations have been restored and become the local store helping to bring new life to hamlets and villages.

Abbreviations indicate:

*Act*: Date of Act of Parliament
*Remains*: Surviving features of note
*Uses*: Purposes to which railway buildings and land have been adapted
*Pass*: Passenger traffic: date of opening or withdrawal
*Gds*: Goods traffic: date of opening or withdrawal

## CHAPTER 2: SHREWSBURY

Shrewsbury was the grand junction for the Welsh Border and Severn Valley, dominated by the LNWR and GWR, individually and jointly, and this section includes the Joint Line branches, highly individual in a variety of ways. They range from that to Minsterley, which ran under the lee of the Shropshire hills and the Ludlow & Clee Hill, which conquered them.

## SHREWSBURY: SHROPSHIRE UNION GOODS YARD

*Shropshire Union Railways & Canal Company*

A small difficult to work yard overshadowed by Telford's prison, where inmates must have found life quieter since shunting ceased.

*ACT*: 3 August 1846 (Incorporation of SUR & CC).
*OPENED*:
*CLOSED*: 5 April 1971
*REMAINS*: Sharply curved, short tunnel, with smoke blackened roof opposite main platforms. Mouth bricked up and use of matching bricks makes position difficult to identify.
*USES*: Station car park. Goods shed at far end in industrial use.

## COLEHAM ENGINE SHEDS

Sheds were beside the S & H south of the station, at Scott Street, Sutton Bridge at junction of the Severn Valley Railway. (499118). GWR and LMS sheds, side by side, and enginemen's lodging house demolished soon after final closure in 1970. Site landscaped in May 1987 at start of comprehensive redevelopment scheme for wider area.

## CRUCKMEOLE JUNCTION - MINSTERLEY    5 miles
*LNWR & GWR Joint*

Single line, totally rural branch, off the Shrewsbury & Welshpool Joint. Cruckmeole Junction was 5 miles from Shrewsbury station.

*ACT*: 29 July 1856 Shrewsbury & Welshpool. Branch vested in LNWR & GWR Jointly on 5 July 1865.
*OPENED*: 14 February 1861
*CLOSED*: 5 February 1951: *Pass.* 1 May 1967: *Gds.* Track retained for a period. Lifted 1973. 12 September 1960: Hanwood Station (S & W) *Pass* 4 May 1964 *Gds*
*REMAINS: Cruckmeole (or Hanwood) Junction* trackbed curving south (431092).
*USES: Plealey Road* station house in private use. Building extended. Small goods shed (419075). Station crossing, with single gate, was not interlocked to its signals. *Pontesbury*: Station house in private use. Goods shed used by local gardeners' association (389063). *Minsterley*: Station house (375051).

## SNAILBEACH DISTRICT RAILWAYS    3 miles
*Snailbeach District Railways Company*

As a narrow gauge line (2 ft 4 in), the SDR does not strictly qualify for inclusion in this book, yet it was inseparable in enthusiasts' eyes from the Minsterley branch - and far more interesting not least because it was in the ownership of Colonel Stephens for a short time.

*ACT*: 5 August 1873 Pontesbury - Snailbeach Mine (3 miles) plus $1^3/_4$ mile extension, never built. 5 August 1891: Shropshire Mineral (Light) Railway authorised to extend SDR. Not built.
*OPENED*: 1877
*CLOSED*: Unused for several years before reopening in 1922. 1946: SDR closed except Pontesbury - Callow Hill Quarry, leased to Shropshire County Council. 1959: Complete closure.
*REMAINS: Pontesbury*: Branch exchange sidings were just west of station (393063). SDR crossed Shrewsbury - Bishop's Castle Road A488 on overbridge at 392061 and ran under Minsterley - Habberley unclassified road at sharp S bend (382043). Lordshill shunt - back in craggy woodland by lane (371017). Callow Hill Quarry was at 384049.
*Snailbeach*: Bridge where SDR passed under road (372023). Engine shed (373021). Also track and mine site nearby and cutting through which line approached shed and mine. Evocative area.

# LUDLOW - CLEE HILL                                      6 miles
*Ludlow & Clee Hill Railway*

Most spectacular of all Welsh border branches in setting and operation with 1 in 20 steam worked section and 1 in 6 cable incline. Far more to enjoy than its comparatively short length might suggest and trackbed remains make the route easy to visualise.
*ACT*: 22 July 1861. 1 June 1867: Working agreement with LNWR and GWR Joint. 1 January 1893: L & CHR absorbed by Shrewsbury & Hereford LNWR & GW Joint.
*OPENED* 24 August 1864: Ludlow - Bitterley, $4^1/_2$ miles. Privately. 1 June 1867: Bitterley - Clee Hill (incline top).
*CLOSED*: 10 May 1960: Incline last used. 7 November 1960: Incline closed officially. Wagons and locomotive brought down during following few days. 15 October 1962: Ludlow (Clee Hill Junction) - Bitterley Yard last used. 31 December 1962: official closure.

*REMAINS*: Middleton: Abutment of bridge across B4364 (538769). Trackbed on tree-covered embankment beside road for about $1/4$ mile.
*USES: Ludlow*: Small engine shed still recognisable as part of main building of Shukers Land Rover Centre on site of goods yard. Housing estate occupies Clee Hill trackbed from S & H junction. Middleton: Siding site use as contractor's yard. *Bitterley*: Cutting on 1 in 20 Yard approach incline heavily overgrown by trees.

Trackbed passes under bridge carrying lane between A4117 and Bitterley village (572769) and virtually disappears among trees which mark the Yard's grave.

Start of incline, which sight of road bridge, clearly traceable at ground level. Shells of comparatively modern brick and concrete roofed buildings hidden among trees. They lie close to stone and brick retaining wall and fence of old sleepers, which formed the northern boundary of railway. Remains of loading dock and short incline to a siding behind the mainly wooden signal box in the middle of the yard and beside the cable incline foot. Box, and also water column by approach incline, long demolished. Incline fenced off and used as sheep pasture. Best relished from steep, hump - back bridge carrying road to houses and CAA radar station. Park well clear of bridge because road is busy (587762). Trackbed in shallow cutting below. Incline course clearly discernable. Bridge is close to summit plateau, where little is left but cleared site of tall brick drum winding house and wooden engine shed. *Clee Hill*: Trackbed leading from incline top to Dhu stone quarries is partly used for new roads to quarry and quarry vehicle park.


## TITTERSTONE QUARRIES - BITTERLEY YARD      $1^{1}/4$ miles

*British Quarrying Co Ltd*

A narrow gauge, 3ft 0in rail system from quarry faces to crushing plant and self-acting incline to Bitterley Yard.
CLOSED: 1952
*REMAINS*: Quarry was at 595776 and incline foot at 574768. *Bedlam*: Incline crossed lane at 585773. *Bitterley*: Incline trackbed on low embankment climbing through fields.


## SHREWSBURY - LLANYMYNECH      18 miles

*Shropshire & Montgomeryshire Railway*

An unforgettable railway in unforgettable countryside.

*ACTS*: 29 July 1862: West Shropshire Mineral Railway: Westbury - Llanymynech (13³/₄ miles). Not built. 5 July 1865: Shrewsbury & Potteries Junction incorporated to build several routes. 16 July 1866: Potteries Shrewsbury & North Wales Railway incorporated by amalgamation of S & NWR and S & PJ. 7 August 1886: Shropshire Railways formed to acquire PS & NWR. 11 February 1909: Shropshire & Montgomeryshire Railway: Light Railway Order.

*OPENED*: 13 August 1866: S & PJ: Shrewsbury (Abbey Foregate) Red Hill (3 miles). S & NWR: Red Hill - Llanymynech (15 miles) - and Nantmawr. 1871: Kinnerley - Criggion. (6 miles). 11 March 1960: Shrewsbury (Abbey Goods) - Severn Valley branch: new connection.

*RE-OPENED*: 13 April 1911: Shrewsbury (Abbey) - Llanymynech. 22 February 1912: Kinnerley - Criggion. 1 June 1941: War Department takes over traffic operation.

*CLOSED*: 21 December 1866 - December 1868. 22 June 1880: Shrewsbury (Abbey) - Llanyblodwell: Line closed by Board of Trade Order. 6 November 1933: regular passenger services withdrawn. Special trains continued. 31 December 1959: Kinnerley - Criggion. 31 March 1960: WD transfers S & MR to BR (Western Region) for dismantling 12 May 1986: Hookagate Rail Welding Depot.

*REMAINS: Shrewsbury*: Bell Lane: Cutting of extension from Abbey Foregate to Shrewsbury & Birmingham in-filled and grassed over. Positional clue is exceptionally wide green verge to east of the road (505124). Trackbed to south beside river Rea is a pleasant footpath incorporating river bridge. (503121). Trackbed visible on both banks. *Shrewsbury West Halt*: At 495114. *Meole Brace Halt*: At 483107. *Hookagate*: High brick abutments flank Shrewsbury & Welshpool line at western end of wood (460095). *Hanwood Road* station was beside A488 (453103) *Cruckton Halt*: At 440113. *Ford*: platform hidden in undergrowth beside A458 (411132). *Shrawardine*: Stone abutments and trackbed of approaches to Severn bridge (389157) *Nesscliff & Pentre*: Platform at 369178. *Criggion branch: Chapel Lane Halt*: At 331183 Crew Green: Station at 327156. *Llandrinio Road*: Platform ends (307157) *Criggion*: Station was at 296151.

*USES: Shrewsbury (Abbey Foregate)*: Oil depot at station, where island platform remains. Coal depot in station yard. *Red Hill*: Station and halt swallowed by wartime interchange and sidings with Welshpool line. Later, Hookagate Rail Welding Depot

established on part of site. *Shoot Hill Halt*: Crossing keeper's house in private use (419125). *Nesscliff & Pentre*: Trackbed converted to road in what OS Maps show as 'Military Training Area (380168). Crossing keeper's house in private use (369178).
*Kinnerley Junction*: Trackbed approaching from Shrewsbury in military use. S & M locomotive shed and Repair Shops in commercial use (338199) *Wern Las Halt*: Crossing keeper's cottage (316204). *Maesbrook*: station in private use. (301207). *Llanymynech*: Platform edge on S & M station site. Cambrian Railways station site is coal depot (271210) *Criggion branch: Melverley*: Viaduct adapted for unclassified road from Crew Green B4393 to Melverley village. Road uses trackbed embankment on both sides of Severn. *Llandrinio Road*: Platform ends (307157).
*Criggion*: Station in private use.

## CHAPTER 3 - SEVERN VALLEY RAILWAY
## SHREWSBURY (SUTTON BRIDGE     39$^1$/$_2$ miles
## JUNCTION) - HARTLEBURY
*Great Western Railway*
This section deals primarily with the two closed sections lying either side of the restored Severn Valley Railway. It includes the trackbed through the Severn gorge, where part can be walked to get between sites of the Ironbridge Gorge Museum.
*ACT*: 20 August 1853: Severn Valley Railway: Shrewsbury - Hartlebury 31 July 1857: SVR leased to Oxford Worcester & Wolverhampton. 1 November 1860: SVR leased to West Midland Railway. 18 July 1872 SVR vested in GWR.
*OPENED*: 1 February 1862
*CLOSED*: 9 September 1963: Shrewsbury (Sutton Bridge Junction) - Bewdley *Pass*. 2 December 1963: Shrewsbury (S & M GF) - Highley (Alveley Colliery). Access retained to sidings at Buildwas for power station boilers. 22 January 1968: Section closed completely. 3 February 1969: Alveley Sidings - Bewdley North closed by BR. 1 February 1965: Stourport - Hartlebury *Gds*. 5 January 1970: Bewdley - Hartlebury - Kidderminster *Pass*. Bewdley South - Stourport *Comp*. 1 October 1980: Stourport CEGB - Hartlebury *Comp*. Official date. Last coal train worked March 1979.
   *REOPENED*: 6 July 1965: Severn Valley Railway Society formed. 23 May 1970: Bridgnorth - Hampton Loade. 12 April 1974: Hampton Loade - Highley. 18 May 1974: Highley - Bewdley.

*REMAINS: Berrington* A458 bridge abutments (554060). *Jackfield* Preserved level crossing with gates. *Bridgnorth*: Bridge across A458 immediately north of station yard long removed, but abutment remains on north side of road, close to mouth of Bridgnorth Tunnel.

*USES: Shrewsbury*: About half mile of trackbed through modern housing estate south from shunt - back to Abbey Goods at Sutton Bridge to (502113) to Sutton Road (505109) has a new line on it: wide, unbroken, white painted on tarmaced surface dividing it into pathway and cycleway. South to A5 trackbed has been converted into a shale path. A5 overbridge close to roundabout demolished and alignment improved. Immediately south, trackbed absorbed into field, though route can be traced by pinpointed bridge on unclassified road from A5 roundabout to Berrington (512103). Berrington: Station house (with platform) in private use (535074). *Cressage* Station house in private use (591042). Long stretches of trackbed between Shrewsbury and Buildwas are in agricultural use. *Buildwas* Level crossing on B4378 to Much Wenlock demolished and road improved beside western boundary of Ironbridge Power Station.

Merry-go-round trains run through large, hanger-like discharge plant built on station site. Most easterly of tall cooling towers lies on trackbed. *Severn Valley Way* footpath starts here, the $^3/_4$ mile to Ironbridge & Broseley station site incorporating *Benthall Edge Railway Trail*. It includes viaduct. The restored Severn Warehouse is on opposite bank of river. At *Ironbridge* the station site has been laid out as a landscaped car park for visitors to the historic bridge only yards away. It was the first iron one in England and cast in Coalbrookdale in 1779. From here the *Severn Valley Way* continues on trackbed passing *Jackfield* (692025). Half a mile beyond is *Coalport* station in private use. It retains a platform and waiting room (701020). This section of the Severn Valley Way is shown on a large scale street plan of Telford, 1986. Beyond Coalport, much of the trackbed is in agricultural use, or providing better road access to isolated farms. *Linley Halt*: in private use (705983). To the south, the trackbed has been incorporated into a golf course (722945) while north of *Bridgnorth* tunnel, a small housing estate is on the trackbed. *Bewdley*: Bewdley South Junction - Mount Pleasant Tunnel - Burlish (1 mile) bought by Severn Valley Railway 1972 for relaying as a stock siding.

*Burlish Halt*: was at 807218. Trackbed towards centre of Stourport-on-Severn developed. Station and level crossing were on A451. Crossing long replaced. Station site may be used for housing.

171

Junction for CEGB sidings was at 815718. Branch trackbed towards Hartlebury, including short viaducts, now a country walk. *Hartlebury* Bridge over A449 demolished 1984 for road improvements. (845718).

# CHAPTER 4 - SEVERN VALLEY: THE BRANCHES
## WELLINGTON - LIGHTMOOR JUNCTION  5$^1/_2$ miles
*Wellington & Severn Junction Railway*

This served the industrialised northern part of a 25$^1/_2$ mile cross-country route completed to the Shrewsbury & Hereford north of Craven Arms in 1867. Part of W & SJ is being revived by enthusiasts of the Telford Horsehay Steam Trust.

*ACT*: 28 August 1853: 1 August 1861: Company leased to GWR: absorbed 1 July 1892.

*OPENED*: 15 May 1857: Ketley Junction - Horsehay Ironworks *Gds* 2 May 1859 *Pass*: 1860 (date uncertain) Horsehay - Lightmoor *Gds* 1 August 1861: Wellington - Lightmoor (reverse) - Shiftnal: *Pass*.

*CLOSED*: 23 July 1962: Wellington - Much Wenlock *Pass*. Ketley Junction - Ketley *Comp* 7 July 1964: Ketley - Horsehay *Gds* 4 January 1981 Horsehay (Adamson Butterley works) - Lightmoor *Comp*.

*REOPENED*: 27 May 1984: Telford HST: Horsehay Yard - Heath Hill Tunnel ($^1/_4$ mile approx). 9 December 1985: Horsehay & Dawley station.

*REMAINS Ketley*: Station was on south side of A5 now A518 Station Road. Platform visible (673110) *Doseley*: Level crossing remains in Holly Road (679061) and Lightmoor Road (684057).

*USES: Ketley* M54 motorway built across trackbed at eastern end of A518 slip roads at junction 6. Trackbed stretching north for quarter of a mile towards Ketley Junction is footpath starting at 675103. *New Dale Halt*: Was at 677095. Trackbed running half a mile across Lawley Common incorporated into Wrekin Way footpath to *Lawley Bank* station site (676088). *Horsehay & Dawley*: Telford HST incorporates station yard and platforms in cutting. Northern end of operating track immediately south of A442. Trackbed from Heath Hill Tunnel - Lightmoor leased by Trust from Telford Development Corporation.

# BUILDWAS-MUCH WENLOCK  3$^1/_4$ miles
*Great Western Railway*

A small company built this short line and provided a valuable lifeline to a busy market town. It had more words in its title than miles in track!

*ACTS*: 21 July 1859: Much Wenlock & Severn Junction Railway. 5 June 1875: working agreement with GWR. 1 July 1896: Absorbed by GWR.
*OPENED*: 1 February 1862 (with Severn Valley: Shrewsbury - Hartlebury).
*CLOSED* 23 July 1962: Wellington - Much Wenlock *Pass* 4 December 1963: Buildwas - Longville *Comp* Engineer retained use until 19 January 1964.
*REMAINS* Trackbed can be roughly traced close to east side of B4378. *Farley Halt* was at 632019 on lane from main road.
*USES: Buildwas*: Two level junction station with lower platforms for SVR long demolished and incorporated into power station complex.

## MUCH WENLOCK - CRAVEN ARMS       14 miles
## (MARSH FARM JUNCTION)
*Great Western Railway*
The Much Wenlock Craven Arms and Coalbrookdale Railway - the Wenlock Railway - also built the one mile link between Buildwas and Coalbrookdale, including the Albert Edward bridge, still used by merry-go-round coal trains to Ironbridge power station.
*ACTS*: 22 July 1861: Wenlock Railway. 1 July 1896: Absorbed by GWR.
*OPENED*: 1 November 1864: Buildwas - Coalbrookdale. 5 December 1864: Much Wenlock - Presthope (3 miles). 16 December 1867: Presthope - Marsh Farm Junction (11 miles).
*CLOSED*: 31 December 1951: Much Wenlock - Craven Arms *Pass*. (17 miles). Longville - Marsh Farm Junction *Comp* (7 miles). 4 December 1963: Buildwas - Longville *Gds* (10 miles).
*REMAINS: Much Wenlock*: Branch bridged B4378 at 624002. Stout Abutments of bridge over A458 (617997). *Westwood Halt* was at 601 984. *Easthope Halt* was at 562959.
*USES: Much Wenlock*: Station sympathetically converted into houses. (625002). Goods yard, which lay between bridges mentioned above, has been landscaped. Traces of overbridge (000620). *Longville*: Station, nameboard attached, in private use. Bungalow built in yard (542937). *Rushbury*: Station in private use (516914). *Harton Road*: House in private use. Station area in farming use (483893).

## HOLLINSWOOD - STIRCHLEY       1¹/₄ miles
*Great Western Railway*

A short freight - only single branch surviving a variety of industries, riddled with level crossings and other operational difficulties. *ACT*:

*OPENED*: 24 February 1908: GWR began branch operation.

*CLOSED*: 2 February 1959.

*REMAINS*: Branch terminus was at 071075. While modern OS maps show traces of the Coalport branch in the Stirchley area there is no trace of the course of the Stirchley branch.

# WELLINGTON (HADLEY JUNCTION) - COALPORT      9¹/₂ miles

*London & North Western Railway*

Remains of the LNWR Coalport branch, which ran just to the west of the Stirchley branch, are easier to find, not least because part of the trackbed forms part of another noted path, The Silkin Way.

*ACT*: 27 July 1857

*OPENED*: 17 June 1861

*CLOSED*: 2 June 1952: *Pass.* 5 December 1960: Stirchley - Coalport East *Comp.* (3¹/₄ miles). 6 July 1964: Wellington (Hadley Junction) - Stirchley *Comp.* (4¹/₂ miles).

*REMAINS*: Much of the route is clearly marked on OS sheet 127. *Oakengates*: Station was at 698109. *Dawley & Stirchley*: Station building demolished. Platforms and goods shed remains (696067).

*USES: Hadley*: Branch bridge over A518, and high flanking embankments long demolished and local environment improved. (680123).

North of Telford Central station (opened 12 May 1986 (703092)) A442 Queensway partly constructed near branch route. *Telford Town Centre*: This lies close to site of *Malins Lee* Station (703087). Telford Town Tram (narrow gauge) ran alongside Randlay Lake in Town Park. Depot was at 700016. Some four miles of trackbed to Coalport East form the Silkin Way. Footpath broken where it crosses Coalbrookdale branch (698053). Short diversion across road bridge. *Blists Hill*: railway tunnel has been infilled to pedestrian - only height as it passes under entrance to Blists Hill open air museum (695035). Nearby, trackbed adapted to give improved access to Museum. Museum incporates relaid brick and tile loading siding, once branch connected. A little further north, *Madeley Market* station is used as offices (700042). Between Blists Hill and Coalport, an angled bridge takes the Silkin Way under the spectacularly restored, though non-operational double - track Coalport or Hay Incline Plane, with a vertical descent of 207 ft. It was built to lift barges between the Canal and the River. (695025). *Coalport East*: Single platform station and engine and carriage shed long demolished and site landscaped beside river. (701021). Bridge which crossed the platform carrying a road to Coalport Bridge extant, also another which crosses road that follows river bank.

## WOOFFERTON - TENBURY                                5¹/₄ miles
*LNWR & GWR Joint*
For exactly a century, this, the most southerly branch of the S & H Joint Line, formed the western end of a route through to the Severn Valley at Bewdley.
*ACTS*: 21 July 1859: Tenbury Railway authorised. 29 July 1862: With the S & H. Tenbury Railway leased to LNW & GW Joint.
*OPENED*: 1 August 1861
*CLOSED*: 31 July 1961: *Pass and completely* Also: Woofferton station (S & H Joint) *Pass.*
*USES*: Woofferton: Timber yard occupies trackbed from junction. Immediately beyond, improvements at junction of A49, A456 and B4362 involved demolition of A49 bridge over branch midway through shallow cutting. *Little Hereford* Level crossing on A456 demolished and road alignment much improved (547682). *Easton Court*: Station house in private use. Platform (550680). *Tenbury Wells*: (as renamed in 1912): Station area cleared and developed as industrial estate (591689). B4214 to Clee Hill climbs on overbridge at east end of estate. Cutting to east in-filled. Trackbed, mostly in agricultural use, easy to trace using OS 138. From Woofferton, it lies immediately north of the A456, after road crosses trackbed, it keeps close company to the south until site of overbridge (570681) when it returns to north side for rest of the way.

## TENBURY - BEWDLEY                                  15¹/₂ miles
*Great Western Railway*
A delightful branch which provided the stem for the Cleobury Mortimer & Ditton Priors Light Railway and also pierced the heart of Wyre Forest, almost inaccessible by road. Many interesting remains and much of trackbed walkable.
*ACT*: 3 July 1860: Tenbury & Bewdley Railway. Worked by GWR

and transferred to it by confirming act of 1869.

*OPENED*: 13 August 1864

*CLOSED*: 1 August 1962: Tenbury Wells - Bewdley *Pass*. 6 January 1964: Tenbury Wells - Cleobury Mortimer *Comp*. (9 miles). 16 April 1965: Cleobury Mortimer - Bewdley (north Junction) *Comp*. (6 miles).

*REMAINS*: Trackbed on north side of A456 between Tenbury Wells and Newnham Bridge, includes bridge close to junction of A456 and minor road (622686). *Bewdley* Pillars of Dowles viaduct across Severn (780764). Abutments of branch overbridge across B4194 close by.

*USES: Tenbury Wells*: Houses on trackbed east of station in Burford - the village in which station was situated. *Newnham Bridge*: Restored station buildings now a shop and station yard a garden centre and road depot of Hereford & Worcester CC. Eastern edge of depot spanned by long bridge carrying minor road. Has plate of The Horsehay Company. Not dated. Site evocative with wide views.

*Neen Sollars*: station in private use. Platform (662720). Cleobury Mortimer: Station house converted to holiday apartments. (702754). *Wyre Forest* Station house in private use (727760). Trackbed incorporates Nature Reserve managed by Worcestershire Nature Conservation Trust. $2^{1}/_{4}$ miles of trackbed owned by Nature Conservancy Council (738761 - 772763). Section includes notable embankments.

# CLEOBURY MORTIMER &     12 miles
# DITTON PRIORS LIGHT RAILWAY

*Promoted by private company*

Light railways fascinated enthusiasts and this one remains as well known long after closure as it did during its lifetime.

*ACTS*: 23 March 1901: Light Railway Order. 1 January 1922: Absorbed by GWR. 1 May 1957: Line taken over by Admiralty from BR (Western Region). 30 September 1957: Admiralty takes over operation.

*OPENED*: 19 July 1908 *Gds* 20 November *Pass*

*CLOSED*: 26 September 1938 *Pass* 16 April 1965: *Gds*

*REMAINS: Cleobury Mortimer*: CM & DP wooden platform adjacent to GWR station platform long demolished. Bridge abutments beside A4117 close to Tenbury branch by The Blount Arms. (702755). Wooden CM & DP platform at GWR station long demolished. Letter box labelled 'Cleobury Town Station' on electricity pole on B4363 (681768).

*Detton Ford*: Grassy platform with wooden edge and hut, beside minor road and former level crossing close to river Rea (665796). *Prescott*: Low railway bridge over river hidden in woods bordering minor road (661811). *Burwarton*: level crossing site at south end of station. Crossed minor road (632855). Cleobury Town. Office building converted into bungalow. Station masters nearby in private use. *Cleobury North*: Trackbed in private occupation on both sides of former crossing of B4364 (624873) *Ditton Priors* former Royal Navy Armaments depot, where railway ended, now a trading estate (612892).

## CHAPTER 5: RAILWAYS OF WORCESTER
## WORCESTER (BUTTS BRANCH JUNCTION)  1 mile
## - RIVERSIDE
*Great Western Railway*

Removal of the branch allowed an immense improvement in the city's congested road system and much improved the riverside environment.

*ACT*: 23 July 1858: Oxford Worcester & Wolverhampton Railway. Diglis branch abandoned and Butts branch substituted. 21 July 1859: Worcester & Hereford Railway: branch to Severn at Worcester (and power to enlarge Hereford station).

*OPENED*: c. 1862

*CLOSED*: c. 1930: Butts terminus - Riverside terminus. 25 April 1953: Racecourse traffic ended. 1 February 1957: Butts Branch junction - terminus.

*REMAINS* Single trackbed descending on arches squeezed between Worcester & Hereford viaduct and Worcester Royal Infirmary. Trackbed severed on east side of Croft Road, where low bridge beside W & H viaduct was removed 2 June 1960.

*USES*: Trackbed obliterated by major road improvements, and coach and lorry parks. Remainder of railway land to Butts terminus by Racecourse landscaped.

## WORCESTER (SHRUB HILL) - HILL  29 chains
## EVANS WORKS

The Vinegar branch. This private line was operated by the GWR and operating difficulties attracted the continual interest of enthusiasts.

*ACTS*: 1 August 1870: The Worcester Railways & Tramway Act.

Hill Evans & Company.

*OPENED*: 28 May 1872, Maintenance agreement with GWR.

*CLOSED*: 15 June 1964

*REMAINS*: From Worcester Goods Yard trackbed descended past front of BRSA club and alignment can be noted from Tolladine Road. Shrub Hill 'Public Road Crossing', in official terms, which was semaphore signalled, is clearly definable beside Great Western hotel; it ran through what is now the car park.

Also traceable are crossing sites in Padmore Street (junction with Cromwell Road), and at the crossing at the works entrance. A railway abutment remains on east bank of Worcester & Birmingham canal.

*USES: Worcester Goods Yard* Start of trackbed descent has been converted into footpath for staff using dmu and locomotive stabling sidings beside former, roofless, engine shed. Bascule bridge abutments cleared for approach road to Shrub Hill Industrial Estate.

## CHAPTER 6: THE MARCHES

Leominster station was the grand junction of the Marches for, in addition to services to Shrewsbury & Hereford, its two branch platforms were the terminus for services to Worcester (24 miles) and the Kington branches, which served Kington (14 miles), New Radnor (20 miles) and Presteigne (18 miles).

WORCESTER (BRANSFORD ROAD $23^3/_4$ miles
JUNCTION) - LEOMINSTER

*Great Western Railway*

A glorious country branch that reached 685 ft above sea level while rolling across hop-growing hills. Remembered with affection by those who sought out the remotest of branch lines.

*ACTS*: 1 August 1861: Worcester Bromyard & Leominster Railway. 1869: Bromyard - Leominster abandoned by Board of Trade Certificate. 12 November 1870: Working agreement with GWR. 30 July 1874: Leominster & Bromyard Railway. 1 July 1888: Worcester Bromyard & Leominster and Leominster & Bromyard vested in GWR.

*OPENED*: 2 May 1874: WB & L: Bransford Road Junction - Yearsett. 22 October 1877: Yearsett - Bromyard. 1 March 1884: Leominster - Steens Bridge. 1 September 1897: Steens Bridge - Bromyard.

*CLOSED*: 15 September 1952: Leominster - Bromyard *Pass and Comp*. 7 September 1964: Bransford Road Junction - Bromyard.

*REMAINS: Bransford Road Junction*: Trackbed diverging right from Worcester & Hereford soon after it crosses three low bridges, including first across river Teme (808527). *Bransford*: A4103 bridges trackbed in cutting. Parking difficult (803528). *Leigh Court* Shell of station building fenced off and incorporated into car park used by angling club. Platform edging and bridge abutments beside river Teme (782537).

*USES: Knightwick*: Station in private use, with plaque and wooden signal. Bridge abutments beside garden (737552). *Suckley*: Station in private use. Platforms amid trees. Overbridge demolished and lane it carried embankmented. Not obvious. Trackbed to west overgrown. *Yearsett* High arch track overbridge (707535). *Bromyard*: Industrial estate on station site. Trackbed converted into $^1/_2$ mile long road. Bromyard & Linton Light Railway (2ft 0in) based at estate entrance. Its trackbed extends east and passes under A44 in deep cutting. *Rowden Mill*: Station restored and owner provides holiday accommodation in former LMS Inspection saloon (628565). *Fencote*: Station house (600589).

*Steens Bridge*: Small housing estate on station site. Three pairs of semi-detached bungalows built on low-edge platform. A44 overbridge demolished to improve alignment. (543583). *Stoke Prior*: Landfill site in widened trackbed cutting where there was a halt. (530567). Beyond Halt branch curved sharply north to run on a separate low embankment alongside S & H main line to Leominster where trains ran into the Down platform, then an island, but since modified as the Down platform without island status. Much of branch trackbed beside S & H absorbed into A49 Leominster by-pass.

## LEOMINSTER - KINGTON                     13$^1/_4$ miles
*Great Western Railway*

Apart from serving a large farming area and a busy market town, this was the stem of a system which mid Victorian railway promoters hoped would take them through to the Cambrian coast.

*ACTS*: 23 May 1818: Kington Railway (3ft 6in). 10 July 1854: Leominster & Kington Railway. 13 July 1863: Company leased to GWR and West Midland Railway.

*OPENED*: 1 May 1820 Kington Railway (tramway). January 1856: Leominster - Pembridge (8 miles). 2 September 1856: Pembridge - Marston Halt (2 miles). 27 July 1857: Marston Halt - Kington *Gds* 20 August *Pass.*

*CLOSED*: 7 February 1955: *Pass* 28 September 1964 *Gds.*

*REMAINS: Leominster*: Two-road engine shed closed April 1962,

179

was on the Down side just north of the station. At Kington Junction, just north of A49 barrier crossing, trackbed heads west through trees (499594). *Upper Marston*: Tall bridge abutments flanking narrow lane. Trackbed on wooded hillside provides good impression of how contractors conquered hilly terrain. Forge Crossing Halt was at north end of lane : see Presteigne branch. *Titley*: Overbridge on minor road across deep, overgrown cutting. (340581).

*USES: Kingsland* Crossing keeper's cottage beside long, straight stretch of trackbed, converted into bungalow (452605) Station house in private use. Goods yard used by saw milling company. (441609). *Pembridge* Station in private use, marked by signal. (389591). *Marston Halt* Keeper's cottage (361582). *Titley*: Station building in private use. Overbridge abutments flank road beside station approach (328581). *Bullock's Mill*: crossing keeper's cottage converted to holiday accommodation. (317572). *Kington*. Original station 1855 - 75, private house, with plaque. Goods shed in industrial use. Yard and rest of station site now Hatton Gardens Industrial Estate. Lies at east end of town (303571).

## KINGTON - NEW RADNOR $6^1/_2$ miles
*Great Western Railway*
*ACTS*: 16 June 1873: Kington & Eardisley Railway: Kington - New Radnor Extension. 1 July 1897: K & ER absorbed by GWR.
*OPENED*: 25 September 1875.
*CLOSED*: 5 February 1951: *Pass* Temporary closure confirmed permanent 4 June. 31 December 1951: Dolyhir - New Radnor *Comp* 9 September 1958: Kington - Dolyhir *Comp*
*USES: Kington*: A44 By-pass road of 1983 follows trackbed, past site of engine shed, closed February 1951 (301570), through deep and widened cutting beside river Arrow on northern edge of town and rejoins A44 at 288570, where trackbed had been converted earlier to improve road for about a mile through Stanner to Burlinjobb. GWR fencing retained. *Stanner*: Station used by County Highways Department. Goods shed in industrial use. *Dolyhir*: Station building inside extended limestone quarry, used as mess room. *New Radnor*: Station site caravan park on south side of A44 village by-pass (217603).

## TITLEY - PRESTEIGNE $5^3/_4$ miles
*Great Western Railway*
The railway did not take the prosperity to Presteigne, County

town of Radnor, that it had been expected to, and Kington, about the same size, with a slightly smaller population, remained a much busier centre and market town.

*ACTS: 31 July 1871*: Leominster & Kington Railway authorised to build Presteign (sic) branch. 23 July 1877: GWR Act included provision for the L & K to make short extension at Presteign. 2 August 1898: L & KR amalgamated with GWR.

*OPENED*: 10 September 1875. (Date per company entry in *Bradshaw's Manual*).

*CLOSED*: 5 February 1951. *Pass* Temporarily withdrawn. Confirmed permanent 4 June. 28 September 1964: *Comp.*

*USES: Forge Crossing*: Keeper's cottage in private use (347591). *Presteigne*: Industrial estate, partly financed by EEC Regional Development Fund, on station site. Trackbed running about $3/4$ mile used for road, with new junction B4362/B4355, where hump-back bridge with sharply curved approaches, was demolished. (321634). School on original station site.


## TITLEY - EARDISLEY                                    7 miles
*Great Western Railway*

A delightful rural route that was a victim of both world wars.

*ACTS*: 30 June 1862: Kington & Eardisley Railway. 1 July 1897: K & ER absorbed by GWR.

*OPENED*: 3 August 1874

*CLOSED*: 1 January 1917 - 11 December 1922 (temporary). 1 July 1940: *Pass and Comp.*

*REMAINS: Titley*: Trackbed on wooded embankment alongside lane off A44. Abutments of overbridge over farm road. (335565). *Eardisley* Trackbed curving sharply west to join Hereford Hay & Brecon trackbed just east of A4111 humped overbridge (313485).

*USES: Lyonshall*: Station in private use. Platform. Private house built in goods yard. (335560). *Almeley*: Station area in farm use. Dock, goods siding, buffer stop. GWR fencing. (329517).


## HEREFORD (BARR'S COURT)                          $27^3/4$ miles
## THREE COCKS JUNCTION
*Midland Railway* (apart from short section at Hereford).

The main 'foreign' company in North Wales was the Great Central; in South Wales it was the Midland, which got access via the

Hereford Hay & Brecon.

*ACTS*: 8 August 1859: Hereford Hay & Brecon Railway incorporated Hereford - Talyllyn ($34^1/_4$ miles). 6 August 1860: Three Cocks - Talyllyn transferred to Mid Wales Railway; .Talyllyn - Brecon to Brecon & Merthyr. 1 July 1874: HHB leased to Midland Railway. 16 July 1885: HH & B amalgamated with Midland Railway. (From 1886).

*OPENED*: 24 October 1862: Hereford - Moorhampton *Gds* 30 June 1863: *Pass* (10 miles) 30 June 1863: Moorhampton - Eardisley (5 miles). 11 July 1864. Eardisley - Hay-on-Wye (7 miles). 19 September 1864: Hay - Three Cocks ($5^1/_2$ miles) - Brecon *Pass*

*CLOSED:* 2 February 1893: MR station Hereford (Barton). 31 December 1962: Hereford - Brecon *Pass*. Eardisley - Three Cocks *Comp* 28 September 1964: Hereford (Moorfields) - Eardisley *Comp* 1 August 1966: Hereford: Brecon Junction - Moorfields Junction *Comp*.

*REMAINS*: Much of their trackbed is overgrown and absorbed into agricultural use. Small stone bridges remain in several places.

*USES: Hereford*: Junction to Barton station leads to Bulmers Railway Centre, where locomotives use half-mile of branch for public trains. Local trackbed also used for housing. *Kinnersley*: station building used as store. (341489). *Eardisley*: Station in private use. Garden of bungalow uses part of platform. Goods shed and loading gauge. (311486).

*Hay-on-Wye*: Station in industrial use. Footpath created on trackbed beside the river in town centre by bridge carrying B4351 *Three Cocks Junction*: Station is within large bottled gas distribution depot.


## PONTRILAS - HAY-ON-WYE $18^3/_4$ miles
*Great Western Railway*

The Golden Valley Railway remained a backwater after promoter's dreams of it being part of a Liverpool - South Wales - Bristol through route evaporated.

*ACTS*: 13 July 1876. 1 July 1899: GVR vested in GWR. Act : 1 August.

*OPENED*: 1 September 1881: Pontrilas - Dorstone ($10^1/_2$ miles). 27 May 1889. Dorstone - Hay.

*REOPENED*: 1 May 1901.

*CLOSED*: Temporarily: 23 August 1897: Dorstone - Hay. 20 April 1898: Pontrilas - Dorstone. 15 December 1941: *Pass* 1 January 1950: Dorstone - Hay *Comp* 2 February 1953: Abbeydore - Dorstone *Gds* 3 June 1957: Pontrilas (Ordnance Storage Depot) - Dorstone *Comp* 31 March 1969: Pontrilas - Pontrilas MOS Depot.

*REMAINS: Pontrilas*: Stone station building on Newport Abergavenny & Hereford (closed passengers 9 June 1958). Bridge over river Dore beside A465, which was improved after demolition of branch overbridge.

*Clifford*: Station buildings (252457). *Hay*: Junction with HH & B beside Wye (234443). Hay station: trackbed of both lines extending 25 chains. *Vowchurch*: Station was at 361365.

*Peterchurch*: Station was at 344385. *Dorstone*: Station was at 344385.

*USES: Abbeydore*: large farm building on station site (385388). Trackbed to north provides access to fields. *Bacton*: Similar access north of station site. (382327). *Westbrook*: station building (277437). *Clifford*: station in private use (252447).


# CRAVEN ARMS (STRETFORD BRIDGE JUNCTION) - BISHOP'S CASTLE

9³/₄ miles

*Bishop's Castle Railway*

'An enthusiast friend once said of the Bishop's Castle railway that it was worth going all round the world to see.' Quote from *The Railway Magazine* January 1933.

*ACTS*: 28 June 1861: Shrewsbury & Hereford at Winstanstow to Oswestry & Newtown near Montgomery, branch to Bishop's Castle. 19¹/₄ miles. 29 June 1865: Chirbury - Minsterley. (9¹/₄ miles). Not built.

*OPENED*: 24 October 1865: Winstanstow - Bishop's Castle. Formal date. 1 February 1866: public traffic.

*CLOSED* 20 April 1935 *Pass and Comp.*

*REMAINS*: Stretford bridge platform, close to S & H, was at 430846. BCR signal preserved in NRM.

*USES: Horderley*: station in private use (410868). *Plowden* station in private use (382877): *Eaton*: Station in private use (375895). *Lydham Heath*: Station site County Council road depot (345905).

*Bishop's Castle*: Station site in Station Street. Goods shed occupied by timber company.


# STAFFORD - WELLINGTON (STAFFORD JUNCTION)

18¹/₄ miles

*London & North Western Railway*

LMS timetables showed branch services in Stafford - Wellington - Shrewsbury - Welshpool context, but not all stopping trains ran through and they were used mainly be people making local journeys from country stations into town.

*ACTS*: 3 August 1846: Shropshire Union Railways & Canal Company: Stafford - Wellington. Also: Wellington - Shrewsbury (joint with Shrewsbury & Birmingham, incorporated same date). 2 July 1847: SUR & CC leased to LNWR.

*OPENED*: 1 June 1849: Stafford - Wellington. Also: Shrewsbury - Oakengates.

*CLOSED*: 7 September 1964: Stafford - Wellington *Pass* 1 August 1966: Stafford (Bagnall's Siding) - Newport (excl) *Comp* 1 July 1968: Newport - Donnington (excl) *Comp* 2 October 1979: Donnington (Exchange Sidings) - NCB Granville Colliery. Wellington (Stafford Junction) - Central Ordnance Depot, Donnington, still open, was singled 25 July 1971 ($2^{1}/_{4}$ miles).

*REMAINS: Stafford*: M6 (Stafford by-pass) crosses above trackbed (897232). Overbridge in cutting to west. *Haughton*: A518 overbridge (855211). *Gnosall*: station yard. Overbridge initialled 'SUR' (818205). *Coton*: A518 overbridge (812204). *Newport (Church Aston)*: overbridge abutment beside A518 (735170).

*USES: Stafford*: Short section from West Coast main line electrified and used as siding. Buffer stops visible from passing trains. Overbridge immediately beyond (910233) *Gnosall*: Station demolished. Down booking office presented to Shrugborough Museum. *Stafford - Newport*: 10 mile footpath being developed by Staffordshire County Council. *Newport*: Station house in private use beside a housing estate extending to trackbed and platform. Former A41 improved by demolition of overbridge beside station. Station crane moved to Blists Hill Museum 1973. (750183). A41 Newport by-pass bisects trackbed east of town. (755184). *Lilleshall*: A518 by-pass on trackbed to *Donnington* where roundabout with tall clocktower is on station site. (706143). Stub of branch enters Central Ordnance Depot beside newly aligned A518 (New Trench Road). (695132).

# WELLINGTON (MARKET DRAYTON JUNCTION) - NANTWICH (MARKET DRAYTON JUNCTION)

*Great Western Railway*                                $27^{1}/_{2}$ miles

A much used secondary route with comparatively closely spaced stations in-filled by halts, yet passenger traffic was always light. Line twice crossed Shropshire/Cheshire border at Coxbank, near Audlem. (655417 and 657411).

*ACTS*: 7 June 1861: Nantwich & Market Drayton Railway ($10^3/_4$ miles). 7 August 1862: Wellington & Drayton Railway incorporated. 30 July 1866: W & DR amalgamated with GWR. 1 July 1897: N & MDR amalgamated with GWR.

*OPENED*: 20 October 1863: Nantwich - Market Drayton. 16 October 1867: Wellington - Market Drayton.

*CLOSED*: 9 September 1963: Wellington - Nantwich *Pass*. 1 May 1967: Wellington - Nantwich *Comp*.

*REMAINS: Longdon Halt*: Was by B5063 at 630149. *Rowton Halt*: was at 627198. *Ellerdine Halt*: was at 626218. *Peplow* station was 625245. *Tern Hill*: Low three-arch bridge over river Tern visible from A53. Low embankments both sides. High abutments of branch overbridge on sharp S bend (631315). *Little Drayton Halt*: was at 660339. *Adderley*: station was at 662402. *Coxbank Halt*: was at 655419, close to bridge abutment. *Coole Pilate Halt*: bridge over unclassified road demolished (648460). Low embankment to south. Halt was sited between road and Shropshire Union can, immediately north of railway bridge over canal, of which Abutments remain.

*USES: Admaston*: The Silkin Way runs on trackbed for about 1 mile north from 636128 to its northern end at Bratton on B5063. *Crudgington*: station demolished c 1978. Trackbed in industrial use, incorporating large creamery. Overbridge on B5062 (628180). *Hodnet*: House on station site (621280). Ornate and substantial goods shed and yard to south. Yard (capacity 87 wagons) used by coal merchant. Steeply-humped bridges north and south of station site on lanes to Stoke upon Tern. Trackbed south to Peplow in agricultural use. *Wollerton*: Halt long demolished and trackbed to south provides access to fields (622297). Two bridges arch trackbed. *Tern Hill*: Overbridge on A41 demolished and road improved. *Market Drayton*: Suggestions that section north to Nantwich should become a walkway were quickly dismissed by local authorities.

Station site in extensive industrial use (672348). A53 By-pass on trackbed for nearly a mile from 651335. Road crosses trackbed at 672351. *Audlem*: Several detached houses on station site (Heywood's Ridge) on south side of A525, where overbridge removed and northern abutment tapered. Low wall on side of road was base of other bridge abutment (655430). *Baddington (Nantwich)*: Trackbed close to Market Drayton Junction in agricultural use. High hump-back bridge on A530 with curved approaches over trackbed by farm. Most northerly bridge on line.

## CHESTER (TATTENHALL JUNCTION) - WHITCHURCH     15 miles

*London & North Western Railway*

While continuous industrial traffic between Merseyside and the Midlands thunders along the A41, in many places only yards away, there is peace to be found by the trackbed, which runs partly under the lee of the wooded, lovely and little known Bickerton Hills.

*ACT*: 16 July 1866

*OPENED*: 1 October 1872

*CLOSED*: 16 September 1957 *Pass*. 4 November 1963: *Gds* Occasionally used for Chester - Crewe passenger train diversions until 8 December.

*REMAINS*: Entire trackbed traceable through the open countryside Branch twice crossed the A41. South of Tattenhall (476570), where there was an overbridge. Near Grindley Brook, the road is carried over the trackbed at a sharp bend (518442). *Grindley Brook*: 30 miles long Cheshire Sandstone Trail to Frodsham, east of Chester, begins just south of site of halt (521435). Route details at noticeboard on A41.

The flight of six Llangollen Canal locks here provide more interest than trackbed, carried across canal on high skew bridge incorporating courses of blue brick. Trackbed on short embankment turns towards Whitchurch and disappears into farmland.

*USES: Waverton*: This station on Chester & Crewe main line was the only non-branch station to be used by its local trains. Closed 15 June 1959 *Pass* 1 March 1965. *Gds*. It is an architecturally interesting station, having been built in 1897 for the Duke of Westminster in keeping with the buildings on his estate. *Tattenhall*: Station in private use. Garden on up platform (479585). Not to be confused with Tattenhall Road, which was on Chester & Crewe main line. *Broxton*: Station and hump back bridge on A534 long demolished and road improved. Cheshire County Council built drivers' rest area on station site. Commercial vehicle and car parks attractively segregated by high earth banks. Birdsong clear against traffic rumble (479543). *Malpas*: Station building charmingly restored as offices and area landscaped. Small industrial estate of single storey buildings on trackbed immediately north includes goods shed. *(498492). Whitchurch*: A49 overbridge

186

(538425). Cutting stretching towards Shrewsbury & Crewe line.

## CHESTER: SALTNEY MARSHALLING YARD ½ mile - SALTNEY QUAY

*Great Western Railway*

Also known as the Dee branch, it serves small wharves and several busy factories. The Great Central Railway's Connah's Quay branch, a few miles further downstream, handled far greater coastal traffic.

*ACT*: 6 August 1844: North Wales Mineral Railway

*OPENED*: 4 November 1846

*CLOSED*: 14 December 1970: Final section: Dee Junction - Spencer's scrapyard.

*REMAINS*: Four span bridge which carried Chester & Holyhead over branch in River Lane, Saltney (386652).

*USES*: Trackbed north of Saltney High Street (A549), which branch crossed on gated crossing beside the Anchor Hotel, used for store development. Concrete single line bridge which carried branch across stream close to its outfall into river Dee now forms leg of one-way system to new supermarket and also factories. (377652). Wharves landscaped and built up as part of flood prevention scheme.

## CHESTER: SALTNEY MARSHALLING YARD & PASSENGER STATION

*Great Western Railway*

Never an easy yard to view from either train or roadside - unlike its neighbour Mold Junction on the Chester & Holyhead. Enthusiasts neglected Saltney Yard in favour of the glamorous GWR scene at Chester (General) station and shed. Yet Saltney Yard was busy enough to be open round the clock, except between midday and midnight on Sundays.

*ACT*: 6 August 1844: North Wales Mineral Railway: Saltney - Wrexham. 28 August 1846: NWMR amalgamated with Shrewsbury Oswestry & Chester Junction to form Shrewsbury & Chester. 1 September 1854: S & C amalgamated with GWR.

*OPENED*: 4 November 1846.

*CLOSED*: 3 April 1967: Saltney marshalling yard. Saltney station: 1 January 1917. Reopened 4 July 1932. 12 September 1960: Final closure *Pass*.

*REMAINS: Saltney*: All marshalling yard buildings demolished 1975 except NWMR workshops of which shell survives, awaiting restoration, in Boundary Lane opposite The Anchor Hotel (387651).

*USES*: 1 November 1985: Yard site of approximately 8 acres advertised for sale by BR Property Board, Birmingham.

## MOULDSWORTH - MICKLE TRAFFORD - CHESTER (NORTHGATE)   3³/₄ miles

*Cheshire Lines Committee*

Nowhere was a sense of historical contrast sharper than at Northgate, a Victorian barn, close to a spectacular stretch of the City walls towering above the Shropshire Union Canal. Northgate was appreciably closer to the City's heart than General station - now Chester - with a main building well matched to the best of Chester's period architecture.

*ACTS:* 5 July 1865: Chester & West Cheshire Junction. 10 August 1866: C & WCJ absorbed by Cheshire Lines Committee.

*OPENED* 2 November 1874: Mouldsworth - Chester (Northgate): *Gds* 1 May 1875 *(Pass)*.

*REOPENED*: 1 September 1986: Mickle Trafford - Chester - Dee Marsh Junction.

*CLOSED*: 12 February 1951: Mickle Trafford East (CLC) *Pass* 1 July 1963 *Gds* 5 April Chester (Northgate) - Chester East Junction: *Gds* 6 October 1969 *Pass* 4 January 1960: Chester (Northgate) engine shed: *steam* 6 October 1969: *comp*

*REMAINS: Chester*: Sandstone and brick abutments of two bridges which carried lines to engine shed, goods yard and banana warehouse across Chester & Holyhead main line are close to east mouth of Windmill Lane tunnel and site of Chester No 6 box, which was above tracks.

*USES: Chester (Northgate)*: Station site sold to City Council 1970. It opened the £5 million Northgate Leisure Centre on 4 April 1977. Renovated retaining wall with 12 brick bays now separate the levels of the Centre car park. Twenty - two acres at north of triangle partly formed by trackbeds of lines from Northgate station to east and west junctions, bought by City Council, January 1982 for council and private housing. Private company began developing Northgate Village, summer 1985 and early in 1988 City Council began building sheltered housing on 'Northgate Triangle', as it is officially known. Land between village and C & H line utilised as municipal car park, which while large, often gets packed. In 1978 an 85ft 60 ton wrought iron bridge which carried tracks from Northgate across the C & H replaced a Cambrian Railways timber bridge across the river Tygwyn north Harlech. Northgate Banana Warehouse (Trafford House in Trafford Street), is in commercial use 'Elder & Fyff's' electricity sub-station is alongside. The western boundary wall of Northgate station in Victoria Road is partly incorporated into boundary wall of modern DIY store.

## CHESTER (EAST & SOUTH JUNCTIONS) $6^3/_4$
## - HAWARDEN BRIDGE (DEE MARSH JUNCTION)
*Great Central Railway*
A route which gave the GCR access to Chester and North Wales. Reopened, as part of the Mickle Trafford - Dee Marsh Junction route (9 miles) for Shotton steelworks traffic, in 1986.
*ACT*: 28 July 1884: Manchester Sheffield & Lincolnshire. Promoted as Chester & Connah's Quay Railway.
*OPENED*: 31 March 1890
*REOPENED*: 1 September 1986
*CLOSED*: 9 September 1968: Chester (Northgate) - Dee Marsh Junction. Dee Marsh (East - North Junctions) *Pass*. 14 May 1984: Mickle Trafford - Dee Marsh Junctions *Gds* Station economies ahead of passenger service withdrawal were: *Chester (Liverpool Road)*: 2 April 1951 *Pass* 5 April 1965. *Gds Blacon* 4 January 1965 *Gds Saughall*: 1 February 1954 *Pass and Comp. Sealand*: 5 April 1965 *Gds*
*REMAINS*: *Chester (Liverpool Road)* Station was on west side of A5116 (Birkenhead Road) (404675). *Blacon*: Station site in wooded cutting. Platform edges. Goods yard overgrown by trees (383682). *Saughall*: Platform edges. Steelpipe company in station yard. Notable row of railway cottages east of station site at end of private road. (357691). *Sealand*: Platform edges on east side of hump back A550 bridge. (334699). RAF Sealand Maintenance Unit had extensive sidings on either side of A550 worked by four small diesel shunters.
*USES*: The reopened line is easy to view from roads, especially in Chester, where it crosses the Chester & Birkenhead within site of Chester station. The route is not road accessible at either Mickle Trafford or Dee Marsh junctions.

## HOOTON - WEST KIRBY $12^1/_2$ miles
*LNWR/GWR JOINT*
One of the most northerly lines in which the GWR had a stake,

this branch became better known and far more popular after closure when it was converted into the Wirral Country Park, officially opened 2 October 1973.

*ACTS*: 17 July 1862 Birkenhead Railway: Hooton - Parkgate. 12 July 1882: LNWR: Parkgate - West Kirby.

*OPENED*: 1 October 1866: Hooton - Parkgate. 19 April 1886: Parkgate - West Kirby. October 1894: Kirby Park. May 1909: Caldy.

*CLOSED*: 17 September 1956 *Pass* 7 May 1962 *Gds* Stations: 1 February 1954 Thurstaston, Caldy 5 July 1954: Kirby Park.

*REMAINS*: Almost entire trackbed has been used as the Wirral Country Park or Wirral Way.

*USES: Hooton*: Most westerly of two branch platforms forms footpath past old brick waiting room. Red station sign. *Hadlow Road*: Station restored as museum and signal box and level crossing gates from Hassell Green on the North Staffordshire Sandbach - Alsager branch added for atmosphere. (331774). *Neston*: Rock cutting trail car park is in Lees Lane (307775). Small housing estate on Neston station site in Station Road (295773): Bidston - Hawarden Bridge - Wrexham line crosses Station Road. *Heswall*: Houses on station site (265279) *Thurstaston*: Footpath passes between platform edges. Large car park and camping site in former goods yard. The Park Visitor centre, which includes railway exhibits, is adjoining station site. Large grassy mounds in field leading to cliff edge hide wartime anti-aircraft gun emplacements. *West Kirby*: Original iron footbridge over trackbed in Ashton Park by lake (216865). Hump-back A540 overbridge demolished and road improved opposite Concourse, including baths and fire station, built on Joint Line station site and Wirral Railway sidings.

# Bibliography

I have been fortunate in having personal memories to bind together much of my research and fieldwork into lines, already long closed, which are slipping deeper and deeper into history. I have also had the pleasure of being able to enjoy reading many books and journals, in particular, those of three organisations of which I am a member: the Branch Line Society, the Railway & Canal Historical Society and Railway Ramblers.

Increasing land values have made trackbeds far more valuable than they often were when tracks were torn from them and their subsequent development can be noted from new editions of maps of several kinds, including street maps.

### Background Books

Appleton, J.H. *Disused Railways in the Countryside of England and Wales* A report to the Countryside Commission (1970).

Bannister, G.F. *Branch Line Byways* (vols 1 and 2) (1986 & 87).

Beck, Keith M. *The Great Western North of Wolverhampton* (1986).

Biddle, G and Nock, O.S., *The Railway Heritage of Britain* (1983).

Beck, Keith M. *The West Midland Lines of the GWR* (1983).

Casserley, H.C. *Railway History in Pictures: Wales and the Welsh Border Counties* (1970).

Christiansen, Rex *Regional History of Railways of Great Britain: Volume 7 The West Midlands* Revised 1983, vol 13 *Thamas & Severn* (1981).

Clinker, C.R. *Register of Closed Passenger Stations and Goods Depots in England, Scotland and Wales* (1978).

Clinker, C.R., *Great Western Railway: A Register of Halts and Platforms 1903-1979*

Daniels G and Dench, L.A. *Passengers No More* (1973).

Elis, Rhys ab. *Railway Rights-of-Way* (Branch Line Society) (1985).

Greville, M.D. and Spence, Jeoffry *Closed Passenger Lines of Great Britain 1827 -1947* (1974).

Hawkins, C. and Reeve, G. *LMS Engine Sheds* (Vol 1) (1981).

Hill, N.J. and McDougall, A.O. *A Guide to Closed Railway Lines in Britain 1948 - 1975* and Amendment Lists.

Industrial Railway Society *Industrial Locomotives of Chester Shropshire & Herefordshire* Handbook (editor: Alan J Bridges) (1977).

Lambert, A.J. *West Midlands Branch Line Album* (1978).

Lewthwaite, G.C. *Branch Line Index* and supplements

Lovett Jones, G. *Railway Walks. Exploring Disused Railways* (1980).

Lyons, E *An Historical Survey of Great Western Engine Sheds 1947* (1972).

Lyons, E and Mountford E.R. *An Historical Survey of Great Western Engine Sheds 1837 - 1947* (1979).

MacDermot, E.T. *History of the Great Western Railway* (Vols 1 and 2). revised by C.R. Clinker.

Railway Clearing House. *Railway Junction Diagrams 1915* (1969)

Salop Record Office *Canals and Railways: A list of plans and related documents deposited at the Shirehall, Shrewsbury* (revised 1969).

Watts, W.W. *Shropshire. The Geography of the County* (1919).

There are, of course, many other sources from which a picture of forgotten railways can be pieced together. *Bradshaw's Shareholders Guides* and *Railway Guide* (public timetables), individual company working timetables and appendices, short train and bus timetables published locally provide fascinating insights into local life, as well as train operation.

The same is true of old guide books, generally railway orientated. In Victorian and Edwardian days they often suggested 'skeleton' or outline tours of many small areas, like the Wye and Severn Valleys, lasting up to a month. Holiday guides published by the larger companies are another source of information and pleasure.

Perhaps the most famous of these was the GWR *Holiday Haunts*. In the back were not only advertisements for British hotels and resorts, but for sea voyages. These railway guides were popular with the big shipping companies. The GWR *Holiday Haunts* of 1921 contained a special supplement headed by steamship companies, including P & O to the Far East, Union - Castle (sic) to South Africa and the Cunard Line 'to all parts of The World.'

Did the guides entice the wealthy travellers with time on their hands to catch boat trains to Southampton rather than stopping trains deep into the remote and lonely countryside around Worcester or New Radnor?

### Chapter 2 - Shrewsbury & District

British Railways Board, *The Reshaping of British Railways* 1963 (The Beeching Report).

Brook F, and Allbutt, M. *The Shropshire Lead Mines* (1973)

Casserley, H.C. *Britain's Joint Lines* (1968)

Cooke, R.A. *Track Layout Diagrams of the GWR and BR WR East Shropshire* (Section 32) (1978).

Morriss, Richard K. *Rail Centres: Shrewsbury* (1986).

Morriss, Richard K. *Railways of Shropshire: a brief history* (1983).

Shropshire Railway Society, *Shropshire Railways Revisited* (1972).

Tonks, Eric S. *The Shropshire & Montgomeryshire Railway* (re-vised 1982).

Turner, Keith & Susan *The Shropshire & Mongomeryshire Light Railway* (1982).

### Chapter 3 - The Severn Valley Railway

Salop County Library, *Handbook to the Severn Valley Railway* 1863, Reprint. Undated.

Wrekin Disrict Council, *Ironbridge and the Wrekin. The Visitor's Guide*

*Chapter 4 - Severn Valley: the branches*

Denton, J.H. *A Tour of the Railways and Canals between Oakengates and Coalbrookdale* R & CHS booklet 1961.

Denton, J.H., *A Tour of Telford's Transport Past* R & CHS booklet 1986

Gammell, C.J., *Great Western Branch Lines 1955 - 1965* (1975).

Ironbridge Gorge Museum Trust, Booklets, various.

Lewis, M.J.T. *Early Wooden Railways* (1970)

Neele, G.P., *Railway Reminiscences* 1904

Price, M.R.C., *The Cleobury Mortimer & Ditton Priors Light Railway* (Oakwood Locomotion Papers) (1963).

Smith, W. and Beddoes, K. *The Cleobury Mortimer & Ditton Priors Light Railway*


*Chapter 5 - Railways of Worcester*

Cooke, R.A., *Track Layout Diagrams of the GWR and BR WR: Worcestershire* (section 33) (1976).

Jenkins, S.C. and Quayle, H.I., *The Oxford Worcester & Wolverhampton Railway* (1977).

Nicholson, R. *Nicholson's Guides to the Waterways* (Vol 3: South West) (1973).

Potts, C.R. *An Historical Survey of Selected Great Western Stations* (Vol 4) (1985).


*Chapter 6 - The Marches*

Ashworth, B.J. *Steam in the West Midlands & Wales* (1975).

Body, Geoffrey, *PSL Field Guide: Railways of the Western Region* (1983).

Clinker, C.R. *The Hay Railway* (1960)

Denton, J.H., *British Railway Stations (1965).*

Griffith, Edward *The Bishop's Castle Railway 1865 - 1935* (revised 1969).

Howse, W.H. *Radnorshire* (1949).

Mowat, C.L. *The Golden Valley Railway* (1964).

Page, James, *Forgotten Railways: South Wales* (vol 8) (1979).

6000 Locomotive Association *Bulmers Railway Centre, Hereford*


*Chapter 7 - North of the Severn - 1*

Christiansen, Rex and Miller, R.W. *The North Staffordshire Railway* (1971).

Hendry, Dr. Preston, and *An Historical Survey of Selected*
Hendry, R. Powell, *LMS Stations* (1982).

Lester, C.R. *The Stoke to Market Drayton Line and Associated Canals and Mineral Branches* (1983).

Talbot, E. *LNWR Miscellany* (volume 2) (1980).


*Chapter 8 - North of the Severn - 2*

Barnard, D.B. *Transport in the Whitchurch Area, Part II Canals & Railways* (Whitchurch Area Archaeological Group) (1985).

Birmingham Locomotive Club, *Industrial & Independent Locomotives and Railways of North Wales* (1968).

Bolger, Paul, *An Illustrated History of The Cheshire Lines Committee* (1984).

Davies, Hunter, *A Walk Along the Tracks* (1982).

Dow, George *Great Central* (vols 2 and 3) (1985 and 1965) editions.

Dyckhoff, Nigel. *The Cheshire Lines Committee: Then and Now* (1984).

Greville M.D. *Chronology of the Railways of Cheshire* (1973).

Holt, G.O. (revised Gordon Biddle) *A Regional History of the Railways of Great Britain: The North West* (volume 10) (1986).

Marshall, John *Forgotten Railways: North-West England* (volume 9) (1981).

Merseyside Railway History Group *The Hooton to West Kirby Branch Line and The Wirral Way* (1982).

Pevsner, Nikolaus, and Hubbard, Edward, *The Buildings of England: Cheshire* (1971).

Somerville, Christopher, *Walking Old Railways* (1979)

# Index

Page numbers in *italics* denote plate pages. See also detailed references to places, branches and associated lines in the Gazetteer. For major LNWR and GWR entries see branches.

# INDEX